"Today, we all understand the Internet business is not the software business. We strive to build networks and platforms."

– Evan Williams,
Founder of Twitter, Medium and Blogger,
"Medium is not a publishing tool"

PLATFORM SCALE

How an emerging business model helps startups
build large empires with minimum investment

Sangeet Paul Choudary

First Edition

ISBN No. 978-981-09-6758-1
Platform Thinking Labs Pte. Ltd.

For Devika

ABOUT THE AUTHOR

Sangeet Paul Choudary is a widely published researcher and advisor to C-level executives globally, best known for his work on platform business models and multi-sided network effects. He is the co-chair of the MIT Platform Strategy Summit, held annually at the MIT Media Labs in Boston. Sangeet also acts as an industry advisor to the Global Platform Data Project at Stanford University and is an advisor at 500Startups in Silicon Valley. He is an Entrepreneur-in-Residence at INSEAD Business School and a Global Fellow at the Centre for Global Enterprise in New York.

Sangeet is an advisor to C-level executives globally and has advised CXOs and board members in multiple industries across Europe, North & South America, Asia and Australia, on the design and implementation of platform business models and network effects.

Sangeet is a regular keynote speaker at leading industry conferences globally (represented by Celebrity Speakers Ltd.) and was invited to speak at the G20 World Summit 2014 events in Brisbane. He has lectured at leading universities in the US, including Harvard Business School, Carnegie Mellon University and the MIT Media Labs. He is a board member (advisory) of CoFounders Lab, the world's largest community of technology entrepreneurs.

At the G20 World Summit 2014 in Brisbane, he was hailed by the Australian media as 'a forefront researcher into how businesses can use metadata and technology' and 'the go-to person when it comes to understanding digital economics'.

Sangeet's work has been featured and recommended on leading publications, including the Wall Street Journal, Harvard Business Review, MarketWatch, Forbes, WIRED Magazine and Fast Company. In the April 2015 issue of Thinkers magazine on 'Redefining Capitalism', he was featured alongside globally leading thinkers like Michael Porter and Don Tapscott. Sangeet is also a contributing author to the book *Managing Startups* (O'Reilly Media, Inc) and the co-author of the upcoming book *Platform Revolution* (W.W. Norton & Company, Inc).

For more details, please visit
http://platformthinkinglabs.com/about/sangeet-choudary

PRAISE

"*A compelling framework for building platforms, networks and marketplaces. Essential reading for every entrepreneur and innovator.*"

– JON ORINGER,
Founder and CEO, Shutterstock

"*The leading resource for understanding business models for the networked age. Highly recommended for entrepreneurs and innovation professionals looking to build new platforms and networked businesses.*"

– PATRICK VLASKOVITS,
New York Times Bestselling Author of The Lean Entrepreneur

"*Many understand the power of platforms. Few understand how they work. Only Sangeet tells you how to build them.*"

– NIR EYAL,
Wall Street Journal Bestselling author of Hooked

"*Sangeet's work brings science and structure to a host of emerging digital business models. A must read for every serious entrepreneur and innovator building marketplaces or platforms.*"

– MICHAEL KARNJANAPRAKORN,
Founder and CEO, SkillShare

"*The go-to authority for the latest on platforms. Impeccably ties theory and business practices with tangible example. His insight and foresight are tremendously helpful.*"

– REUVEN GORSHT,
Global Vice President, SAP

"*The bible of digital media and emerging business models. I would strongly recommend Sangeet's work on this topic to CIOs and Innovation leaders waiting to unlock growth using digital.*"

– UMANG BEDI,
Managing Director, South Asia, Adobe

"Unquestionably the paramount mind in platform thinking."

– ANDREW GUNSBERG,
Television Host of Australian Idol, The Bachelor,
Live To Dance, The Hot Hits Live from LA

"The go-to person when it comes to understanding digital economics."

– ABC MORNINGS RADIO TALK SHOW,
Australian Radio, at the G20 World Summit 2014

"An excellent source for managers to develop platform thinking and stay up-to-date on the dynamics of platform-based markets."

– PROF. FENG ZHU, PROFESSOR,
Harvard Business School

"A forefront researcher into how businesses can better use metadata and current technology."

– 4BC 1116 NEWS TALK,
Australian Radio, G20 World Summit 2014

"Sangeet is one of the deepest thinkers I know. He has helped countless startups understand and unlock their core value as platform businesses. His work sits next to Clayton Christensen and Geoffrey Moore."

– MENG WONG,
Co-founder, JFDI

"One of the best innovation strategists in the world and an expert on building platforms. His work is a must-read for entrepreneurs, investors, and innovators worldwide."

– KEVIN DEWALT,
Former EIR at NSF and Founder, SoHelpful.Me

"Sangeet's work provides amazing insight into the success and failure of todays business models, a resource that entrepreneurs and innovators cannot afford to ignore."

– FANG SOONG CHOU,
General Partner, PixVine Capital

"Sangeet's platform analysis covers the topic with a depth that's unique and desperately needed. It's forced me to rethink how I would structure digital business models to leverage the gains from being a platform v product."

– GEORGE BABU,
Founder of Rypple, acquired by Salesforce

"Sangeet's insights reflect his wisdom across not only platform economics but wider digital disruption issues."

– CAT MATSON,
Panel Moderator, G20 Summit Global Cafe,
Chief Digital Officer, City of Brisbane

"Should be part of the curriculum of every business school throughout the world."

– KJETIL OLSEN,
Vice President - International, UpWork

"I've assigned this as mandatory reading for my C-team."

– GARY FORNI,
CEO, TuffWerx and former Global Director of Marketing, Intel

"A must-read for anyone in the 'platform' business.

– AVROM GILBERT,
COO of Seeking Alpha

TABLE OF CONTENTS

Platform Scale (*n*): Business scale powered by the ability to leverage and orchestrate a global connected ecosystem of producers and consumers toward efficient value creation and exchange.

carriers produce

service, capacity,

facilities

value creation

* the governance curates participants on the platform + govern the interactions that ensure

PREFACE

Eating The World

In the late summer of 2011, Marc Andreessen, co-founder of Netscape and the venture capital firm Andreessen-Horowitz, opined in a *Wall Street Journal* op-ed that "software is eating the world." Andreessen was referring to firms like Amazon and Google that displace traditional industry leaders with new business models. Ever since, the phrase has become a rallying cry for every new startup hoping to build the next big thing.

Software has been around for several decades now, but its ability to "eat" the world – to disrupt and reorganize traditional industries – has become most apparent over the last decade and a half. During this period, software has "eaten" media, telecom, professional services, and retail and is increasingly "eating" banking, healthcare, education, energy, transportation – practically everything imaginable.

Yet it isn't software itself that is eating the world. It is the ability of software to orchestrate people and resources, make intelligent decisions, and enable a connected global workforce to create value that is the real force driving disruption today. Uber orchestrates the physical movement of cars and travelers connected to the Internet, with its algorithms making intelligent decisions. Facebook intelligently identifies the content that is most relevant to a particular user, while Reddit organizes users around the world toward an editorial function. Airbnb isn't merely an app or a website; it is a central market-making mechanism that allows the creation of an alternate market for accommodations. Likewise, Amazon has done much to change power structures in the publishing and retail industries. The Nest thermostat demonstrates software's ability to add a brain to physical objects. Nest's thermostats make intelligent decisions, constantly learning from their surroundings and from the collective behavior of other connected thermostats.

Observed closely, the nature of software hasn't changed. However, its ability to organize labor and resources and make intelligent managerial decisions has changed significantly over the last decade and more. The democratization of connectivity and the rise of data-driven decision-making systems are leading to the emergence of a new range of business models. These new software-enabled business models are "eating" the world.

We are no longer in the business of building software. We are increasingly moving into the business of enabling efficient social and business interactions, mediated by software.

The systems mediating these interactions follow the platform business model: a plug-and-play business model that allows connected users and things to plug in and orchestrates them toward efficient interactions. Some of us continue to believe, erroneously, that building superior technology will determine business success in the future. Instead, as this book illustrates, leveraging technology – often commoditized – to orchestrate connected users toward new and efficient value-creating interactions holds the key to the business models of the future.

This book explains the inner workings of these new business models and their ability to scale rapidly. The platform business model is powered by a new set of factors that determine value creation and competitive advantage. These factors are rapidly changing how entire industries operate. Upstarts are disrupting deeply rooted traditional industries by leveraging platforms. The decline of Nokia and Blackberry and the challenge of Uber and Lyft to the taxi industry worldwide bear testament to this shift. Meanwhile, individuals and niche brands are gaining rapid market access by leveraging platforms for global reach. Teenagers are building highly monetizable media empires on YouTube, while many freelancers make a better living on Upwork than they ever did or could at a traditional firm.

My fascination with platforms emerged from a desire to understand business success and failure in the context of emerging digital business models. *Platform Scale* is an outcome of this growing fascination to unpack the inner workings of business models in a networked world.

The ideas in this book aim to illustrate the importance of these models, the forces that power their rapid scale, and the factors that will make them the dominant business models in a networked world. While the effects throughout society are self-evident, the causes are deeply contested and only superficially understood. *Platform Scale* serves to create a lens to analyze these changes and apply them to future platform-scale businesses.

This book is structured into six sections covering various aspects of platform scale. Section one introduces the concept of platform scale – the mechanism by which these new business models scale rapidly – and explains the shift in business thinking needed to manage businesses with platform scale. Section two lays out a stepwise framework for the business design of platform business models. Section three examines the core managerial decisions involved in managing platform scale businesses. Section four explores solutions to a problem specific to getting started with platform scale: the chicken and egg problem. Section five lays out the science of viral growth in a world of networks. Section six takes the counter view on platform scale and identifies conditions where scale can work against platform businesses. Finally, the epilogue proposes a framework for applying these principles in large, traditional, incumbent business organizations.

As the world becomes more connected, the systems that best harness these connected users and objects toward efficient social and business interactions will win. To successfully do so, these systems will need to understand and leverage platform scale.

AN INTRODUCTION TO INTERACTION-FIRST BUSINESSES

ENABLE INTERACTIONS

We are not in the business of building software,
We are in the business of enabling interactions.

1.1

THE REVOLUTION WILL BE PLATFORMED

An emerging family of business models has gained rapid traction over the past decade. Businesses like Uber, Airbnb, and Twitter that were founded less than a decade ago have rapidly grown to gain global adoption and built multi-billion dollar business empires. Over the same period, companies like Google, Facebook, Apple, and Amazon have demonstrated rapid valuation gains, becoming some of the highest-valued companies in the world. These businesses seem to follow a different playbook to achieve scale. The traditional principles of scaling a business no longer seem to apply, something that leaves incumbents confused. This introductory chapter explains how the mechanics that drive business scale are changing and how the new rules of scale create tremendous opportunities for businesses to innovate and transform themselves.

PIPES TO PLATFORMS: A SHIFT IN BUSINESS DESIGN

The Internet restructures the mechanics by which businesses create and deliver value. This has important implications across industries and gives rise to a whole new design for business. We are in the midst of transformative shift in business design as business models move from *pipes* to *platforms*. Pipes have long served as the dominant business design for the industrial economy. Firms build products or craft services, push them out, and sell them to customers. Value is produced upstream and consumed downstream, creating a linear flow of value, much like water flowing through a pipe. In effect, pipes were designed to enable the flow of value in a straight line.

Pipes appear in nearly every area of modern industry. The traditional manufacturing supply chain runs on a pipe model. Every consumer good that finds its way into our hands comes down a pipe that constantly adds value to the product. Our service organizations work like pipes; they aggregate the resources for service provision and deliver those services to clients. Traditional media – television, radio, and newspapers – are pipes pushing content to us. Our education system often works like a pipe where teachers push "knowledge" to receptive students. There is a linear movement of value from a producer to one or many consumers in all examples of pipe businesses.

Early digital business models also followed the pipe design. The first media companies on the Internet worked like pipes. Amazon's e-commerce store started as a pipe. Single-user software-as-a-service runs like a pipe, where the software is created by the business and delivered to the consumer. Even today, many businesses continue to see the Internet as a pipe, one of many delivery channels.

However, three forces today – increasing connectedness, decentralized production, and the rise of artificial intelligence – are driving a whole new design for business. The emerging design of business is that of a platform. Some of the fastest-scaling businesses of the last decade – Google, Facebook, Apple, Uber, and Airbnb – leverage the platform business model. These businesses create a plug-and-play infrastructure that enables producers and consumers of value to connect and interact with each other in a manner that wasn't possible in the past. Facebook provides an infrastructure for users to connect with each other and enables interactions between them. Uber coordinates drivers and passengers toward economic exchanges. Many businesses today act as platforms enabling interactions among their participants.

Platforms allow participants to co-create and exchange value with each other. External developers can extend platform functionality using its APIs and contribute back to the very infrastructure of the business. Platform users who act as producers can create value on the platform for other users to consume.

This changes the very design of the business model. While pipes created and pushed value out to consumers, platforms allow external producers and consumers to exchange value with each other. In this new design of business where the firm is no longer the producer of value, platforms perform two specific roles:

1. They provide an open, participative, plug-and-play infrastructure for producers and consumers to plug into and interact with each other.
2. They curate participants on the platform and govern the social and economic interactions that ensue.

Today, social platforms like Facebook, YouTube, and Twitter allow users to create content and interact with each other. Marketplaces like eBay and Etsy facilitate remote interactions. Some platforms, like Tinder and Airbnb, facilitate in-person interactions. Others, like Uber and Munchery, manage the coordination and movement of real-world resources in real time. All these platforms perform the two key roles mentioned above. They provide an open, plug-and-play infrastructure and govern the interactions that ensue once participants come onboard the platform.

The enablement of interactions between external participants is a core aspect of the platform business model. *Enabling interactions on a plug-and-play infrastructure requires a multi-directional flow of value between different participants.* This is different from pipes, which solely create and push value out to consumers in a linear flow of value. The rise of platforms demonstrates that we are in the midst of a fundamental change in the very design of business.

As we note above, the mechanism of value creation on a platform is very different from that in a pipe business. To understand this better and the implications that this has on business scalability, it is helpful to understand the three key shifts that are brought about by a shift from pipe to platform business models.

PIPES TO PLATFORMS – THREE PRIMARY SHIFTS

The movement from pipes to platforms is manifested through three key shifts in the way that a business works.

a. *Shift in Markets: From Consumers to Producers*
In the traditional view of the market, the consumer was located at the end of the pipe. The pipe would deliver products and services to the consumer. The consumer's relationship with the business was straightforward. The business built what the consumer wanted, and the consumer paid for the good or service, often with money but also with attention and engagement. The functions of production and consumption were clearly demarcated. On platforms, the business does not create the end value; rather, the business only enables value creation. As a result, participants on the platform take on production as well as consumption roles. Sellers on eBay, drivers on Uber, and video creators on YouTube act as producers and create value on the platform. While pipes could focus solely on their consuming users, platforms need to focus on producers as well as consumers. If the platform cannot entice a group of producers to act and engage consistently, it is unlikely to be successful at creating value.

b. Shift in Competitive Advantage: From Resources to Ecosystems
Pipes competed through resource ownership and control. This led to the rise in popularity of the vertically integrated business as well as the idea of scaling through mergers and acquisitions. In a world of pipes, firms compete based on the control and ownership of internal resources and intellectual property.
This traditional view of competitive advantage – that bigger is better and the more you own, the more you win – has broken down. Domination through the possession of vast monetary or physical resources – a hallmark of the pipe world – does not apply to the world of platforms. Airbnb and

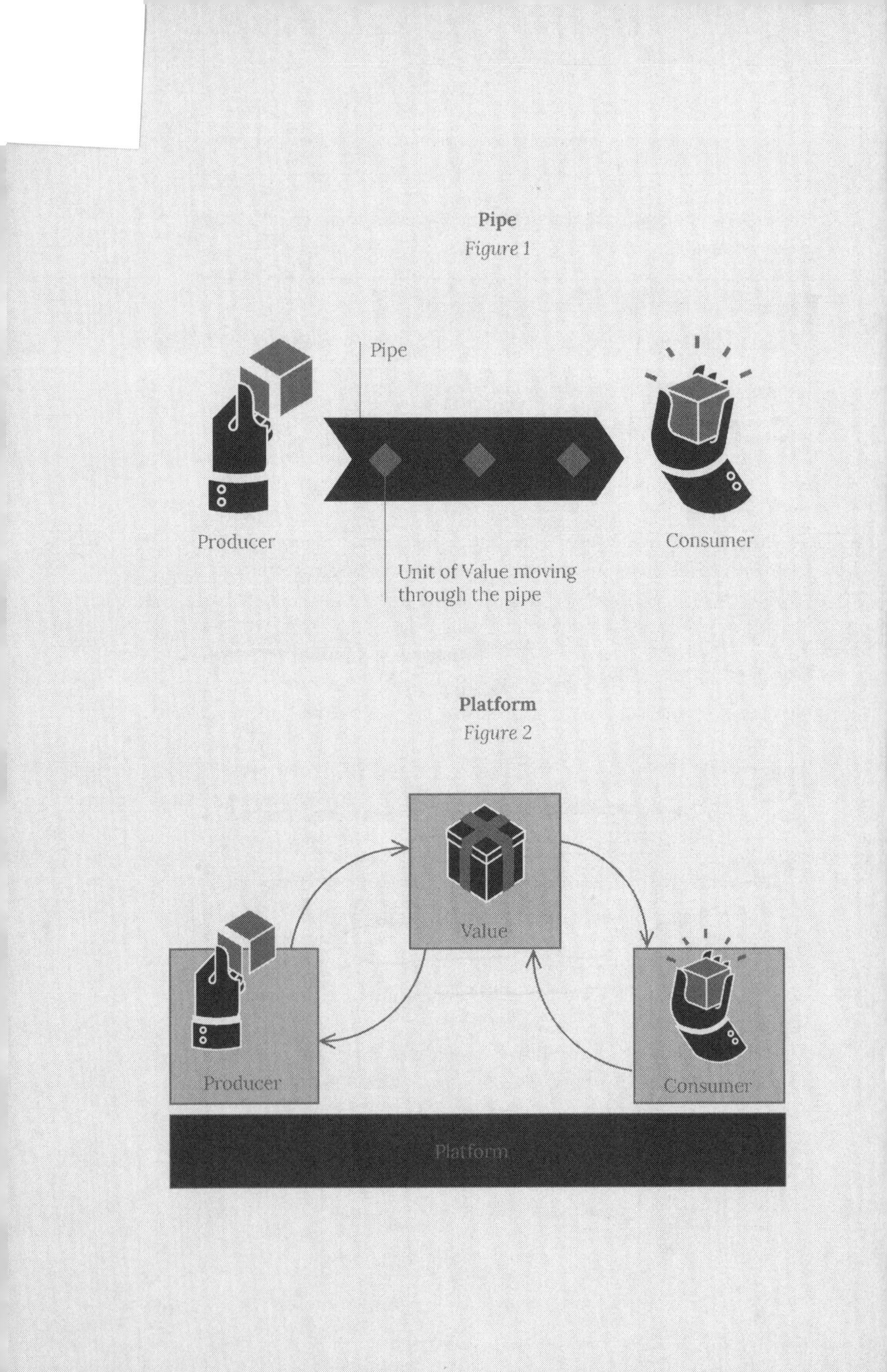

Pipe
Figure 1

Platform
Figure 2

Uber aren't multi-billion dollar businesses because of the employees and resources they control in-house but because of the ecosystem of producers and consumers that they succeed in attracting, curating, and cultivating. Platforms successfully orchestrate value-exchanging interactions in this ecosystem using data about the various ecosystem participants. Ecosystems are the key enablers of value creation on platforms and a new source of competitive advantage. *Platform giants will create massive value, not through their access to physical resources but through leveraging data to orchestrate physical and digital resources across their ecosystem.*

c. Shift in Value Creation: From Processes to Interactions

Media companies have historically relied on the process of sourcing and disseminating media. This has been partially replaced by interactions between users on various social networks, such as Twitter and Facebook. These platforms focus on matching the right content with the right consumer based on certain parameters that the platform determines in real time.

In linear pipes, value creation is centered on an end-to-end process that shifts value down the pipe, from the producer to the consumer. On platforms, the interaction between producers and consumers, facilitated by the platform, determines value creation and exchange.

Lack of resource ownership, as previously mentioned, works in tandem with the movement from processes to ecosystem interactions. On Airbnb, resources are owned by hosts; on Uber, resources are owned by drivers. Platforms enable value creation and exchange by matching the most relevant resources from producers in the ecosystem with the consumers on the platform that need those resources.

Value is no longer created and scaled merely through processes that organize internal labor and resources. Instead, value is created and scaled through interactions that orchestrate users and resources in the ecosystem. While inventory-intensive companies like hotels have focused on maximizing capacity utilization (process focus), emerging platforms like Airbnb and Uber focus on improving the algorithmic matching of supply and demand (interaction focus).

The three shifts detailed above change the mechanics by which firms create value, interact with markets, and build competitive advantage. Eventually, the shift from pipes to platforms changes how a business creates and scales value.

As we move from a world of pipes to one of platforms, the rules of business scale – the guiding principles of how a business grows over time to create greater value – change. To better understand these new models of growth, it is important first to explore the history of business scale in the context of the shift from pipes to platforms.

A BRIEF HISTORY OF SCALE

The ability of a business to scale is determined by its ability to *aggregate* the inputs to business – labor and resources – and coordinate them *efficiently* toward value creation and delivery.

Pipe Scale

In a world of pipes, businesses achieved scale by aggregating labor and resources internally and used value-creating business processes to transform these inputs into functioning products and deliverable services. As these organizations grew larger, they increased process efficiency and managed value creation through command-and-control hierarchies.

In a world of pipes, aggregation also helped firms exchange created value for commercial gain. The pipe world aggregated attention around specific mass media channels. The purchase of goods and services was aggregated at retail stores. Value would flow down the pipe to consumers aggregated at these end points.

The aggregation of value creation inside factories and service organizations, coupled with the aggregation of demand at specific points of sale, serve as a hallmark of pipe design.

Pipe scale (n): *Business scale powered by the ability to coordinate internal labor and resources toward efficient value creation and toward delivery of the created value to an aggregated consumer base.*

The management of pipe scale involves the design and optimization of this linear flow of value from the business to the consumer.

Over the past hundred years, large organizations have mastered the art of building and scaling pipes in this manner. As a result, these companies have consistently succeeded in creating massive business value that has stood the test of time, until now.

Platform Scale

The mechanics of achieving aggregation and efficiency are undergoing a radical transformation. As we move to a world of platforms, we see a more decentralized form of aggregation emerge. Inputs to business – labor and resources – no longer need to be aggregated internally; pervasive connectivity allows the aggregation of labor and resources even when they exist externally. This ability to aggregate resources without the need for physical concentration and centralized control leads to a new design for platform business models.

As the world becomes more connected, we're seeing the rise of **platform scale**. The fastest-scaling businesses today build and manage platforms that allow external producers and consumers to plug in and create and exchange value with each other directly.

Platform scale (n): *Business scale powered by the ability to leverage and orchestrate a global connected ecosystem of producers and consumers toward efficient value creation and exchange.*

The management of platform scale involves the design and optimization of value-exchange interactions between producers and consumers.

Pipe scale leveraged internal processes and resources to create value and defined mass media and retail as the two points at which "big business" would talk to consumers. Platform scale leverages a global ecosystem of interacting producers and consumers who are always on, ever producing and consuming, and collectively have the potential to power transformative business models. As businesses move from pipe scale to platform scale, they will reduce focus on the ownership of resources, which formed the basis of traditional competition, and will instead compete on their ability to facilitate interactions between producers and consumers in their ecosystem. Below, we explore the many manifestations of platform scale that we see around us today.

MANIFESTATIONS OF PLATFORM SCALE

The implications of platform scale aren't restricted to specific industries. Much of the disruption that we see around us today may be accounted for by a universal shift from linear to networked business models, from pipe scale to platform scale. As we note below, this shift is already playing itself out across multiple industries.

a. Social media – Pipes give way to social participation

The vast majority of traditional media – TV, radio, newspapers – work like pipes, pushing content to consumers. YouTube, podcasts, and Medium use the platform model. These platforms constantly encourage producers and consumers of content to interact with each other.

The democratization of content production tools and the shift in media distribution power from journalists to user-producers led to the shift from traditional to social media. As with other shifts to platform scale, emerging media platforms rely less on the ownership of resources (content) and more on their ability to orchestrate interactions between producers and consumers of content.

b. The on-demand economy – Service delivery on platforms

A hotel leverages pipe scale. It invests in acquiring and owning more rooms and optimizing its business to maximize occupancy.

Airbnb solves the same needs, leveraging platform scale. It doesn't own any rooms, nor does it need to create more rooms physically to scale. Airbnb demonstrates that value lies not in owning resources but in managing the exchange of services in the ecosystem. Airbnb scales an ecosystem of service providers, most or all of which are distributed and autonomous.

Unlike hotels, which invest in resource creation, platforms like Airbnb invest in creating better trust mechanisms that identify and differentiate good behavior from poor behavior and minimize interaction risks. This shift in service delivery, from process-driven pipes to interaction-enabling platforms, is visible across several services verticals. Platforms like Uber, Upwork, LendingClub, and Munchery leverage ecosystem interactions to scale while relinquishing resource ownership.

c. The app economy – Leveraging platforms for innovation

Platforms are changing how firms innovate today. Handset manufacturers like Nokia and BlackBerry would build new handsets leveraging pipe control. They would curate and source apps contractually and pre-load them on handsets. Apple and Android changed the rules in much the same way that Airbnb and YouTube did, by using a networked platform to disrupt a controlled pipe. External developers plug in to the platform and create apps on top of it. Consumers moved to platform phones whose functionality could easily be extended using apps created by external developers. *The disruption of Nokia and BlackBerry demonstrates that firms must leverage platforms for innovation.* Today, banks, retailers, and businesses across diverse industries are following the Android playbook to use platforms for innovation.

d. The intelligent Internet of Things

Nest's thermostats constantly create data, as do GE's machines and Nike's shoes. These products aren't merely physical products anymore; they plug in to platforms. These objects feed data into central platforms, and every individual object connected to the platform learns from the community of other objects connected to the platform. *As we move from pipes to platforms, the business model of consumer goods will also move from one centered on product sales to one centered on platform-enabled connected services, where products work as part of an ecosystem.* Understanding platforms is critical to unlocking these new business models.

Nike's FuelBand and connected shoe have transformed it from a company that only sells shoes to a company working on unlocking new engagement and monetization using a data platform. In a similar manner, GE is transforming its business model by digitizing its machines and managing their behavior over platforms.

e. Products and services as platform-powered communities

This new scale isn't merely restricted to large platforms disrupting traditional industries. We see platform scale powering specific single-purpose applications. Instagram aggregates the world's photography while also aggregating the community's attention for commerce. CrossFit isn't merely a service franchise; its rapid growth may well be attributed to the connected community that has emerged around its services. Nest, unlike every other physical thermostat, aggregates data about energy consumption across all thermostats in an area and provides consolidated analytics and insights to utilities. *Today's products and services benefit from platform-powered communities.* A traditional camera, gymnasium, or thermostat would never have employed such business models, but in a constantly connected world, they provide enormous value to all connected parties.

f. 3D printing – The distributed factory

With the rise of the Internet, manufacturing firms have increasingly relied on external innovators for sourcing industrial design. However, there has never been a concerted shift toward distributed manufacturing because the costs of manufacturing at these individual distributed locations would be too high compared to manufacturing centrally. *With the rise of the 3D printer, there are an increasing number of indicators that some forms of manufacturing will move from pipes to platforms, leading to the creation of entirely new markets.* Industrial designers will sell directly to consumers in much the same way that graphic designers currently do on platforms like Threadless and 99Designs. Collaboration models in industrial design and assembly will become networked as well.

g. Crowdsourcing and the Wikipedia of everything

The coordination of production has traditionally required a supply chain of integrated, top-down processes and controls. Wikipedia reconfigured this linear process and allowed it to be managed cyclically on a network. Wikipedia allows anyone to contribute content to a self-policing/semi-autonomous editorial base that works together to create a constantly changing document on the platform. Similarly, Waze, an Israeli traffic prediction app, crowdsources driving information from multiple drivers while simultaneously using algorithms to determine authenticity before distributing traffic conditions to the wider community.

Wikipedia and Waze reimagine the organization of the traditional production function, away from supply chains and onto platforms. They provide an early glimpse into a future where value creation may not need a supply chain, instead being orchestrated via a network of connected users on a platform.

h. Cryptocurrencies

Platform theory helps to explain the workings of cryptocurrencies, like Bitcoin. Decentralized management – through mechanisms like the blockchain – has the potential to change governance structures for the next generation of platforms, much like social feedback tools power curation on many of the current generation of platforms. While we do not explore Bitcoin in detail in this book, the principles laid out apply equally well to understanding all emerging platforms that the book may not explicitly cover.

PLATFORM SCALE IMPERATIVE

At their core, platforms enable a plug-and-play business model. Other businesses can easily connect their business with the platform, build products and services on top of it, and co-create value. Platforms primarily benefit not from internal production but from a wider source of open co-creation and open market interactions. This ability to drive interactions through a "plug-and-play" infrastructure is a defining characteristic of platform scale.

We are still in the early innings of exploring the platforms made possible by new forms of aggregation and efficiency. There may be numerous ways in which the old conflicts with the new. While additional rules and regulations that ensure safety and efficiency in the new model are necessary, they are likely only to regulate and channel the transformation, not stop it from happening.

As the world becomes more connected, the platforms that harness these connections and the ensuing interactions into effective business models will win.

1.2

THE PLATFORM MANIFESTO

A Shift In Thinking For An Age Of Platforms

As the design of business transitions from pipes to platforms, we realize that business principles that applied in a world of pipes no longer apply in a world of platforms. The mechanisms by which value creation is achieved through aggregation change in a world of platforms. Value creation still requires the aggregation of resources and labor, but the design and methods of achieving this aggregation change. As a consequence, business principles that governed decision-making in a world of pipes may no longer apply in a world of platforms.

The platform manifesto, presented in this chapter, lays out the shift in mindset needed to manage this new world. The manifesto explains the shift in business principles while acknowledging that value creation and delivery are still centered on a business's ability to aggregate.

THE ECOSYSTEM IS THE NEW WAREHOUSE

Businesses have traditionally relied on internal labor and owned resources to scale value creation. As the world becomes more networked, businesses can leverage a new source of scale: *an external ecosystem of users and partners connected to the business over the Internet.*

Amazon started out as a traditional online store but aggregated additional supply-side scalability as it moved toward an online marketplace model. This marketplace model leveraged warehouses and inventory, distributed across an ecosystem of partner merchants, to serve consumers. More recently, many e-commerce shops in India have also realized the need to shift from stores to marketplaces, from pipes to platforms. The ecosystem stores the inventory while the platform manages the matching of this distributed inventory with demand. The platform may even manage or orchestrate the physical delivery of goods from the warehouses, but it doesn't own significant portions of the inventory that it sells. When Amazon enabled the liquidation of inventory owned by its partner merchants, it started leveraging the ecosystem as a distributed warehouse.

Hotels own inventory, but Airbnb works as a virtual accommodation provider, leveraging rooms in its ecosystem. This enables Airbnb to expand fast and operate without fixed costs. Traditionally, media houses have prided themselves on owning content or sourcing the best content contractually. YouTube and Soundcloud have unlocked an entire ecosystem of content creators who participate on the platform. These thriving ecosystems of creators enable the platforms to compete credibly with traditional media houses for consumer attention.

The evolution of online news and publishing is no different. Huffington Post started out with a traditional media model, creating most of the content in-house, but it scaled by building out an ecosystem of contributing writers. Later, Forbes, WIRED, and a host of other traditional media companies took a similar path. *The ecosystem-based view of value creation is in stark contrast to the traditional resource-based view of value creation, where control of resources was an important source of competitive advantage.*

THE ECOSYSTEM IS ALSO THE NEW SUPPLY CHAIN

Resources and labor have traditionally been organized around internal processes to power value creation. Pipes organized processes as supply chains that would move value from the producer to the consumer. With the rise of platforms, the ecosystem is the new supply chain.

The costs of coordinating labor and resources toward value creation are declining rapidly as new coordination tools enable a distributed ecosystem to work together to create value. We saw this first in the creation of open-source software, where an external ecosystem of contributors worked together to improve the software as a large, globally distributed team. Wikipedia brought this ethos to publishing and media by organizing a distributed network of content creators and content editors, toward the common goal of creating credible and citation-rich content.

Viki is a Singapore-based company that leverages an ecosystem for a task that has normally been performed using internal processes or contractual arrangements. Viki sources soap operas and movies in Asian languages and orchestrates a global ecosystem of translators to create subtitles for the content. Viki's software powers the subtitle creation, editing, and confirmation process and is reminiscent of the open-source tools used by Wikipedia. The process of adding subtitles has historically relied upon internal management but is now achieved by orchestrating a complex ecosystem of creators and editors via a software platform.

Quirky, A New York based "invention company," is trying to re-imagine manufacturing on an open platform. The entire manufacturing supply chain, from design to production, packaging to distribution, is managed via a platform across a multitude of different parties.

As noted in Chapter 1 of this section, we've always used aggregation to enable the coordination of value-creating processes. However, the precipitous drop in the costs of coordination and distributed production enables platforms to achieve aggregation across many types of activities more effectively and efficiently than a command and control hierarchy ever could.

THE NETWORK EFFECT IS THE NEW DRIVER FOR SCALE

The notion of the ecosystem as the new source of supply and value creation demonstrates an important shift in a networked world. Scale is no longer achieved purely through accumulation of labor and resources within a business or through non-scalable contractual relationships outside the business. Instead, *scale is achieved by leveraging interactions in the ecosystem.* A new breed of startups is building large empires with minimum investments, leveraging value created and exchanged in the ecosystem.

Platform businesses scale through network effects. Network effects make the platform more valuable as more value is created and exchanged by the users of the platform. This, in turn, attracts even more users, scaling the value creation further. Greater value creation attracts greater value consumption, and vice versa. The network effect creates positive feedback that enables systems to scale faster as they grow. These concepts are explored in detail in subsequent chapters in this section.

DATA IS THE NEW DOLLAR

In the quest to maximize shareholder value, organizations have traditionally been optimized to absorb revenue. Sales professionals are measured and incentivized based on the revenue they help the organization absorb. *In the quest to transform into platforms, organizations must shift from a culture of dollar absorption to a culture of data absorption.* Business units should be measured not just in terms of dollars absorbed but also in terms of monetizable data absorbed. As companies like LinkedIn demonstrate, more data absorbed from users yield more ways of making money. LinkedIn absorbs more data from its users than Monster ever did, and this helped it create a larger job market than Monster's.

Ecosystem interactions are orchestrated using data. Supply is matched with demand using data. Platform users are served in a highly personalized manner by leveraging data. Toyota, GM, and Ford are transforming themselves to become data-acquiring companies, as they move toward re-imagining cars as platforms. Their cars constantly stream data about usage, which helps these brands better predict after-sales service. Data captured from cars also help insurance companies personalize their premiums better.

COMMUNITY MANAGEMENT IS THE NEW HUMAN RESOURCES MANAGEMENT

Community management is often viewed as an extension of marketing. If a linear world demanded marketing and customer relationships to manage and influence an audience, popular thinking would have us believe that a networked, participatory world should shift the focus of marketing to community management. But a community isn't simply a more participative audience. A *community must be scaled in a platform business, in much the same way that a workforce of employees is scaled within an organization.* Community management requires structuring and managing incentives for participants, enabling the learning and development of producers, and creating a host of other support infrastructure that the human resources department would traditionally provide to an organization internally. Managing community incentives and governance is as important as managing internal employee conduct and compliance.

The first non-founding employee at Instagram was neither an engineer nor a designer, nor even a marketer. The Instagram founders understood the importance of managing ecosystems and communities. Employee #1, Josh Riedel, was a community manager, tasked solely with managing the growing community of content creators on Instagram.

Community management is all the more important when one considers the fact that service marketplaces, like Airbnb, compete with traditional service providers, like hotels. Traditional service providers invest heavily in training and managing incentives for their staff. To provide a service quality at par with traditional service providers, today's service marketplaces must ensure that they invest in community management and development, much the same way that hotels invest in employee training. Most on-demand labor platforms today must redesign community management as a human resources management function for an age of open platforms.

LIQUIDITY MANAGEMENT IS THE NEW INVENTORY CONTROL

Inventory-intensive businesses constantly monitor metrics like inventory turnover. They balance the risks of carrying idle inventory with the goal of offering a minimum guarantee to satisfy demand. In an ideal business, supply should consistently match demand. Both idle supply and unfulfilled demand are undesirable scenarios.

Platforms do not hold inventory, but they must work similarly toward avoiding idle supply and unfulfilled demand. Producers will abandon the platform in the absence of relevant demand. Consumers searching for items become discouraged unless they are matched with relevant supply. Matching supply and demand isn't merely an exercise in efficiency; it is the only way that a platform can hold the two sides together.

Platforms must focus on liquidity management to ensure that both producers and consumers find value in using the platform. High liquidity ensures that the demand on the platform is reliably served with supply and that the supply created on the platform is liquidated with demand efficiently. A platform must ensure that there is enough supply available to meet the demand on the platform. *At all points in its life cycle, the platform must ensure that there is enough overlap between supply and demand to ensure that demand doesn't go unfulfilled.*

Platforms achieve this through a range of mechanisms. In its initial days, Facebook focused on creating a social network within closed college campuses because of the high overlap of users who already knew each other within a campus. Facebook expanded by creating closed but highly liquid networks of users. Despite all its criticism, Uber's surge pricing is the platform's effort at real-time liquidity management. As demand outstrips supply, the ride pricing changes to attract more drivers onto the road. This, in turn, increases supply. Surge pricing is an example of how liquidity management works in today's world. Uber, though, has much to learn about communicating the mechanics of surge pricing effectively to consumers, who often view it as a price-gouging tactic.

CURATION AND REPUTATION ARE THE NEW QUALITY CONTROL

Platforms cannot control quality as pipes did. Pipes relied on hierarchical control and strict quality control mechanisms. Gatekeepers would determine what would be accepted and what would be rejected. When platforms relinquish control to the ecosystem, they lose control of the value-creation process. A *world of platforms needs new mechanisms for quality control that separate the good from the bad while encouraging active participation by an ecosystem of producers.* The rigidity of the traditional quality control process often discourages external producers from participating.

The importance of quality control on an open-access system cannot be overstated. Open systems encourage unrestricted production, leading to abundance, which can lead to a dip in quality and higher search efforts for consumers. Hence, quality control is critical to separate the best from the rest and serve consumers the most relevant content. Some platforms require initial screening of producers to ensure a minimum quality threshold; for example, Uber conducts background checks on drivers. Many platforms determine producers' (or consumers') reputation and quality by aggregating social signals from the community. When hosts and guests rate each other on Airbnb, both sides create signals of quality. On Yelp, consumers rate restaurants, and those that are rated the highest end up getting more business. Amazon has replaced the traditional editorial gatekeeping with a mix of screening and social curation. The platform prevents books from being hosted unless they fulfill certain criteria. However, the books that are hosted are exposed to the market based on social signals (ratings) and customer decisions (purchases). Voting mechanisms on YouTube and Quora work similarly. Quality is controlled through a combination of editorial and social inputs, aggregated by algorithms.

USER JOURNEYS ARE THE NEW SALES FUNNELS

In a linear world, customers are led through sales funnels. Frameworks representing the customer purchase path – such as the AARRR (acquisition-activation-retention-revenue-referral) framework that tracks usage metrics – are often designed as funnels.

In a networked world, purchase paths are no longer linear. Instead, users interact with a business across multiple experiences and channels before making a purchase. Even industries like retail, which have lived by the funnel and tracked footfalls religiously, are moving to measure engagement across multiple touch points.

In a world of multi-device, multi-channel journeys, the browse and buy experiences are decoupled. It is important to ensure that actions taken by users at various points on this journey are leveraged to personalize their experience at every other point. Businesses must invest in integrating these user touch points together. A platform serves as an integration layer that connects multiple touch points with the user.

Every business that wants to benefit from multi-channel integration and serve the user across this journey must integrate its touch points with users using a platform. Once integrated, there should be a continuous flow of data across these touch-points to deliver highly personalized experiences. The platform acts as a sink that constantly absorbs data from the user and consequently delivers highly personalized experiences. Connectivity by data serves as the binding agent between the users' immediate experience and their journey with the business.

DISTRIBUTION IS THE NEW DESTINATION

Pipes have always worked by defining destinations. In a world of pipes, consumers would meet businesses at specific destinations. Consumers had to visit a retail outlet to purchase a product or sit in front of a television to consume an advertising message. However, in an age of always-on connectivity, users are always connected to businesses, sometimes on multiple channels simultaneously. Viewers use additional screens while watching television.

In such a world, businesses must stop thinking in terms of destinations and start thinking in terms of distribution. The business should no longer focus simply on drawing users to a destination. Instead, *a business should work on identifying new ways to distribute its experience into the context of the user.*

BEHAVIOR DESIGN IS THE NEW LOYALTY PROGRAM

In a world of pipes, businesses achieved customer retention and stickiness through a combination of loyalty programs and lock-ins. Lock-ins lured customers into long-term relationships with the business that were rarely beneficial for customers. In a world of open-access platforms, we move from lock-ins to opt-ins. Platforms are self-serve systems and can ill-afford to lock users in. *To ensure that producers and consumers participate regularly and often, platforms must invest in behavior design.* By creating a new habit, Facebook, Instagram, and Pinterest ensure that users stick around of their own accord. To create new behaviors, the platform should constantly reward desirable actions and discourage undesirable ones. Today's leading platforms – Pinterest, Airbnb, Uber, Twitter – created new behaviors that had never existed in the past.

In addition to behavior design, network effects also create stickiness. As the value of the platform increases with greater participation, consumers and producers are organically incentivized to stay engaged on the platform because the platform provides increasing amounts of value to both parties.

DATA SCIENCE IS THE NEW BUSINESS PROCESS OPTIMIZATION

Pipes achieve scale by improving the repeatability and efficiency of value-creation processes. The world of pipes required process engineering and optimization. Process engineers and managers helped improve internal processes and make them more efficient.

In a platformed world, value is created in interactions between users, powered by data. *Data science improves the platform's ability to orchestrate interactions in the ecosystem.* As value creation moves from organizational processes to ecosystem interactions, the focus of efficiency shifts from the enhancement of controlled processes to the improvement of the platform's ability to orchestrate interactions in the ecosystem.

SOCIAL FEEDBACK IS THE NEW SALES COMMISSION

In a world of pipes, employees are incentivized to help the business achieve its goals. Organizations design inorganic incentives like sales commissions and employee bonuses to encourage employees toward specific actions. In a world of platforms, where users start performing the roles traditionally performed by employees, new types of incentives must be architected. In addition to traditional inorganic incentives, *social feedback is a key source of user incentivization on platforms.* Producers on a platform may participate more often when explicit social feedback from consumers is communicated back to them. Readers share Buzzfeed and Upworthy articles because of the social feedback that results from such an action. Instagram users share their creations for social feedback. All these actions are designed to help the platform achieve its goals.

ALGORITHMS ARE THE NEW DECISION-MAKERS

Algorithms are increasingly taking over managerial functions of resource allocation and decision-making. *On platforms, algorithms are the arbiters of both resource allocation and reputation assignment.* For example, Uber's algorithms dispatch vehicles to travelers while maintaining a driver/passenger rating system. A traditional taxi service would have leveraged a layer of middle managers to perform a similar function. *Algorithms also replace traditional gatekeepers.* In the traditional publishing industry, an editor would have made decisions on which books were taken to market. In a traditional funding model, a credit scoring agent would have made a decision on what should be funded. On Amazon or Kickstarter, the book that should go to market or the project that should be funded is increasingly decided by algorithms that leverage a complex set of social inputs. Self-policing communities and the algorithms that nudge them along are the new decision-makers.

REAL-TIME CUSTOMIZATION IS THE NEW MARKET RESEARCH

The Facebook newsfeed is a highly customized gossip column that rearranges itself in real time based on user preferences and actions. Pipe businesses have traditionally been slow to respond to consumer demand, but in a world where data flows constantly from users to business, we are increasingly seeing the real-time personalization of experiences. *Platforms rely on real-time customization to serve the most relevant content from producers to interested consumers.* Producers also benefit from real-time customization as the platform gradually opens or closes access for producers based on their past actions and performance on the platform.

Conversely, excessive customization may also pose a challenge by constantly showing more of what a user has enjoyed in the past to the detriment of the overall experience. Platforms must ensure that they balance relevance with serendipity.

PLUG-AND-PLAY IS THE NEW BUSINESS DEVELOPMENT

In the world of pipes, business development was based on contractual integration. All business eventually required the integration of information and resource flows, but this was achieved through intensive integration operations. In the world of platforms, APIs, and self-serve interfaces, the very nature of business development has fundamentally changed. Increasingly, APIs *are enabling a new form of business development.* Prospective partners can plug and play, obviating the need for complex integration and, in some cases, complex contractual agreements. The API is the contract and the integration interface. Depending on how open the business is, anyone can use its APIs and create value for the business.

Many technology companies prioritize acquisition targets based on how well they are integrated with their existing API. Large companies encourage startups to participate in their developer partner networks and often acquire the most successful startups for those networks. Acquiring a company that has already built on one's API reduces the cost of post-acquisition integration.

The iPhone's app store introduced business development on steroids. Nokia, BlackBerry, and traditional carriers sourced their apps contractually, whereas the iPhone created an open platform, allowing anyone to create apps for it. Increasingly, many industries that have traditionally been considered non-tech, including retail, transportation, and consumer goods, are opening up APIs to encourage innovation by coalescing an external ecosystem of developer-partners.

THE INVISIBLE HAND IS THE NEW IRON FIST

The business processes that enabled pipe scale have historically been managed via hierarchies. As value creation in a platformed world moves to networks, we need a new form of management and culture, both inside and outside the organization. Hierarchies are based on rules and compliance, which require a unidirectional flow of information from the top down. This iron fist is giving way to the invisible hand. This is most evident in the rise of on-demand labor platforms where the invisible hand of algorithms and APIs dispatches supply to meet demand. *The invisible hand – typically taking the form of algorithmic decisions – nudges producers to continue creating value on the platform.* In a networked age, we are moving from a world of command and control to a self-serve world where user participation is encouraged through an invisible hand powered by data, APIs, and algorithms.

PLATFORM SCALE IMPERATIVE

A world of pipes creates value through linear processes managed through command-and-control mechanisms, contractual integration, and internal labor and resource allocation. Platforms move away from closed, controlled processes to open, enabled interactions. The management of platforms must be designed around the goal of enabling interactions between producers and consumers in a platform's ecosystem. The platform manifesto lays out the changes in business principles that are occurring as we move from a world of managing processes to a world of enabling interactions on plug-and-play platforms.

The Platform Manifesto

1. *The ecosystem is the new warehouse*

2. *The ecosystem is also the new supply chain*

3. *The network effect is the new driver for scale*

4. *Data is the new dollar*

5. *Community management is the new human resources management*

6. *Liquidity management is the new inventory control*

7. *Curation and reputation are the new quality control*

8. *User journeys are the new sales funnels*

9. *Distribution is the new destination*

10. *Behavior design is the new loyalty program*

11. *Data science is the new business process optimization*

12. *Social feedback is the new sales commission*

13. *Algorithms are the new decision makers*

14. *Real-time customization is the new market research*

15. *Plug-and-play is the new business development*

16. *The invisible hand is the new iron fist*

1.3

THE RISE OF THE INTERACTION-FIRST BUSINESS

A Fundamental Redesign Of Business Logic

Platforms compete with each other on the basis of their ability to enable interactions sustainably. Platforms do not compete merely on the strength of better features or larger user bases. They build sustainable businesses when producers and consumers participate regularly in interactions. Uber repeatedly enables interactions between drivers and travelers, resulting in rides being exchanged for money. Facebook and Twitter repeatedly enable interactions between content creators and content consumers. Amazon scales by enabling economic interactions amongst its ecosystem of merchants and buyers.

The importance of understanding the platform business, as an *enabler* of interactions, cannot be overstated. In a connected world, businesses will increasingly focus on enabling interactions between users.

The goal of the platform is to enable these interactions between producers and consumers - repeatedly and efficiently.

This chapter explains how interaction-first thinking will increasingly drive business design and lays a foundation for the key ideas explored throughout the book.

UNDERSTANDING INTERACTIONS

An interaction involves an exchange of value for some form of social or economic currency. A producer of value may create and deliver value to a consumer who is willing to offer the relevant social or economic currency in exchange.

Producers and Consumers

Every interaction involves two participating roles.

The **producer** creates supply or responds to demand on the platform. The video creator is a producer on YouTube. A freelancer is a producer on Upwork. The **consumer** generates demand or consumes supply on the platform. The video viewer on YouTube and the client requesting work on Upwork perform the consumer roles on each platform, respectively.

These terms refer to *roles*, not user segments. On eBay, the same user may perform the buyer and seller roles in different interactions. Every user tweeting on Twitter acts as a producer, while the same user performs the consumption role while reading a tweet stream.

Understanding the producer and consumer roles separately informs the design of incentives and the creation of tools that encourage active participation on the platform for the respective roles.

Value and currency

The concepts of value and currency apply to all social and economic interactions. Producers create value in the form of goods or services. The exchange of value may involve the exchange of physical goods (e.g., eBay and Etsy), virtual goods (e.g., Medium, YouTube, and Facebook), standardized services (e.g., Uber and Airbnb), non-standardized services (e.g., TaskRabbit and Upwork), or data (e.g., Waze and Nest).

Consumers may offer economic currencies like money or some other

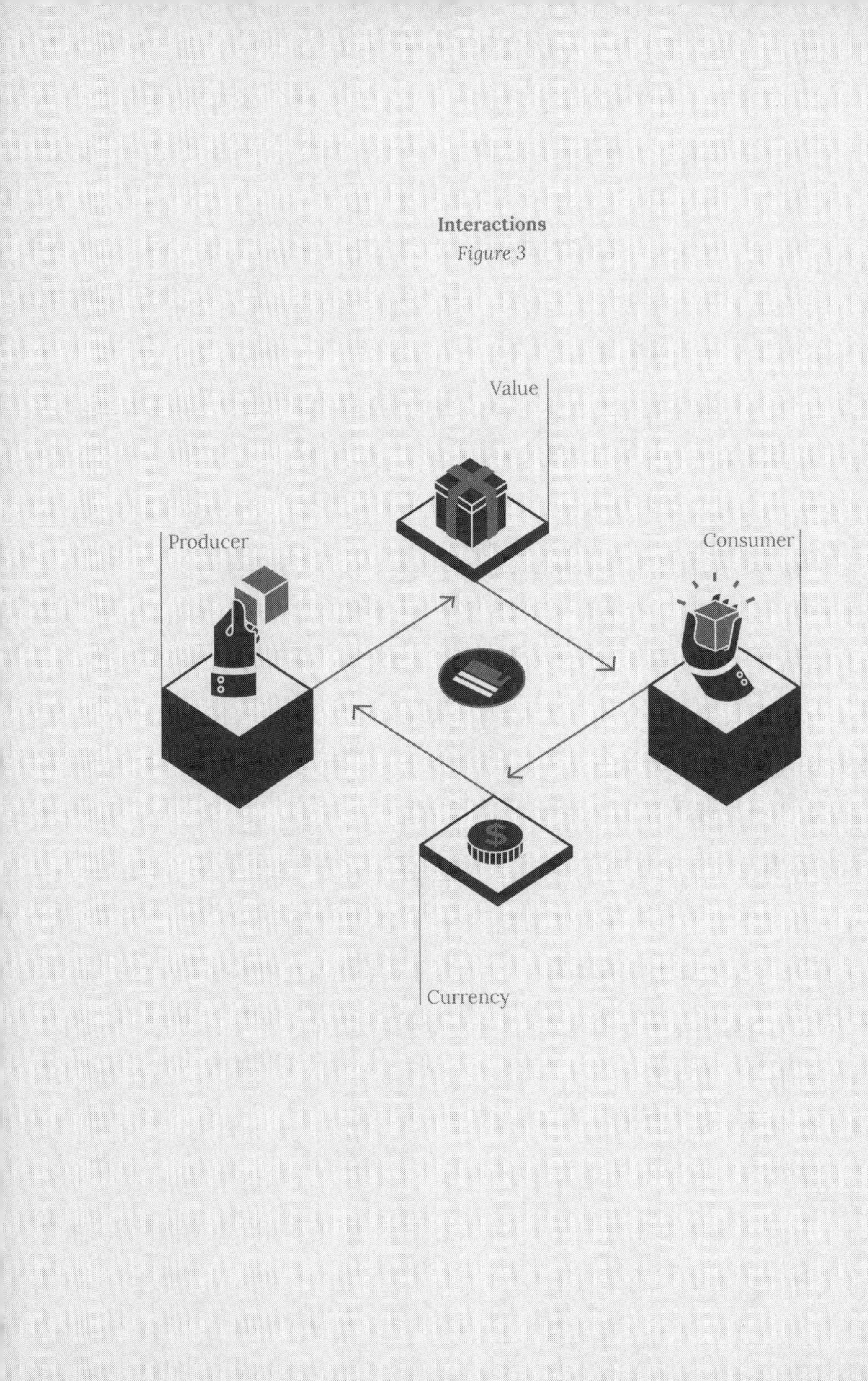

Interactions
Figure 3

tradable item in exchange. In social interactions, consumers may offer social currencies like attention, reputation, influence, or goodwill.

The platform as an enabler of interactions

Platforms enable interactions when they enable the exchange of value and currency between producers and consumers.

A platform offers an underlying infrastructure on top of which producers may create value. Google's Android platform allows app developers to build apps on top of it. Medium allows the creation of value in the form of articles. Airbnb allows anyone with a spare home to publicize its availability. Uber allows drivers to signal that they are available to offer a ride. Every platform allows producers to create and/or signal value in a much more efficient manner than they would have in the past. In this manner, platforms aggregate supply.

Platforms also aggregate demand and allow consumers to "pay" for value through some form of currency. This may involve the exchange of money in some cases. In others, the platform works on communicating the exchange of social currency in one or more forms back to the producer. Medium helps writers gain exposure to an audience, while Yelp helps restaurants build a reputation. Twitter allows users to build a following and gain influence, while Facebook enables users to connect and strengthen relationships with every status update or shared content. These platforms transfer social currency from consumers to producers, which encourages producers to participate further and create value repeatedly.

THE DESIGN OF PLATFORMS AS INTERACTION ENGINES

The interaction-first view posits that the interaction between producers and consumers is the core mechanism of value creation and exchange on platforms.

Linear pipe businesses are built around a core value-creation process. These businesses scale by increasing the repeatability and efficiency of this value-creation and delivery process. Pipes focus on optimizing process flow.

In contrast, platforms must focus on optimizing the flow of value and currency in the ecosystem of producers and consumers. Platforms are interaction engines that scale when they optimize the interaction flow. A platform's goal is to maximize the repeatability and efficiency of the core interaction. Implementing strategic choices that improve a platform's ability to enable interactions is an imperative priority. Every choice that reduces its ability to enable the core interaction must be avoided.

The interaction-first view has important implications for the design and management of platforms. Below, we explore seven specific principles that guide the design of interaction-first businesses.

1. Plug-and-play business design

Platforms must create a plug-and-play infrastructure to encourage interactions. Producers and consumers should be able to plug in to the infrastructure and interact with each other.

Platforms should be built to encourage open participation. Removing barriers to production and consumption helps the platform to scale interactions. To enable open participation, platforms need to remove friction in access and usage. Incentives must be architected into the platform to attract producers and consumers repeatedly. Platforms must also invest in behavior design to create new habits that repeatedly bring producers and consumers back to the platform.

However, open participation leads to the creation of noise. This makes the platform ineffective at enabling interactions. First, open participation may encourage undesirable behaviors by allowing access to all kinds of users. Hence, platforms must architect some form of access control, especially for producers who create value on the platform. Second, open participation leads to an abundance of content, which could increase the efforts required by consumers to find the most relevant items. Hence, platforms need to implement and strengthen consumption filters that determine which items should be served to which consumers. *The design of access control and consumption filters helps with the governance of interactions.*

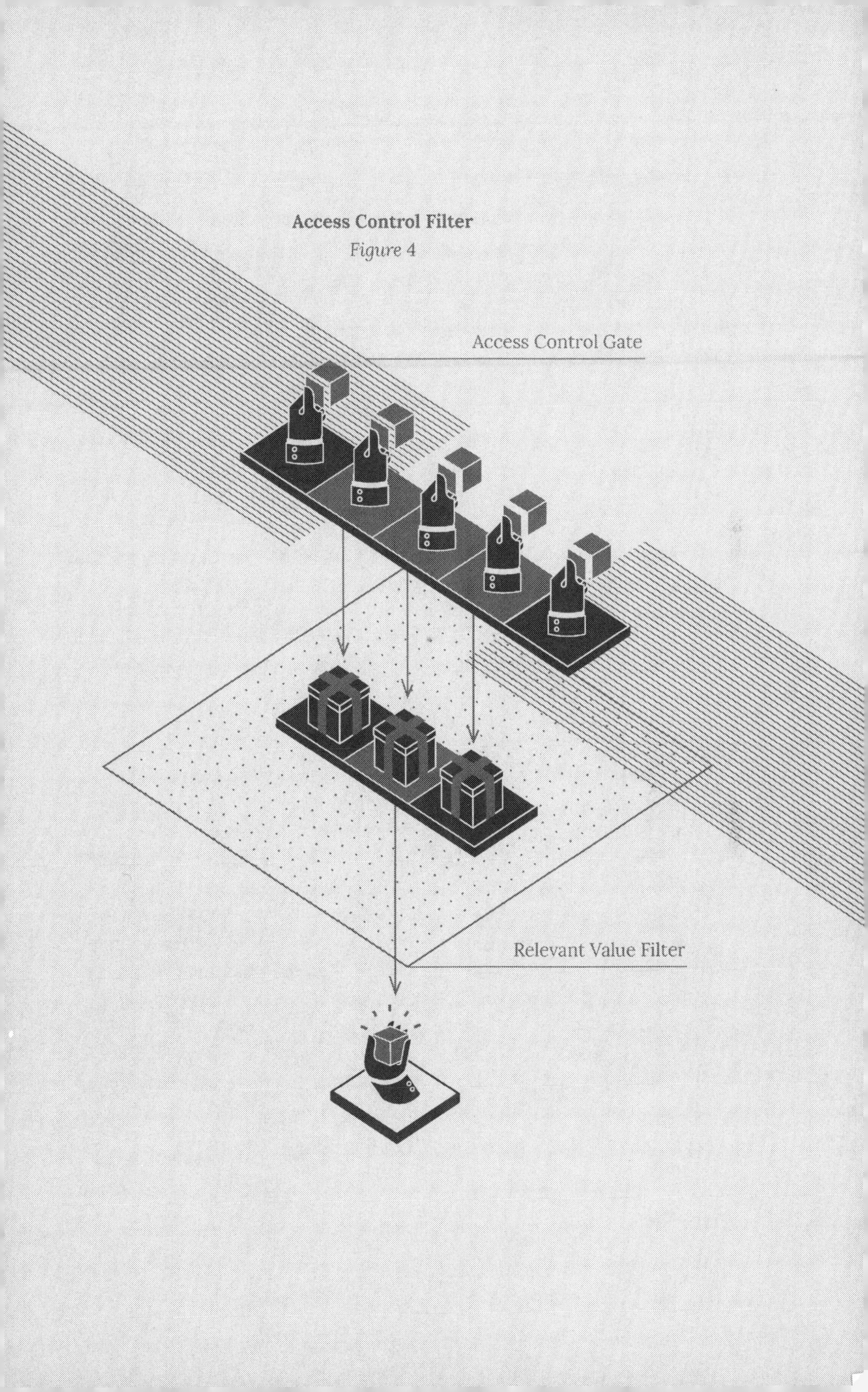

Access Control Filter

Figure 4

The two conflicting priorities of open participation and governance introduce unique challenges for a platform business. Platforms must be carefully architected. Building a plug-and-play business model that orchestrates an external ecosystem requires careful design considerations. This cannot be achieved through tactical tricks and hacks.

2. *Balancing value creation for both producers and consumers*
Pipe businesses can scale well by optimizing the experience for their customers or users. Focusing on the user or customer at the end of the pipe helps to increase the repeatability and efficiency of the value-creation process and successfully scales a pipe. In contrast, platforms must focus on value creation for *both* producers and consumers. Optimizing the experience for a producer may lead to a poor experience for a consumer. For instance, removing barriers to production may help producers but lead to the creation of noise for consumers. In the same way, optimizing the experience of consumers may discourage producers. Consumers in a marketplace may benefit from competitive bidding among producers, but producers may not find it beneficial.

3. *Strategic choice of "free"*
On the Internet, "free" is often the refuge of those who haven't figured out their revenue model. But "free" is not a strategy by itself; it can only be part of a larger strategy that involves some form of monetization made possible by offering some value for free. For example, brands have always provided free samples to encourage trial before purchase.
Most large platforms today – Facebook, Google, Twitter, WhatsApp – started out free, and many remain free. This often serves as license for emerging startups to claim that their choice of "free" offerings is strategic. On platforms, "free" is strategic only if it follows at least one of the following two principles:

a. *It increases the repeatability of interactions.* If the provision of free services to consumers, producers, or both increases the repeatability of interactions, the choice of "free" is strategic.
b. *It involves the capture of monetizable data.* Facebook and Google offer

free services but capture monetizable data: user interests and search keywords, respectively. Advertisements are served in real-time based on this captured data. Platforms that offer services for free must capture data and user engagement in a manner that can be monetized. On most platforms, at least one role is subsidized to participate on the platform. Producer participation may be subsidized, and producers may get free access to the production tools to encourage value creation on the platform. Likewise, consumers may be allowed free access to the platform. This helps the platform build a base of consumers that subsequently attracts producers onto the platform. A systems view is required to balance subsidies and prices to ensure that interactions ensue.

4. *Pull, facilitate, and match*

Pipes focus on enabling repeatable processes. Platforms focus on enabling repeatable interactions. Pipe businesses build a business engine that works on the following three-pronged model:

a. *Source.* The pipe sources inputs into the business.
b. *Assemble.* The pipe leverages value-creating processes to create value from inputs.
c. *Deliver.* The pipe delivers value to the user and/or customer.

These three activities - source, assemble, and deliver - are increasingly made more efficient, leading to higher repeatability of the core process. Platform businesses do not focus on any of these activities. With the goal of enabling interactions, platform businesses have three rather different priorities:

a. *Pull.* The platform must pull producers and consumers to participate on the platform.
b. *Facilitate.* It must facilitate interactions between them.
c. *Match.* It must match demand with supply to ensure that the right producers and consumers interact with each other.

The platform achieves this by:

1. Architecting incentives that repeatedly pull these participants to the platform.

Pull, Facilitate, Match

Figure 5

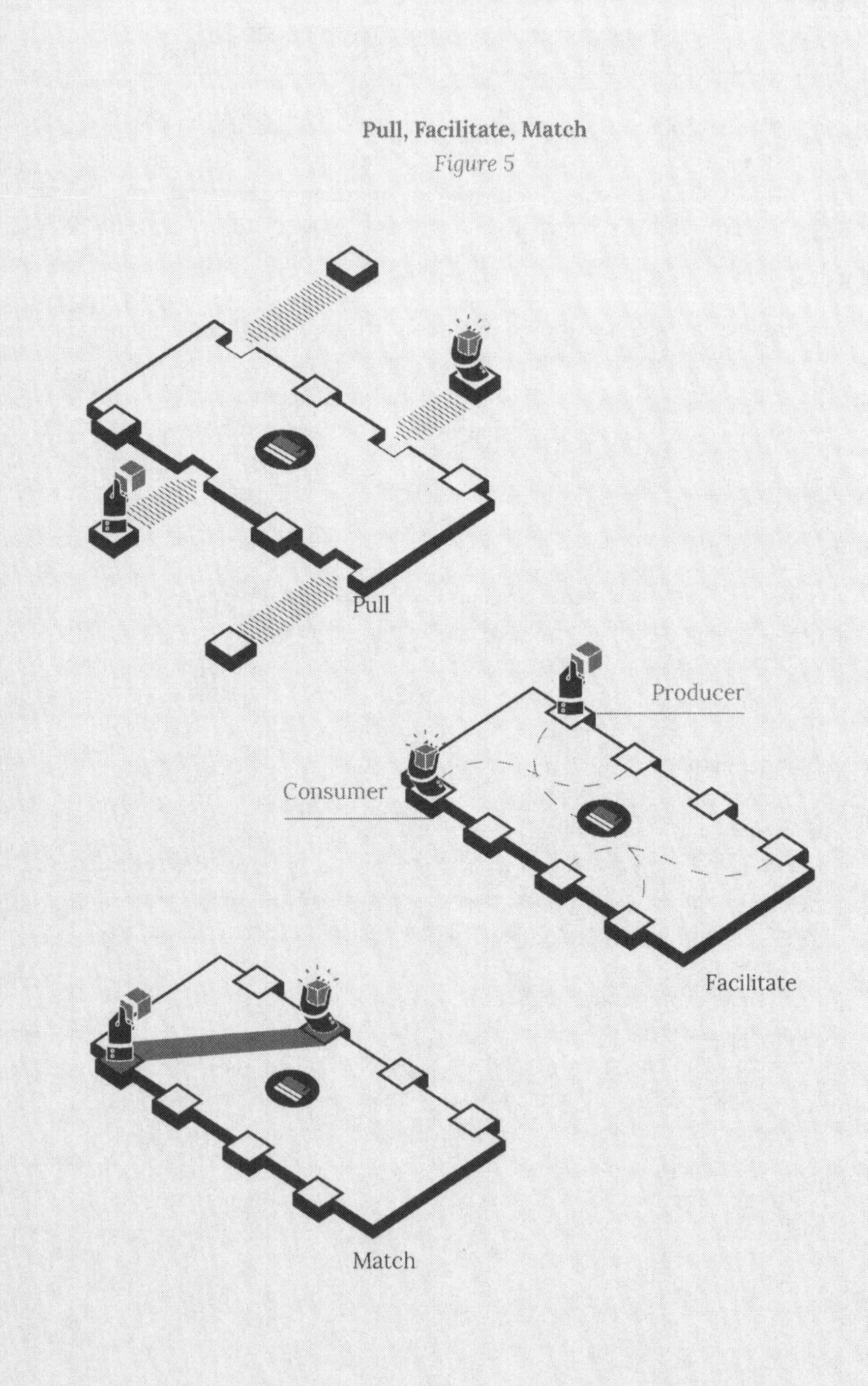

2. Providing a central infrastructure that facilitates the creation and exchange of value.
3. Matching participants with each other and with content/goods/services created on the platform.

5. *Layering on new interactions*
Platforms scale by adding more interactions and layering on edge interactions around a core interaction. All platforms are centered on a core interaction that enables every other (edge) interaction. LinkedIn, for example, has multiple interactions, such as recruiters serving jobs to candidates and thought leaders publishing posts for readers. However, the central purpose of LinkedIn continues to be centered on enabling professionals to connect with each other. LinkedIn's failure to power this core interaction would lead to the failure of all edge interactions that the platform enables.

6. *Enabling end-to-end interactions*
Platforms create efficiencies in interactions by aggregating demand and supply and ensuring that the most relevant users are matched with each other. Most platforms create significant value by performing this matching function.
Increasingly, platforms are expanding beyond the matching function to enable the end-to-end interaction. Uber doesn't merely match the driver to the passenger. It also tracks the duration of the ride and uses that information to charge the passenger accurately and transfer the money back to the driver. Finally, it allows the two sides to rate each other – the exchange of social currencies – to determine signals of quality that it can leverage in subsequent interactions. Efficiencies created in the interaction extend beyond the matching of supply and demand.

7. *Creation of persistent value beyond the interaction*
On many platforms, interactions also enable the creation of lasting and persistent value beyond the single exchange. Airbnb hosts and guests rate and review each other during every interaction, creating *reputation* that enables future transactions. Twitter followers may choose a new account

to follow based on a tweet they read, thereby building that particular account's *influence*. Reddit enables the development of crowd opinion on news articles by aggregating reader inputs and creating *authority* and *visibility* for articles. TripAdvisor brings reviewers and travelers reading reviews together to determine the *reputation* and *quality* of an establishment. In all these examples, value created during individual interactions persists to create cumulative value. This is explored in further detail in subsequent sections.

PLATFORM SCALE IMPERATIVE

A business that goes about building a platform the way it would build a pipe is setting itself up for failure. Many business leaders erroneously apply the pipe execution model to building platforms. The media industry is struggling to come to terms with the fact that the model has shifted. Traditional retail, a pipe by most measures, is being disrupted by the rise of marketplaces and in-store technology. Platforms require completely different mental models to succeed. They need interaction-first thinking. Pipes rely on user-first thinking, not interaction-first thinking. In user-first thinking, the single user's perspective rules all business decisions. This perspective works well when value flows linearly from the business to its users.

As businesses move toward enabling interactions between producers and consumers of value, they must adopt interaction-first thinking.

In interaction-first thinking, the focus on users does not cease but becomes subservient to the focus on interactions. Single user benefits may be overruled if the interaction between users suffers. However, an interaction is truly desirable when it creates value for all participating users while maximizing the efficiency of the interaction. A business that enables desirable interactions will ensure a desirable user experience as well.
For example, a user-first business focuses on the activation and engagement of users. In an interaction-first business, these are consequences of the

main goal rather than the goal itself. User engagement is an outcome of the platform's ability to enable interactions sustainably and efficiently. The movement from the pipe-based, user-first view to the platform-based, interaction-first view is best captured through the following shift:

We are not in the business of building software.
We are not in the business of selling products and services.
We are in the business of mediating and enabling interactions!

1.4

THE PLATFORM STACK

A Framework To Explain All Platforms

Many businesses today leverage platform thinking. Companies across industries are actively building platforms. While all of them function as plug-and-play business models that facilitate interactions, individual platforms may often seem vastly different.

From the perspective of software developers, Android, Salesforce, and Facebook Connect are all platforms, yet they are vastly different. Medium and WordPress are called blogging platforms, but they have little in common with software development platforms. YouTube, Facebook, and Instagram are described as social platforms, while Uber, Airbnb, and their ilk are referred to as "marketplace platforms." All these businesses are vastly different from each other.

To complicate matters further, the Nest thermostat is called a platform. Nike is working on a platform to connect its shoes, while GE claims to be using a platform approach to manage its factories. The Internet of Things and Bitcoin may have nothing in common, but they are both platforms.

While all of the above subscribe to the general definition of the platform as a plug-and-play business model that enables interactions, each is vastly different from the others. This chapter proposes a unifying architectural framework to explain the different configurations of platforms.

THE PLATFORM STACK: AN ARCHITECTURAL FRAMEWORK

Across all platforms, the following three distinct layers emerge repeatedly:

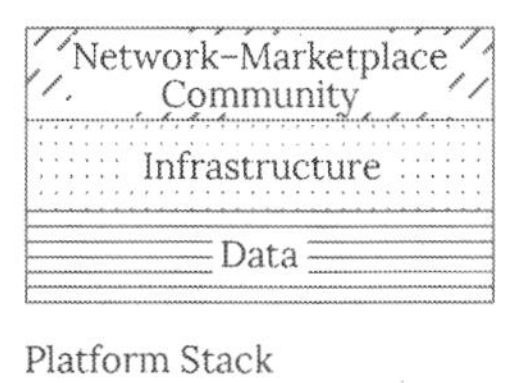

Platform Stack
Figure 6a

a. Network-Marketplace-Community layer

The first layer of a platform is the network or community layer, comprised of the participants on the platform and their relationships. Social networks may require users to connect with each other explicitly. Marketplaces may not require users to form explicit connections but may regularly match buyers and sellers, allowing them to interact. Some platforms may have an implicit community layer. For example, users of Mint.com are not connected to each other, but every user's financial analytics is benchmarked against that of similar users. Every user benefits implicitly from the community without the requirement to connect with others explicitly.

The external network of producers creates value in the network layer. To enable this value creation, platforms need a second layer: infrastructure.

b. Infrastructure layer

The infrastructure layer encapsulates the tools, services, and rules that enable the plug-and-play nature of a platform business. In itself, this layer has little value unless users and partners create value on the platform. External producers build on top of this infrastructure. On Android, developers build apps. On YouTube, video creators host videos. On eBay, sellers host product availability.

On development platforms like Android, the infrastructure layer may be very dominant. On other platforms, like Instagram, the infrastructure layer may be thinner. The infrastructure layer provides the infrastructure on top of which value can be created.

Large-scale value creation leads to the problem of abundance. With an abundance of production, search costs increase for consumers. Too many videos on YouTube may make it harder for consumers to find the best ones. To solve for this, platforms need a third layer: data.

c. Data layer

The final platform layer is the data layer. Every platform uses data in some way. Data allows the platform to match supply with demand. The data layer powers relevance, matching the most relevant content/goods/services with the right users. In some cases, the data layer may play an even more dominant role. The Nest thermostat is a data-intensive platform, where the value is created entirely through the data aggregated across thermostats.

PLATFORM CONFIGURATIONS

While platforms function across these three layers, the degree to which each layer dominates may vary. The platform stack helps to reconcile the differences between different platforms while acknowledging the similarity of the business model across all these instances. To understand different types of platforms, it is helpful to explore three basic configurations of the platform stack further.

Basic configuration 1: The marketplace/community platform

Airbnb, Uber, and most marketplace platforms have a thick marketplace/ community layer. The network is the key source of value. Online communities like Reddit, social networks like Twitter, and content platforms like YouTube benefit from thick community layers.

Arguably, all layers play a role, even if one is more dominant than the others.

The stack helps to illustrate that every platform will have its unique configuration of the three layers.
Certain platforms, like Craigslist and some online forums, focus almost exclusively on the marketplace or community layer, with almost no infrastructure play and without much leveraging of data.

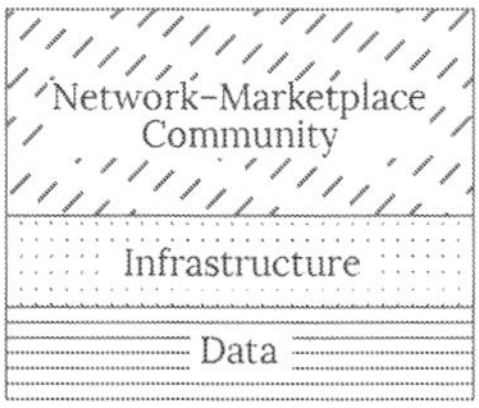

Network-Marketplace
Community
Infrastructure
Data

Platform Stack
Figure 6b

Basic configuration 2: The infrastructure platform
Development platforms like Android provide the infrastructure on top of which apps may be created. In tandem with the Play marketplace, Android's development infrastructure is the key source of value for developers. More traditional views of development platforms focus almost entirely on the infrastructure layer, without a marketplace for apps.

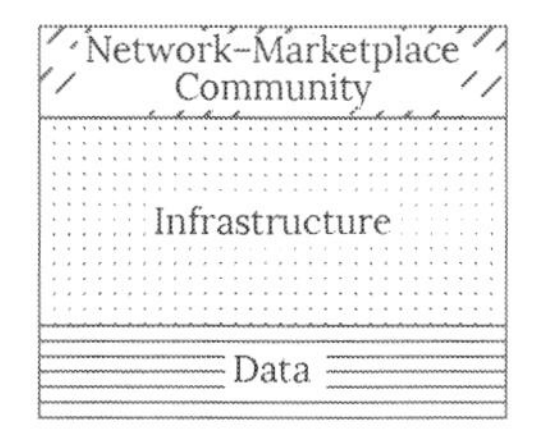

Platform Stack
Figure 6c

As a publishing platform, WordPress provides infrastructure exclusively. It doesn't provide network benefits or any value through data. Medium, in contrast, has a different focus and configuration.

Basic configuration 3: The data platform

The third - and least evident - basic configuration is the one where the data layer plays a dominant role. The data layer plays an important role on every platform. Facebook uses data to fashion newsfeeds, and Airbnb uses data to match hosts to travelers. But on certain platforms, the data layer

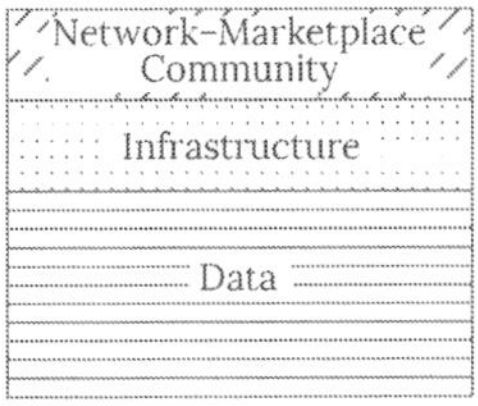

Network-Marketplace Community

Infrastructure

Data

Platform Stack

Figure 6d

itself constitutes the key value created on the platform. Some of them may not even seem like platforms, but, as explored below, they follow the same stack while focusing almost exclusively on the data layer:

- *Wearables.* Nike's shoes and FuelBand constantly stream data to an underlying platform that integrates the user experience across the shoe, the wearable, and the mobile apps. Wearables like Jawbone create value through the data platform. The wearable produces data constantly, and the platform provides analytics back to the user based on the data. Additionally, the platform also pools data from many users to create network-level insights. Wearables benefit from implicit network effects.
- *Nest Thermostat And The Internet Of Things.* The Nest thermostat uses a data platform to aggregate data from multiple thermostats. This aggregation of data enables analytics for thermostat users and powers

services to the city's utilities board. The Internet of Things will give rise to new business models in similar ways through the creation of data platforms.

- *Industrial Internet.* GE's focus on the industrial Internet is another example of a data platform. Machines embedded with sensors constantly stream activity data into a platform that helps each machine learn from other machines and provides network-wide intelligence. These machines benefit from implicit network effects, and every machine learns from the community of machines it is connected to.
- *Enterprise 2.0.* Andrew McAfee highlights the rise of social software in the enterprise and how it's replacing traditional enterprise systems. Enterprise-wide social software needs an underlying data platform to aggregate the many workflows and knowledge exchanges within an organization. The streaming and aggregation of data from multiple input points and the subsequent provision of services to multiple stakeholders is an outcome of a central data platform.
- *Omnichannel Customer Journeys.* Retailers like Burberry and Target use an underlying data platform to unify customer journeys across the store and other remote touchpoints. Actions that a user takes on an app lead to a change in the in-store experience and vice versa. An underlying data platform manages the users' interactions with the store. Over time, this data can be used to create explicit communities by connecting users with similar shopping behavior in the same area with each other. Data platforms function like a pool into which different sources bring data and from which different sources extract insights.

USING THE STACK

The platform stack demonstrates that a taxonomy of platforms doesn't require us to define different families of platforms. Well-defined boundaries do not exist. Development platforms build out marketplaces. Marketplaces open up APIs for developers. Platforms do not fall in different families; they are best represented as different configurations of one stack. This is illustrated further through a set of case studies below.

a. Airbnb vs. Craigslist

The platform stack may be used to visualize the competition between Craigslist and Airbnb.

With respect to the platform stack, Craigslist demonstrates a strong network/marketplace with immense network effects. However, Craigslist does very little on the infrastructure (with no handling of payments and no facilitation mechanisms like trust) and doesn't use data to increase relevance for buyers.

Airbnb started out with poor network effects but with better use of data and a more robust infrastructure to enable interactions between hosts and guests. It enabled end-to-end transactions and invested in the creation of trust mechanisms. Over time, it has built arguably much stronger network effects within the travel and accommodation vertical and has a treasure trove of data that constantly improves its ability to enable desirable interactions.

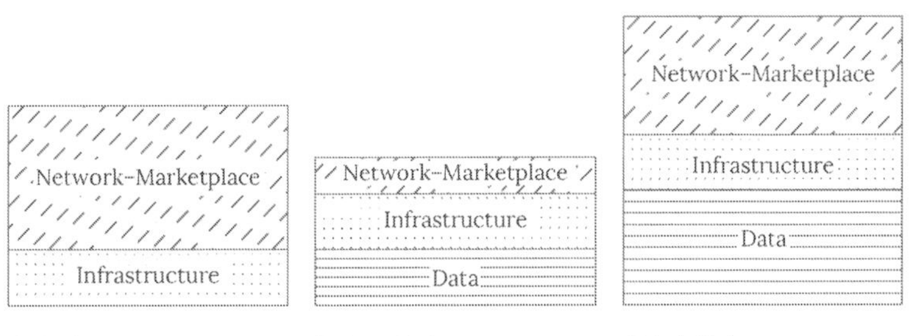

Figure 6e

b. YouTube vs. Vimeo

In its early days, YouTube's hosting and bandwidth infrastructure – coupled with its Flash-based in-browser, embeddable player – formed a compelling value proposition for content creators. As YouTube gained traction, the focus of the platform moved from improving video hosting (infrastructure layer) to improving the matching of videos with consumers (data layer) and increasing viewer engagement (network layer). Vimeo, instead, focuses its platform on content creators and provides them with superior video hosting infrastructure (HD player, a better embeddable player). This has helped the two co-exist despite YouTube's dominance.

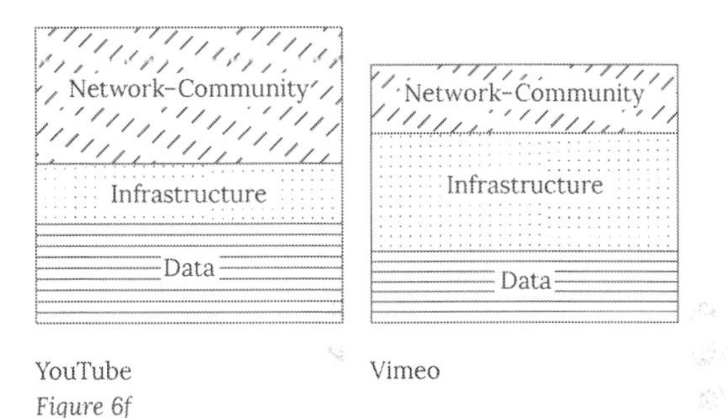

Figure 6f

c. Microsoft windows (pc) vs. Android + Play store

Most development platforms boast a strong infrastructure layer and invest in developing a developer ecosystem. However, the rise of app stores has created an entirely new platform configuration that creates an active marketplace for developers to sell in. The platform serves not just as a technical infrastructure but as an infrastructure for running an entire business.

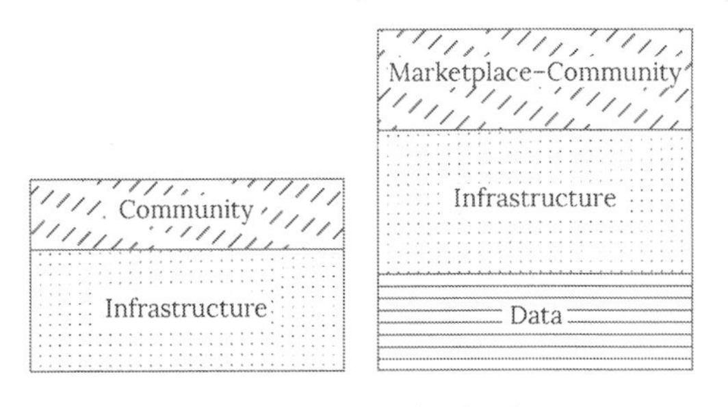

Figure 6g

d. Medium vs. Wordpress

WordPress provides a technology infrastructure for publishers. Medium focuses more on powering a community around ideas than on building better publishing tools. It keeps the technology infrastructure simple – easier plug-and-play – and allows writers and curators to build influence through their content. In the network layer, writers can build a following among readers. The platform also leverages data to help readers discover the most relevant content. In doing so, Medium has built a much more comprehensive platform stack than any blogging platform before it.

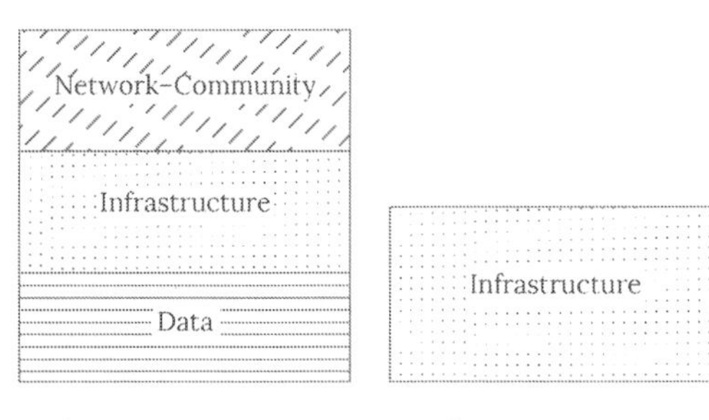

Figure 6h

e. Facebook vs. Myspace

MySpace and Facebook are two social networks with vastly different platform stacks. Facebook's largest draw, arguably, is the newsfeed. By focusing on the use of data to drive higher community engagement, Facebook built an entirely different business. When MySpace started feeling the heat from Facebook, it tried to respond with feature and functionality changes that mimicked Facebook's infrastructure but couldn't build out the rest of the stack quite as effectively. Facebook has done much to strengthen the data layer by creating the Social Graph and the Open Graph. Most social networks before Facebook were largely focused on building community. Facebook, instead, through Connect, has ended up creating a social data layer for the Web.

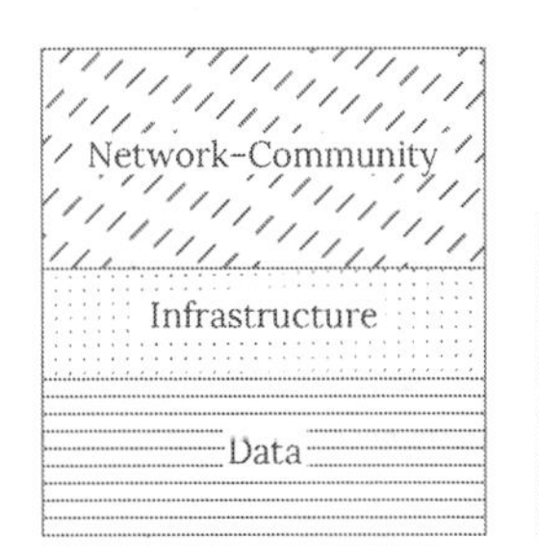

Facebook Myspace
Figure 6i

f. Mint vs. Quicken

Quicken isn't a platform; it's a software tool. The platform stack illustrates how platform-based business models beat software product-based business models. Quicken provides a tool to manage finances. In its initial days, Mint did the same but provided it for free. This allowed Mint to gain traction through a superior tool. However, moving forward, Mint expanded to fill out the rest of the platform stack. Today, Mint enables an implicit network of consumers, who benefit from social analytics that benchmark their spending habits vis-a-vis that of their peers. It also powers a marketplace that allows financial institutions to sell their offerings to these consumers. All of these functionalities are enabled through a constant stream of data coming in from consumer accounts connected to Mint.

g. Instagram vs. Hipstamatic

Hipstamatic and Instagram are deceptively similar. Both allow users to take photos and apply beautiful filters. But there's a difference.

Hipstamatic provided the technology to take beautiful photos using filters. As a software creator, not a platform business, it based its revenue model on charging for the app and for premium filters. On the other hand, Instagram focused on the network layer through its Facebook integration and, over time, built out the entire platform stack. The core value provided by

Instagram – and the reason it succeeded despite a late start – was the network and community for sharing pictures. Ironically, one of the most popular hashtags on Instagram was #hipstamatic, indicating that, while pictures were taken using Hipstamatic, they were being shared on Instagram.

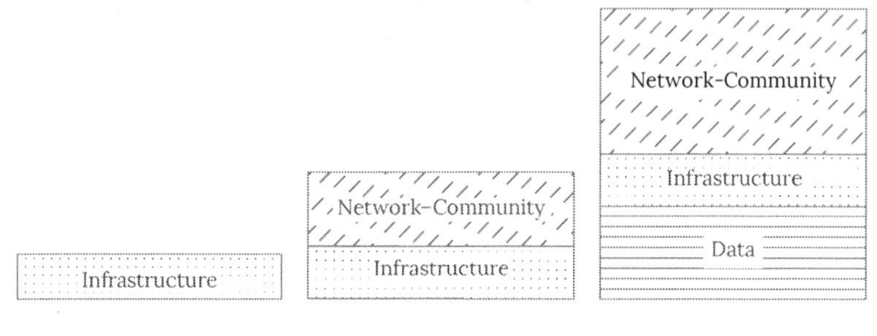

Figure 6j

h. Flickr vs. Facebook photos

Despite Flickr's earlier start and dedicated photo-hosting infrastructure, Facebook hosts the largest number of photos today. Flickr still attracts a large base of users with its storage infrastructure. But a larger base of users uses Facebook to generate conversations around photos.

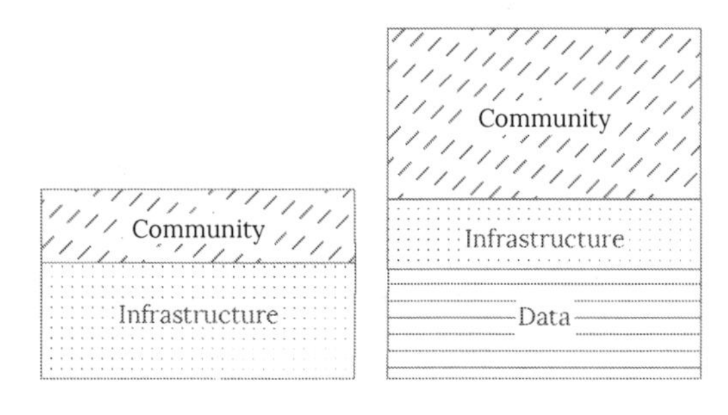

Flickr Facebook Photos

Figure 6k

i. LinkedIn vs. Monster

When LinkedIn launched as a professional social network, Monster may not have seen it as a potential competitor. It was fixated on fighting other job portals. Job portals utilize basic data to help active job seekers find jobs and to help recruiters find resumes. LinkedIn uses much deeper data collection to match users with jobs. By building out a network of professionals, it helps activate passive job seekers who wouldn't visit job portals. LinkedIn has effectively created a larger market of professionals by building out an entirely different stack.

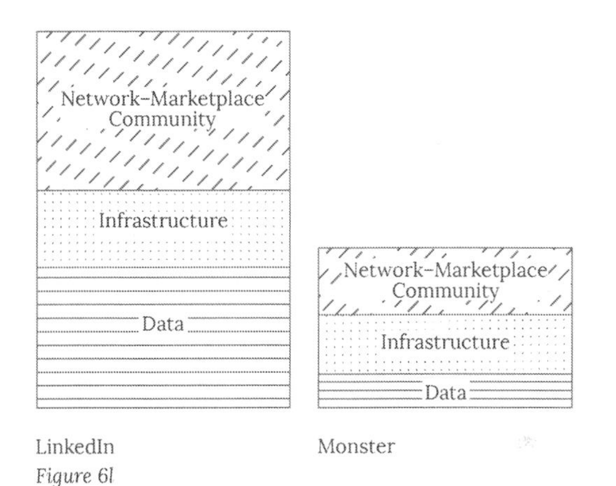

LinkedIn Monster
Figure 61

PLATFORM SCALE IMPERATIVE

The platform stack helps in understanding different types of platforms. More importantly, it helps in defining and executing new platform ideas. It helps in figuring which layers a platform should differentiate itself in and how. The stack helps platform builders understand the key drivers of value and benchmark a platform on those parameters against competition and substitutes without losing themselves in the quagmire of features and functionalities. As we note in Section 2, successful platform businesses require robust architecture, and the platform stack is our first step on the road to designing platforms.

1.5

THE INNER WORKINGS OF PLATFORM SCALE

The Five Ingredients Of Platform Scale

The platforms of the last decade and more have repeatedly sported growth trajectories that are colloquially referred to as "hockey-stick curves." These growth trajectories sport a short gentle start and an inflection point, followed by a steep, non-linear slope. Their resemblance to the shape of an ice hockey stick gave them the name. Venture investors see these graphs often as startups pitch for the funding needed to get past the inflection point. Arguably, actual growth curves have several inflection points, but the overall shape of many such curves, past the inflection point, is non-linear. Businesses that achieve platform scale show such growth trajectories. These businesses start slow, reach an inflection point, and gain rapid traction. The user base, the rate of value creation, and, in many cases, the revenues follow such growth trajectories. Understanding the factors that drive platform scale helps entrepreneurs and managers architect the platform in a manner that is best suited for leveraging these factors.

The importance of the right business architecture for achieving platform scale is explained in detail in Section 2. Startups may often implement tactical "growth hacks" without understanding the real drivers of platform scale. This is ineffective in achieving sustainable scale and does not create the conditions by which the platform can seemingly scale of its own accord. Sustainable platform scale depends on the platform's ability to foster activity in an ecosystem of producers and consumers, and it is achieved only through the right business design and architectural decisions, not through superficial "growth hacks."

The preceding chapters explained how the repeated participation of producers and consumers leads to platform scale. This chapter explores the key drivers that make platform scale possible.

A QUICK NOTE ON PIPE SCALE

Pipes rely on internal processes to create and deliver value. These processes require a setup cost. Factories must be set up to build goods. Subsequently, these processes involve a marginal cost – the cost associated with running through every additional cycle of the process. There are marginal costs associated with production. These involve sourcing, assembling, and preparing the final good or service. Marginal costs associated with distribution are incurred as value is delivered to the consumer. As pipes scale, they try to minimize the marginal costs of production and distribution. They also invest in branding activities that build a brand and eventually help them price better. These factors improve the marginal economics of the business.

This overview of the drivers of pipe scale, while not exhaustive, helps contrast it with platform scale, as illustrated below.

FIVE DRIVERS OF PLATFORM SCALE

The factors that drive platform scale are very different from those that drive pipe scale. Five specific factors, unique to platform scale, work together to drive the rapid growth trajectories observed with today's leading platforms.

1. *Minimal marginal costs of production and distribution*

Platforms benefit from unique marginal economics. Unlike pipes, the marginal cost of scaling both supply and demand is minimal on platforms. A hotel chain expands by setting up more hotels and creating more rooms. It incurs marginal costs in maintaining and managing these rooms on a daily basis. In contrast, Airbnb expands with near-zero marginal costs. New rooms are added and maintained by hosts. Airbnb doesn't incur additional costs associated with servicing new rooms. Airbnb does invest in community management to ensure that hosts follow best practices. It also offers insurance cover to hosts to encourage them to participate on the platform. However, compared to a hotel, the marginal costs of value creation are drastically lower for Airbnb.

Only platforms benefit from superior marginal economics of scaling supply. However, both platforms as well as pipes that use the Internet benefit from low marginal costs of scaling demand. Traditional newspapers incurred high marginal costs of delivery associated with the distribution of physical newspapers. Online news is distributed with near-zero marginal costs of distribution. Hence, efficient pipes can benefit from lower marginal costs of distribution, too. Amazon and Netflix have superior distribution economics compared to their traditional counterparts.

The unique driver of platform scale is the ability to leverage better marginal economics on both supply and demand. Both value creation and consumption scale efficiently compared with pipe scale.

Better marginal economics is only the first source of platform scale. Platforms also benefit from a second source of unfair advantage: network effects.

2. Network effects powered by positive feedback

In a connected network of producers and consumers, greater value creation leads to greater value consumption and vice versa. The two roles fuel each other. A virtuous feedback loop sets in as a platform scales the network of producers and consumers around itself. Coupled with the minimal marginal costs of scaling, this enables platforms to build large businesses with comparatively small investments.

Uber serves as a great example to demonstrate how network effects work. The availability of more cars on the platform attracts more travelers and vice versa. More intricately, the factors that drive scale are not the numbers of cars and travelers but the levels of participation of the two sides. Higher participation from drivers is useful only if it results in higher ride availability and, consequently, lower waiting time for passengers. Similarly, higher participation from passengers is useful to drivers only when it translates into more requests and lower downtime. As demand increases, more drivers join in. In this manner, network effects are powered by a self-reinforcing feedback loop.

Network effects are observed across platforms. The presence of more buyers attracts more sellers on Etsy and eBay. The posting of more videos on YouTube leads to more views and viewer feedback, which in turn leads to the creation of more videos. The creation of more articles on Medium invites higher viewership, which encourages higher participation by writers. When combined with near-zero marginal economics of scaling, network effects demonstrate a unique advantage that platforms have over pipes. These two factors allow value creation on platforms to be scaled at a rate that is impossible and unforeseen on pipes.

As producers participate more often, they attract consumers, who in turn attract more producers. This may often not be as easy as it sounds. Unlike pipes, which rely on employees and partners to scale value-creating processes, platforms rely on users who are often not contractually bound to the platform. In such cases, platforms rely on an additional source of platform scale: behavior design.

3. *Behavior design and community culture*

The central challenge in managing user and partner participation on a self-serve system is compliance. In a traditional organization, compliance is achieved through a hierarchy and a set of rules. How does one achieve this for an open system where participants in the system are not bound contractually? How does one get them to participate as often as needed to maintain a healthy and active ecosystem?

To understand the importance of behavior design, it is helpful to reflect on the download and usage of apps on mobile phones. One may download 50 apps but use only 10 of them on a daily basis, and a smaller number of apps are used multiple times a day. These daily usage apps have succeeded in changing behavior.

Behavior design involves the creation of subtle cues that nudge the user toward the desired behavior. Through subtle cues, notifications, and feedback, users are encouraged to take small steps toward desired actions. Undesirable actions are, in turn, discouraged. Over time, a new behavior sets in.

Before designing behaviors for a platform, it is important to determine how often producers and consumers must participate to enable an active and liquid ecosystem. This should be contrasted with how often these participants would themselves want to participate in those actions. If the gap is too large, the platform may have to invest significantly more in behavior design.

One might well argue that not all platforms rely on behavior design. Wikipedia, for example, is infamous for having created a virtual – and often rigid – hierarchy in its ecosystem of contributors. It ensures compliance through a close-knit community and through a virtual hierarchy.

Behavior design ensures compliance and regularity at the user level. Community culture, often complementing behavior design, ensures compliance at the community level. Through community feedback, a user is made more aware of behaviors that are accepted and encouraged. Users who fail to act in accordance with the community's norms are flagged, and their ability to participate in further interactions is restricted.

Behavior design ensures that producers and consumers participate often and that the platform fosters high activity. However, as platforms scale activity and achieve scale, they often suffer from the problem of abundance. As the number of videos on YouTube increases, its ability to serve the most relevant videos to users must also improve. This leads us to a fourth driver of platform scale: learning filters.

4. *Learning filters*

Facebook's most important feature may well be the newsfeed. The newsfeed filters and serves content based on its judgment of what is most relevant to a particular user. Its ability to filter relevant content improves with greater usage. The news feed is a filter that learns. As a user uses the feed more often, it captures signals on what the user finds desirable (or undesirable) and leverages the data to strengthen the filter further.

Abundance is a characteristic of most platforms. Platforms that allow open participation and production have the potential to gain traction rapidly among producers. This leads to the problem of abundance. This, in turn, makes filters extremely valuable. Without strong filters, higher abundance leads to lower relevance. Lower relevance discourages consumers from participating on the platform, which in turn leads to producers abandoning the platform. Weak filters can weaken network effects, while strong filters constantly strengthen it.

Filters that learn help the platform to scale its ability to deliver value. Platform scale requires scalable relevance and the preservation of an experience that users find valuable.

Platforms that fail to scale relevance often fail despite achieving scale. Scale, ironically, is their undoing. While the impact of filters may not be as obvious as the impact of network effects on platform scale, the strength of a platform's filters determines the platform's ability to continue succeeding after achieving scale. We now explore the final ingredient that contributes to platform scale.

5. *Virality*

All networked and connected systems benefit from virality, a phenomenon where the user of a system brings in new users in the course of using the system. Platforms benefit from virality, but pipes that leverage the Internet can also benefit from it. Instagram serves as a great example of viral growth, as explained in further detail in Section 5. Every time a user clicks a picture on Instagram and shares it with friends on Facebook, the platform is exposed to new users. This is a unique driver of growth that is very different from traditional word of mouth, where users would recommend an offering. Virality doesn't require a user's recommendation. As explained in detail in Section 5, any networked offering can be architected to be viral so that the offering is exposed to more users every time it is used.

PLATFORM SCALE IMPERATIVE

The drivers of platform scale mentioned above are unique to a networked and data-rich world with open, participative systems. Network effects and virality can be achieved only on networked systems. Open, participatory systems enable minimal marginal costs of production and consumption. Data-rich environments help to create strong filters and implement behavior design. In particular, network effects and minimal marginal costs of production are drivers that are unique to platforms. The best platforms implement all of the above drivers into their business architecture. Platform scale is achieved not through marketing initiatives and growth hacks but through a series of architectural considerations while designing the platform that optimize the platform for high participation by producers and consumers. The drivers of platform scale must be architected into the platform. The section that follows lays out a detailed framework for architecting toward platform scale.

CONCLUSION

The Quest For Platform Scale Starts With Architecture

An enduring theme throughout Section 1 is the contrast between pipes and platforms and the corresponding contrast between pipe scale and platform scale.

Platform scale leverages the ability of networked platforms to create and scale value outside the organization in an open ecosystem. Amazon's transition from a pure-play e-commerce retailer to a marketplace, allowing the participation of external merchants with distributed warehouses, is one of the best examples of stepping on the gas and scaling value creation outside the bounds of the traditional organization. But how does one get started with platform scale?

The traditional rules of scaling organizational processes, resources, and labor work well for pipes but do not apply to platforms. Scaling is not a marketing or user acquisition or retention problem. This isn't merely an issue of scaling the ability to generate and fulfill demand. Achieving platform scale requires the ability to scale value creation to scale value exchange – the ability to scale production and consumption simultaneously – and to repeat the two so that each reinforces the other. Hence, a superficial understanding of growth hacks and viral loops isn't sufficient while building platforms. Subsequent sections may address some of these tactical issues, but achieving platform scale requires a deep understanding of the fundamental business design and architecture principles that help achieve scale in platforms.

The quest for platform scale starts with understanding the design principles that enable value creation through ecosystem interactions. To enable this, the platform must be created with an interaction-first approach rather than a technology-first one. We explore this in detail in Section 2.

Most entrepreneurs and managers looking to build the next Airbnb for X or Facebook for Y, dive into the problem headlong by building technology. Instead, technology should be built only after understanding the interaction that needs to be enabled. Without this in mind, one often ends up with a platform that nobody wants to use.

Build platforms with an interaction-first, not a technology-first mindset!

DESIGNING THE INTERACTION-FIRST PLATFORM

The design of the platform business model involves the design of a core interaction followed by the design of an open infrastructure that will enable and govern this interaction.

INTRODUCTION

Building Interaction-First Platforms

Design before you optimize!
Scalable and sustainable business models need to be designed before they can be optimized. Optimizing poor design just makes a poorly designed system worse. The discipline of testing and measuring, championed by the Lean Startup movement, is an extremely important one. Entrepreneurs approach solution development by testing the key hypotheses that could lead to business failure.
While the discipline of testing is important, the single most important decision in testing is the choice of the hypothesis to be tested. Without clarity on the most important hypotheses, one can waste a lot of time testing irrelevant hypotheses and optimizing poor design.
Laying out the overall architecture of the platform helps us understand the key points of failure for the ensuing platform business and shows us what needs to be tested. Business design and architecture for a platform is a necessary focus that needs to work in tandem with prototyping and testing. In the relentless quest for platform scale, most platform implementations

fail because of poor design decisions. The blind pursuit of scale often leads to behaviors that may create results in the short run but are detrimental to long-term sustainable growth. Marketers often tend to focus too heavily on top-of-the-funnel metrics - indications that confirm that potential users are visiting the platform and even taking initial steps but prove inconclusive in determining the impact on real business goals. Moreover, a culture of hacking growth to see rapid, magical results often undermines the design decisions that are required for the sustainability of this growth.

Scalable and sustainable business models need to be designed before they can be optimized. Design and architectural issues are especially complex in the case of platforms because of multiple factors:

- *Multiple user roles*: A platform must cater to multiple user bases, each of which may perform one or more roles in the system. It needs to balance value, costs, and incentives across all these user bases and roles. Failing to achieve this balance for one user base often leads to failure of the overall platform.
- *Open architecture*: Platforms are open systems that allow users to contribute and add value. They need to ensure that users participate regularly on the platform to ensure a vibrant cycle of value creation.
- *Quality control and relevance*: The open and frictionless nature of a platform leads to conflicting priorities. Being open and frictionless, platforms invite abundance. YouTube's content and eBay's listings speak of abundance. It is important to ensure that a platform offers quality and relevance to ensure that the abundance does not overwhelm consumers. This priority is in conflict with being open and participative and needs to be carefully architected.
- *User-generated value*: Since users create all the value, a platform often starts with no value. Design decisions, again, are critical to ensure that platforms attract usage, even at a low value.

Optimizing poor design decisions on a platform can often lead to rapid failure as the platform loses network effects and becomes less valuable for users. A platform needs to manage all design decisions using a central organizing principle: *all design decisions should ensure the repeatability and sustainability of the core interaction that the platform enables.*

Chapter 1 provides a framework for understanding value creation on platforms. Using this context, Chapter 2 starts with the atomic unit of value creation: the core value unit on the platform, and Chapters 3 to 6 structure the core interaction between producers and consumers on the platform around this core value unit. Chapter 7 lays out strategic priorities for platform builders to encourage repeatability and the efficiency of this core interaction. Subsequently, Chapter 8 brings the concepts of this section together into a visual framework for designing platforms. Finally, Chapter 9 takes the opposing view to architecture to account for emergence, an actual phenomenon driving platform scale that is often dismissed as mere luck. Across the contrasting focus on architecture and emergence, this section lays out a comprehensive view of platform design and architecture. This section explores the design frameworks needed to design scalable platforms. Through the remainder of this book, we explore a host of strategies to execute towards platform scale. As we will frequently discover, all these strategies must stem from and reinforce the central architecture of the platform.

THE NEW NEW VALUE

How Small And Simple Ideas Create Massive Value Through Ecosystems

The list of seemingly simple ideas starts with the following:
You can use this to type 140 characters.
Just like your phone camera, but with filters.
Just like SMS but does not cost anything.
Rent out your spare mattress.
Looks like other taxi companies but with a better mobile app.

Some of the most prominent examples of platform scale sound like simple ideas with inexplicably high valuations. The technology capabilities to type out 140 characters or to order a cab at the push of a button do not seem overly complex. To make things more confusing, Instagram's handful of software developers seems to be powering a business that is valued much higher than many software giants that employ thousands of employees. Digg, once valued at several tens of millions of dollars, eventually sold its technology for a mere half a million dollars. Clearly, technology alone isn't driving value.

The value created because of platforms, as we noted in Section 1, has little to do with the technology and much to do with the value that an external ecosystem of participants creates and exchanges on the platform. Through this chapter, we explore various metaphors to understand value creation on platforms. Understanding value creation helps us unpack the various elements that need to be considered while architecting a platform.

PLATFORMS AND VALUE CREATION

The value of a platform is created by the interactions on top of the platform. The value is in neither the technology nor the rate of user adoption. Value lies solely in the activity an ecosystem of connected users powers on the platform. What matters about WhatsApp is not the fact that it is a "simple messaging app" nor just the fact that it has several hundreds of millions of users but the fact that this network of users creates tremendous value through interactions, enough to hook more than 70% of its user base on a daily basis.

The one metric that platforms should really be judged on is the rate at which value is created on the platform. Airbnb is valuable when it powers a liquid marketplace, with millions of transactions. Twitter is valuable when tweets are created, retweeted, and responded to.

We've noted throughout this book that the platform serves as an infrastructure on which value is created. Through this chapter, we try to understand this relationship and this model of value creation in an open ecosystem.

LEGO: WHEN PLATFORMS BECOME CHILD'S PLAY

When building entire towns and physical spaces out of LEGO, one tends to create a base first and then build out other elements (like buildings and trees) on top of this base.

Platforms work in a similar way by providing an underlying infrastructure on which others build and add value.

Android provides the underlying infrastructure for creating applications. YouTube provides the base for creating videos and running virtual media companies. Etsy provides a base for creating product listings and effectively running shops.

Across these examples, the base has no value without the value built on top of it. The platform becomes more valuable as more units of value are added on top of it. These units become the source of supply or inventory for the platform.

Since LEGO is physical and has tangible building blocks, one is tempted to think in terms of content platforms or app platforms where content or apps created on top of the platform have some tangibility. However, this metaphor extends to anything that can be added to the platform that increases its value. For example, Uber drivers stream their availability and location, thus adding value (and inventory availability) to the platform.

Value. The units added on top of the platform represent inventory. These units are the units of value and scale the overall value created on the platform.

Platform. The platform provides the infrastructure and tools on which others can build or add value. The platform often has little or no value of its own.

A *Maker Moment.* Imagine your platform as an infrastructure. What needs to be created on top of it that will serve as inventory? What would you call supply on your platform?

FedEx: movement on a network

Let's move away from the notion of the platform as an underlying infrastructure and think of it as a network of transfer, allowing value to be exchanged between producers and consumers. This is a concept that is equally important to understand when designing platforms.

FedEx works like a network; it delivers packets from a source to a destination. Here's how FedEx gets it right (simplified for illustration):

1. FedEx gathers from the sender (source) about the recipient (destination). The data may include address and other contact information.
2. It converts the data into an internal code to give routing instructions to everyone involved in the transfer.
3. The network leverages the code to deliver the package to the destination.

Networks like FedEx have two key aspects. First, packages are moved around. Second, these packages carry information that enables the network owner to send them to the right destination.

Routing, a concept from network theory, is the process of selecting the best path on a network. Every platform manages routing; the transfer of packages from source to destination.

Twitter transfers tweets from tweet creators to tweet readers. YouTube transfers videos from video creators to video viewers. LinkedIn transfers jobs from recruiters to professionals. Airbnb transfers apartment availability from hosts to travelers. All of these platforms rely on the ability to transfer information correctly from the source to the destination.

While it is important to think of YouTube as an infrastructure on which users host videos, it is also important to recognize YouTube's role in serving videos to the right consumers. This is where the platform needs data to recommend and serve videos accurately.

Value. Every value unit carries data about the unit to match it with the most relevant consumer. Units that cannot be matched do not contribute to activity on the platform.

Platform. The platform uses the data on the unit to match goods and services with the right consumers as well as to match users with each other.

A *Maker Moment.* What data should these units have for them to be matched to the right consumers on the platform? Conversely, what data would you capture about consumers to make this possible?

SPARKS, CATALYSTS, AND REACTIONS

The units of value created on the platform are a prerequisite to sparking an interaction between a producer and a consumer. Uber drivers must be available to be matched to travelers. Listings must be set up on eBay or Etsy to enable any commerce. Service providers must be available and active on TaskRabbit for service requests to be fulfilled.

In all these instances, the presence of value units sparks interactions among external producers and consumers. These units of value are required as a prerequisite to enable value exchange on top of the platform.

Value. The unit starts an interaction between producers and consumers on the platform. Value is created through interactions. Hence, constant unit creation is critical for ensuring activity on the platform.

Platform. The platform regulates and manages activity by creating conditions for interactions. There should be a minimum number of consumable units at all points on the platform.

A Maker Moment. What is the prerequisite for powering interactions on the platform? What is the supply that needs to exist for interactions to be sparked?

SOCCER: THINKING SOCIAL AND INTERACTIONS

In a game of soccer or ice hockey, the state of play always has a central point of focus: the ball or the puck. Spectators do not view the stadium or rink as a whole; they are solely fixated on three things:

- The ball or the puck
- Who has control over it now
- Who is likely to receive/intercept it next

The ball or puck is the center of a social interaction here. A social interaction between two or more parties always has a center. The initiator and the recipient of the interaction are determined relative to this center.

Every platform facilitates interactions between producers and consumers. These interactions always occur around a center, much like the game centers around the ball or puck. Much like the rules of play in a game and the role of the referee, the platform's purpose is to provide the conditions that are necessary for such interactions to occur efficiently.

Value. Interactions are the fundamental units of activity and value creation on the platform. Interactions always occur around a center.

Platform. The platform brings together producers and consumers. It sets the rules of play and creates conditions for interactions to occur.

A Maker Moment. What are the rules of play for producers and consumers to interact with each other? Which interactions would you encourage? Which ones would you discourage?

THE NATURE OF ORDER: ASK THE ARCHITECT

When thinking about design – of products, platforms, or business in general – I've always found it useful to learn from those who do this for a living: architects. While the physicality of real-world design is different from the architecture of building digital systems, the fundamental aspects remain the same.

In *The Nature of Order*, Christopher Alexander makes a great case for inverting how we think about design. To design a building, one shouldn't start with thinking about the building. When architects get down to thinking on paper, they start with a center and build things around and in relation to that center.

Alexander's actual argument is much more nuanced, but the notion of thinking in terms of centers instead of wholes is an important one. When we look at a website or an app, we see it as a whole. We don't see a center. The more complex a system is, the more difficult it is going to be to understand it as a whole. Thinking in wholes leads us to start thinking about features.

When building a platform, it is important that features are not the starting point. Features should instead be built around a center. The center determines how platform users will interact and guides the choice of features on the platform.

Every feature of YouTube, Airbnb, or Threadless is built in relation to the video, apartment listing, or shirt design, respectively. Features are built around these centers.

In the early days of any Internet startup, thinking in terms of features often led to clunky and unusable technology. This is especially true when building platforms that need to encourage both production and consumption functions. The closer one aligns each feature around a center, the more intuitive the platform's usage is.

This ties in to how we think about pipes (linear businesses) as well. Toyota builds a factory starting with the car (end product) and its production in mind. If it adds elements to the factory without the car in mind, it ends up with "bloatware." The same thing happens on digital platforms.

Value. The units are the centers relative to which the platform should be architected.

Platform. Platform design should start with a center, not with features. The center should determine which features are brought in and which are kept out.

A *Maker Moment.* How would you rethink your features if you were to design them around a center?

PLATFORM SCALE IMPERATIVE

The true value of platforms lies in the value created by external producers and exchanged with consumers on the platform, not in technology, nor in user adoption. Value creation is achieved through units of value added on top of the platform. These units serve as the fuel that runs the platform and makes them worth billions of dollars. Subsequent chapters in this section explore these units of value and the role they play in platform architecture in greater detail.

UBER'S DRIVERS, GOOGLE'S CRAWLERS AND GE'S MACHINES

How Core Value Units Power The Platform Economy

What do Google's crawlers, Uber's drivers, and GE's machines have in common? Or for that matter, Elance's freelancers, Dribbble's designers, and Twitter's tweeters?

In a world of platforms, these producers create the fuel needed to facilitate the economic and social exchanges that power business and society.

The first chapter of this section illustrates how a platform enables the creation of value by an external ecosystem of co-producers. To achieve this, the platform acts as an infrastructure, and producers plug into this infrastructure and create value on top of it. The design of platforms should center on the goal of value creation enabled by them. In this chapter, we explore one of the most foundational concepts of platform mechanics: the core value unit.

THE CORE VALUE UNIT

The core value unit is the minimum standalone unit of value that is created on top of the platform. *It represents supply or inventory created on top of the platform.* Without this supply, the platform has very little value in and of itself.

A platform may have more than one form of value unit. In such cases, the platform may have to be designed, keeping each form separately in mind.

UNDERSTANDING THE CORE VALUE UNIT

The concept of the core value unit is best understood by looking at various examples of platforms. A marketplace like eBay has no value without the product listings on the marketplace. These listings are required to power interactions. Similarly, Instagram will cease to be valuable without a constant stream of selfies and pictures. Airbnb needs to have apartments available on the platform to deliver value.

To understand the concept of the core value unit, let's revisit the platform stack. The platform stack lays out the three layers of every platform business model.

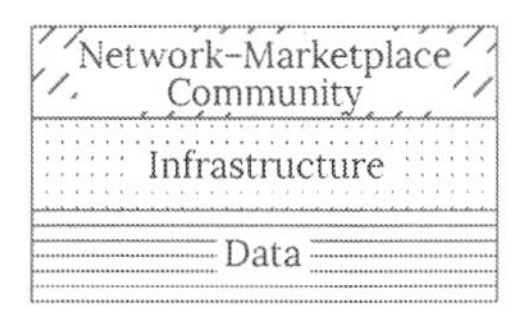

Platform Stack
Figure 7

We noted while analyzing the platform stack that different platforms have different configurations of these three layers. On a platform like eBay, the network/marketplace layer may dominate, whereas, on a platform like Android, the infrastructure layer may be the most important. Let's understand the core value unit in light of these different configurations.

PATTERN 1: NETWORK/MARKETPLACE/COMMUNITY-DOMINATED

Platforms that have a dominant network/marketplace/community may involve the creation and exchange of goods and/or services. On such platforms, the core value unit may take on three forms:

1. *Goods.* If the platform powers a marketplace for the exchange of goods, the listing that describes the good to be exchanged forms the core value unit. Without these listings, the platform has little or no value; eBay and Etsy are examples of such platforms
2. *Standardized Services.* If the platform powers a marketplace for the exchange of standardized services, the listing that describes the service forms the core value unit. Standardized services cannot be customized and are sold "off the shelf." A ride on Uber is a standardized service. The availability of accommodations on Airbnb is standardized. The availability of the service denotes the core value, and the listing is the core value unit.
3. *Non-Standardized Services.* In contrast to the above, the service offered by a plumber on TaskRabbit cannot be standardized. In such cases, the listing describes the service provider. The availability of the service provider (not a specific service) and her active participation on the platform denote value. The profile listing for the service provider is the core value unit on such platforms.

Non-standardized services can also be standardized in some scenarios. A designer may offer a non-standardized service on Upwork. However, Fiverr, a platform that allows services of exactly $5 (and multiples) to be sold, allows the designer to standardize the service as a $5 Fiverr gig.

PATTERN 2: INFRASTRUCTURE-DOMINATED

The concept of a core value unit is much simpler to understand in cases where the platform acts as the underlying infrastructure on top of which value is created. Apps form the core value unit on a development platform. The minimum unit of content constitutes the core value unit on a content platform. Articles on Medium, videos on YouTube, and the ephemeral messages on Snapchat, all denote the core value units for the respective platforms.

There is an additional complexity when understanding value on infrastructure platforms. While a single selfie on Instagram – the core value unit – is created by a single producer, a single article on Wikipedia may be created by multiple producers.
When multiple producers collaborate to create value, as on platforms like Wikipedia or Quirky, the actions of all producers need to be designed for. The concept of the core value unit is easy to understand on infrastructure-dominant platforms because the relationship between the infrastructure and what is created on top of it is very tangible. Tangibility helps us understand the concept better, and this becomes a challenge when we consider data platforms.

PATTERN 3: DATA DOMINATED

What is the equivalent of an app or a video for the Nest thermostat?
The Nest thermostat is like every other thermostat except that it also streams data on its usage. This data helps the thermostat become more efficient over time, contributes to other connected thermostats becoming more efficient over time, and has even been used to create services for third parties. How does one think of a core value unit in a scenario where there is no infrastructure and no explicit community or marketplace?
On data-dominated platforms, the data itself is the source of value. Let's move away from the Internet of things for a moment and look at another data platform family: retail loyalty platforms. Retail loyalty platforms capture a consumer's interests based on past consumption to offer him/her more shopping deals in the future. On a retail loyalty platform, the data profile of the consumer is the value unit. It is the core source of value to a retailer interested in targeting that consumer.
In similar fashion, a usage data profile created by a thermostat on Nest is the core value unit on the Nest platform.
Omni-channel shopping platforms track and aggregate customer actions across multiple channels. On such platforms, data created by the shopper are used to serve deals back to the user or to integrate her shopping experience across channels. On all such platforms, shoppers create value and

merchants consume value. The data profile that a shopper creates is the core value unit on such a platform.

CORE VALUE UNITS AND PLATFORM SCALE

There are several properties of core value units that affect platform scale. Understanding these properties helps us understand key execution priorities in the quest for platform scale:

1. The core value unit is the scaling variable of the platform. The more units there are on the platform – and the higher the quality of these units is – the more valuable the platform will be. *To achieve platform scale, focus on increasing the quality and quantity of core value units on the platform.*
2. As platforms scale, they achieve abundance. To deliver value, they need to have strong filters that deliver only the most relevant value to users. We explore this in detail later in this section.
3. The core value unit is required to spark interactions. Interactions are enabled by the platform.
4. The design of the platform should center on the value that is created on the platform.

The core value unit serves as the starting point for all platform design and architecture.

CORE VALUE UNIT: THE FUEL THAT RUNS THE PLATFORM ECONOMY

The value proposition of a platform revolves entirely around its core value units. From a producer's perspective, a platform is:

1. An infrastructure to create or store value: Android provides an infrastructure for the creation of applications. YouTube provides an infrastructure to host videos.
2. A marketplace to find an audience for the goods/services represented by the value units: Airbnb acts as a marketplace for listings that represent rooms; Uber serves as a marketplace for information that represents available taxis.

From a consumer's perspective, a platform is a repository of value units that filters the most relevant units to the consumer.

The value proposition for both roles revolves entirely around the value units. A platform without units has little or no value. A platform that fails as an infrastructure or a market for value units will not attract producers. A platform that fails to serve the right units to consumers will fail to retain them.

THE UNIQUE CHALLENGE OF PLATFORM BUSINESSES

It may be evident by now that the concept of the core value unit is central to all information businesses. Even when information businesses behave like pipes, they transfer value units from the point of production to the point of consumption. The difference, though, is that these units are not produced by external producers. For example, Google's crawlers crawl the Web to create the Web page indices (value units) that make Google valuable as a search engine. The concept of value created on technology and the relationship between value and infrastructure are the same even though the indexed pages are being created by Google's crawlers, not by external users.

Value units are especially interesting in the case of platforms. Unlike pipes, platforms don't control the quality and quantity of their core value units. *Platforms are information factories without control over inventory.* They can create the factory floor, i.e., provide the infrastructure. They can create a culture of quality control, but they do not employ an iron fist in controlling the amount and quality of what is produced and consumed. The challenge of building and managing platforms is that one does not exert direct control over the source of value.

As a result, focus on the core value unit is especially important when running a platform. Who can create value units, how they are created, and what differentiates a high-quality unit from a low-quality one are all critical design decisions when building a platform. As we progress through this section, we will increasingly note that all platform design decisions are built around the core value unit.

PLATFORM SCALE IMPERATIVE

The age of the industrial economy accorded inordinate power to those who held the means of production. In the age of platforms, production is decentralized. Whether it is the decentralization of manufacturing through 3D printing, the decentralization of marketing and journalism through social media, or the decentralization of service providers in the collaborative economy, the means of production are no longer limited to large companies or entities. *With decentralized production, the platforms that enable and aggregate this production are the new winners.*

In a platformed world, the people and processes that determine quality and quantity of value units determine success. Google's ability to serve results and solve the world's problems collapses if its crawlers don't work well and its algorithms (filters) fail to serve the most relevant results. Uber's ability to serve consumers collapses if there aren't enough drivers available within a particular area. Instagram's ability to engage users in conversations and keep them away from competing platforms collapses if users stop taking selfies. The core value units power the platform economy. *Any strategy for achieving platform scale should start with a focus on the core value unit.*

BUILDING AN INTERACTION-FIRST PLATFORM BUSINESS

A Factory-Style Approach To Designing A Data Business

What does the traditional world of manufacturing have in common with how networked platforms work? How can a basic understanding of factory design help us change the way we think about designing Internet platforms, marketplaces, and social networks? Everything old is new again. The basic principles of factory design help us create a framework for understanding platform design.

BUSINESS DESIGN FOR FIFTH GRADERS

At a fairly abstract level, the goal of all business is the creation of value and the capture of some part of this created value.
If we revisit pipe thinking and consider the example of manufacturing, value is created in a factory. We explored this when we looked at how value is created by aggregating resources and processes towards value creation. The factory achieves its goal by setting up a linear sequence of value-creating actions and aligning labor and resources around them towards the

creation of the end product.

There is an end-to-end process that is responsible for value creation.

On closer observation, we note that every similar process involves the movement of a unit of production (and consumption). This unit moves through this sequence of value-creating actions and gathers value. Finally, in the hands of the consumer, this unit delivers value to the consumer. In exchange, the consumer pays with some form of currency, typically money.

This unit is the object manufactured by a plant. It is the car running through Toyota's assembly line or the toothpaste tube being filled at Colgate-Palmolive.

This object is the basic unit of production and consumption in the industrial world.

The design of a manufacturing plant involves the following steps:

1. Start with the object you're creating: the product.
2. Lay out the steps required to create it (value-creating actions).
3. Design the process that encapsulates this flow of action.
4. Design a factory (and organization) that can execute this process.
5. Enable the exchange of value for some form of currency.

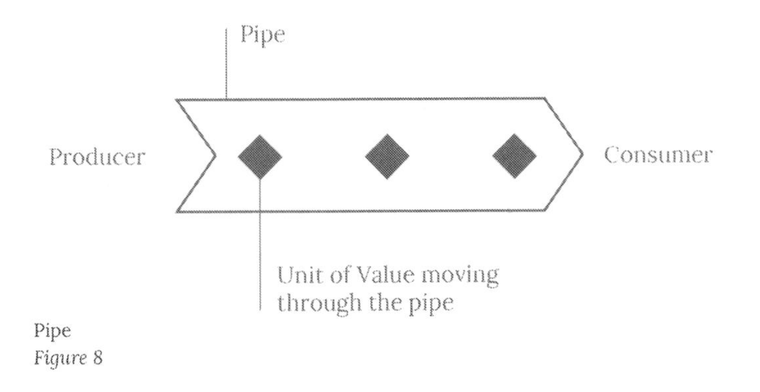

Pipe
Figure 8

The factory design enables the process.
The process design enables value creation.
But all of this starts with the unit of value being created. The process of value creation and the entire business model is designed around this center. Business design doesn't work in the opposite direction. One doesn't start with building a factory and an organization and then figure out how to leverage them to squeeze out a product.

BUSINESS DESIGN FOR A PLATFORMED WORLD

The fundamentals of business design do not change in the shift to platforms. Everything old helps us to understand the apparently new.
Business design, as we noted, doesn't start with the factory; rather, it starts with the unit that is produced. Unfortunately, many networked platforms today start with 'factory design'. They start out by designing the features and functionalities on the website or app that an end user would use to produce or consume value. Instead, this should be the last step in platform design. To understand business design for platforms, let us revisit the pipe *(see Figure 8)*.
Now, let us observe how this changes for platforms:
Two key changes take place in the move from pipes to platforms.
First: *The locus of value creation shifts from inside the pipe to outside the platform.*
Second: *The producer role shifts from inside the pipe to outside the platform (see Figure 9a).*
(Note: The platform may act as the producer in some cases, but most platforms will allow for external production in some way or other.)
These are the two fundamental shifts that we need to be aware of when designing platforms. Against that context, platform design should follow the following principles.

1. *Start With The Core Value Unit*

The design of all platforms should start with the core value unit. *(see Figure 9a)* Start with the unit. When designing Twitter for X, look at what the

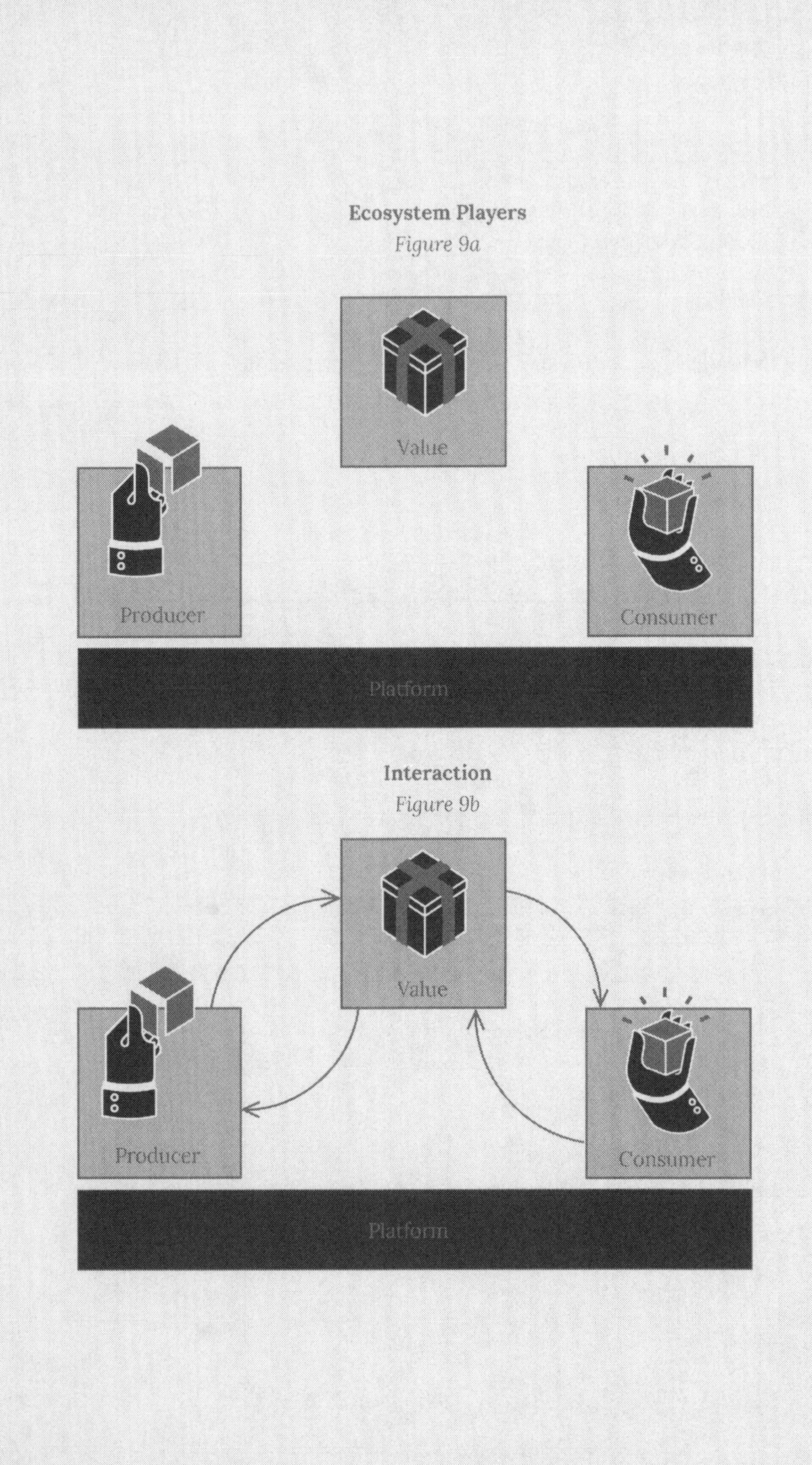

Ecosystem Players
Figure 9a

Interaction
Figure 9b

tweet for X looks like. When building Uber for Y, focus on the equivalent of the ride. What is the unit of supply on the new platform? What will it take for the platform to encourage its repeated and regular production? *Start with the core value unit – and build out from there.*

2. Build The Core Interaction Around The Core Value Unit

In the case of pipes, one starts with the unit and then moves on to designing the process of production and distribution.

Similar to process design for pipes, platforms are built around a set of actions that enable the creation, curation, and consumption of value.

These actions constitute the core interaction: a set of actions that the platform needs to enable repeatedly to ensure value creation and exchange.

Every platform enables at least one interaction between producers and consumers *(see Figure 9b).*

Producers upload videos and consumers view them and vote on them. This is the primary interaction on YouTube. On Kickstarter, producers start projects and consumers consume them and back them with money.

In all interactions, the producer creates value for the consumer and the consumer "pays" for it using some form of currency. Currencies may range from actual money to attention, reputation, influence, and even data. For instance, video viewers on YouTube "pay" for videos through attention (views), reputation (votes), and influence (channel subscriptions).

A platform may have multiple value units and multiple interactions, but there will specifically be one that is core to the value proposition of the platform. Users do not use YouTube primarily to create and consume comments; they use it to create and consume videos. Commenting may serve as an edge interaction on YouTube and doesn't centrally dictate the design of the platform. In most cases, the core value unit and the core interaction are readily obvious. In subsequent chapters, we explore a few cases where they are not.

One important difference between pipes and platforms is worth noting. Consumers don't add value in real time to the product in the case of a pipe. Value creation is the sole prerogative of the producer. On platforms, consumers may add value as well. A producer may take a picture on Flickr, but consumers may tag it and help it get discovered. A producer may upload a video on YouTube, but consumer votes determine how often it is consumed. There are various ways in which consumers add value to the core value unit on platforms.

3. Design The Platform Around The Core Interaction

The third and final step in the architectural journey requires us to lay out the platform. Once we identify the core value unit and design the core interaction as a set of actions, platform design follows.

The goal of the platform is to enable the core interaction between producers and consumers.

The core interaction sets up a framework for evaluating every feature or functionality that one may want to implement. The prioritization of features and functionalities, as well as community management and marketing initiatives, should be determined based on their ability to make the core interaction more efficient and repeatable *(see Figure 9b).*

OF SYSTEMS AND INTERFACES

A common fallacy in a lot of software management is the temptation to start with the interface rather than the heart of the system. YouTube, for instance, is a complex system but has many different interfaces/functionalities for creators, viewers, brands, advertisers, media houses and other stakeholders on different channels.

When designing a platform, one must distinguish between the system and the interfaces. The design of the interfaces should be consistent with the design of the system. This, in turn, is achieved by starting with the core value unit and the core interaction that are enabled by the platform.

PLATFORM SCALE IMPERATIVE

In summary, there are three key principles in platform design:

1. Platform design should start with defining the value that is created or consumed: the core value unit.

2. The core interaction – the set of actions that enable the creation and consumption of that value – should be laid out around the core value unit.
3. The design of the platform's features, functionalities, and management should stem from the design of the core interaction.

Everything old is new again! The answers lie in using the old to interpret the new!

UBER, ETSY, AND THE INTERNET OF EVERYBODY

A Visual Guide To Networked Businesses

A network connects diverse participants and enables them to exchange value with each other. Fax machines, telephone networks, stock exchanges, and credit card networks have done exactly that. With the Internet, we now have a universal network that connects everyone with everyone (well, almost). Networks inherently bring a unique challenge. When value moves in a straight line (as in the case of pipes), it can move in only one direction. On a network, however, value can flow in any direction. Networks function well when the right value is transferred to the right destination.

VALUE TRANSFER AND BUSINESS DESIGN

We've looked at FedEx as a network that delivers packets from a source to a destination, leveraging data. The goal of the network is to transfer the packet from the source to the destination with minimum failure. False positives deliver packets to the wrong doorstep. False negatives prevent the right recipients from receiving the packets intended for them.

Most platforms work in a similar manner. Every platform is responsible for the transfer of core value units from a source to a destination. Regardless of what these platforms do, the success or failure of their business model depends on their success or failure in making this transfer happen. To understand the importance of value transfer on platforms, it is important to understand the structure of interactions.

THE ANATOMY OF AN INTERACTION

All economic and social interactions involve the exchange of three fundamental things:

1. Information
2. Goods/services
3. Currency

All platform businesses require the exchange of information, goods/services, or currency.

Across all platform-enabled interactions, we note the following three points. First, some or all of these exchanges may occur through the platform. Some exchanges that do not occur through the platform may still be tracked by the platform.

Second, the exchange of information always occurs through the platform. The exchange of goods/services and currency may or may not occur through it.

Finally, all other exchanges are triggered following the initial exchange of information.

The configuration of different platforms may vary significantly depending on which exchanges they capture and which ones they don't. Below, we explore a few common configuration patterns for platform businesses.

PATTERN 1: INFORMATION + CURRENCY

Airbnb's business model requires three exchanges:

1. Transfer of information on accommodation availability from host (producer) to traveler (consumer)
2. Transfer of money from traveler (consumer) to host (producer)

Pattern 1

Figure 10

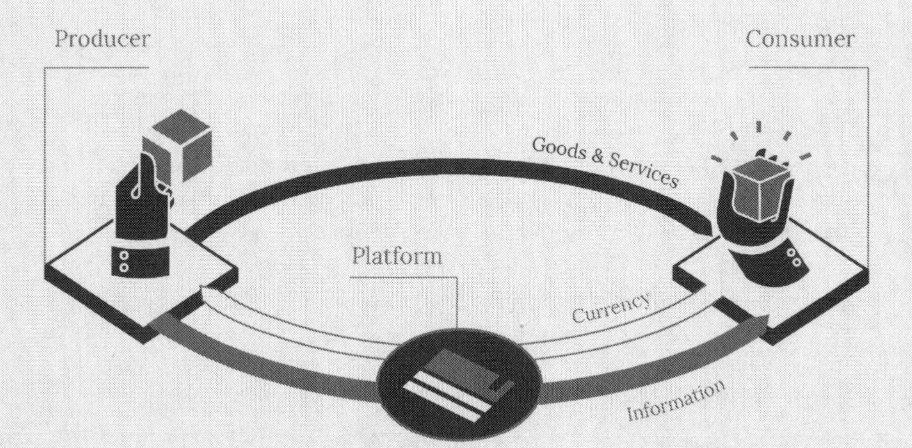

3. Transfer of accommodations-as-a-service from host (producer) to traveler (consumer)

These flows, when visualized, appear as follows: TaskRabbit, a marketplace that allows consumers to find service providers, follows a similar pattern where information and currency (money) flow through the platform but services flow outside of the platform (*see Figure 8a*).

Let's look at a variant of this model: a marketplace for physical products, e.g., Etsy (*see Figure* 9). Etsy's business model involves three key exchanges:

1. Transfer of listing information from seller (producer) to buyer (consumer)
2. Transfer of money from buyer (consumer) to seller (producer)
3. Transfer of physical goods from seller (producer) to buyer (consumer)

Again, the transfer of goods/services occurs outside the platform, while the transfer of money is captured on the platform. In scenarios where the transfer of money occurs internal to the platform, platforms often take a transaction cut. *The platform's monetization options are dictated by which transfers can be captured and/or tracked by the platform.*

PATTERN 2: INFORMATION ONLY

Several platforms do not capture the exchange of money. These platforms often monetize by charging a premium listing fee or a lead generation fee. Craigslist and most other classifieds websites only allow the listing of information. The flow of goods and services, as well as that of money, is neither controlled nor tracked by the platform (*see Figure* 10).

Local commerce platforms like Yelp or India's Justdial enable consumers to connect with local businesses. The money transfer between the participants occurs outside the platform. As a result, their monetization models are based on subscription, paid promotion, or lead generation fees. Groupon, another local commerce player, is slightly different. It enables the transfer of money both on the platform (up to the value of the deal) as well as off the platform (if the transaction exceeds the value of the deal). One may buy a Groupon for a restaurant but exceed the value of the coupon while dining at the restaurant and pay the remainder directly to the merchant. Hence, money is transferred both through and outside of the platform.

Pattern 2

Figure 11

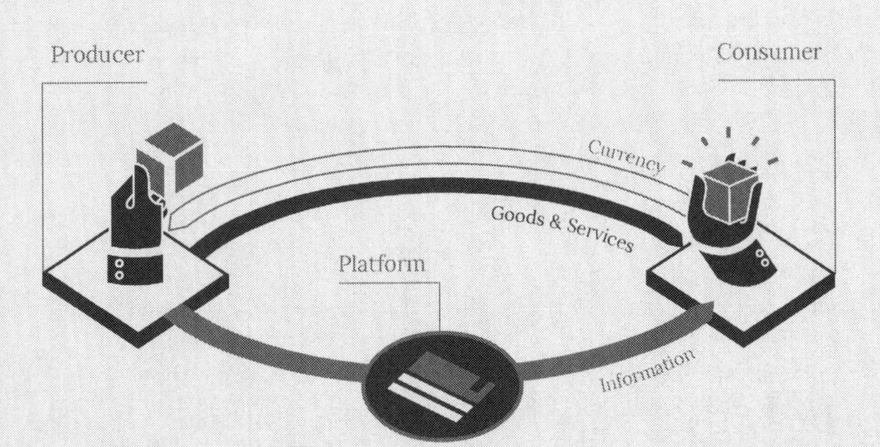

PATTERN 3: INFORMATION + GOODS/SERVICES + CURRENCY

In certain cases, the exchange of goods and/or services may be captured by the platform. Given the digital nature of Internet-enabled platforms, this configuration applies to the exchange of virtual goods (including content) and to services that can be delivered digitally. Clarity is a platform that connects experts with advice seekers through a consulting call. The model works as follows:

1. Transfer of a call request from requestor (consumer) to expert (producer);
2. Transfer of services from expert (producer) to requestor (consumer) via a call;
3. Transfer of money from requestor (consumer) to expert (producer).

All three transfers occur through the platform. The call is enabled by Clarity, and the exact duration of the call is tracked. The subsequent billing for the call is charged on the basis of the exact call duration *(See Figure 11)*.

Uber's business model requires three exchanges:

1. Transfer of information on cab availability from driver (producer) to traveler (consumer) in response to the transfer of a request;
2. Transfer of transportation-as-a-service from driver (producer) to traveler (consumer);
3. Transfer of money from traveler (consumer) to driver (producer).

It is important to note that, even though the transfer of goods and services occurs outside the platform, the platform is best able to manage the transaction if it can track this transfer in some way. Uber is aware of the locations through which a ride moves, which in turn helps it bill on exact usage and determine completion of the ride. We see a similar model at work in the case of virtual goods *(see Figure 11)*. On the Kindle Store, readers buy books from authors. The exchanges facilitated are as follows:

1. Transfer of information from e-book author (producer) to e-book searcher (consumer);
2. Transfer of money from e-book searcher (consumer) to e-book author (producer);
3. Transfer of e-book from e-book author (producer) to e-book searcher (consumer).

Pattern 3

Figure 12

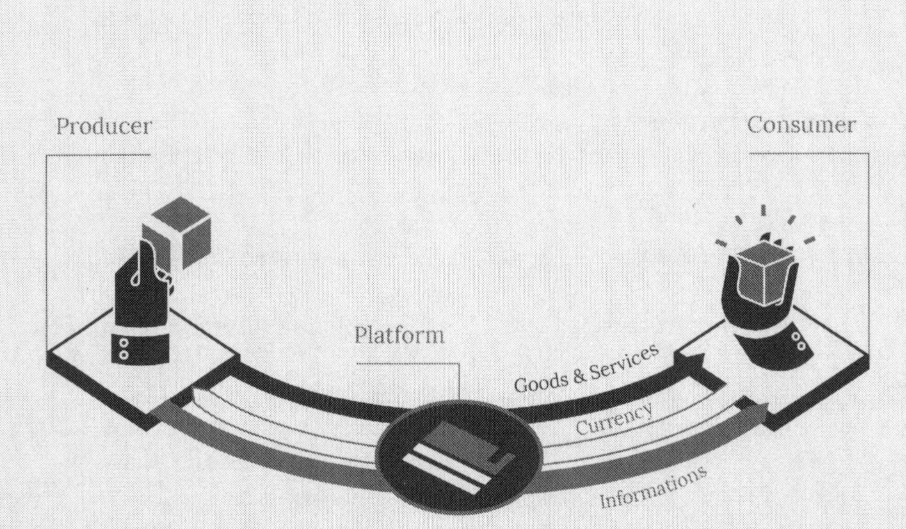

PATTERN 4: ALTERNATE FORMS OF CURRENCY

Not all interactions involve the exchange of money between participants. Other forms of currency may be offered in exchange for the goods and/or services provided. Stream readers on Twitter pay with their attention. By following the tweeter, they also provide her with greater influence. Readers and questioners on Quora pay with views as well as votes. Votes lead to higher reputations for the answer creators. On Quora, votes also lead to the accumulation of credits that can be used to promote more content in the future. Hence, readers pay content creators through a combination of attention, reputation, and influence on Quora. Communities like CouchSurfing work similarly to Airbnb but without the exchange of actual money. In such cases, goodwill and reputation are generated and transferred within the community.

PLATFORM SCALE IMPERATIVE

Every platform-mediated interaction starts with the exchange of information. The transfer of information signals the presence of supply and matching supply with demand. Further, it enables the two sides to make a decision about exchanging goods/services for some form of currency. Enabling this exchange of information is critical to achieving platform scale.

In Chapter 1 of this section, we noted the platform's role in acting as a base on which units of value are created. In this chapter, we noted the platform's role in transferring the units to the right consumers and matching supply with demand. Through the rest of this section, we work off these two roles of the platform to build out a framework for the platform's overall architecture.

PERSONALIZATION MECHANICS

How Filters Drive Value In The Abundance Economy

Platforms allow large-scale production through an external ecosystem of producers. Inevitably, this leads to abundance as more producers come on board. In tandem with enabling efficient production, the platform must also ensure that it enables efficient consumption. As abundance increases, the effort that consumers invest in finding the most relevant content also increases. This chapter explores how platforms solve the abundance problem by creating and managing consumption filters.

PERSONALIZATION MECHANICS

Uber drivers announce their availability and coordinates by streaming their locations. Drivers create value on the platform: information about their location and availability, which helps them to be matched to the right consumer. When a consumer pulls out a phone and requests a cab, he/she creates a filter – the location and time of request. All drivers available on Uber at that time are passed through this filter, and the one most relevant to a consumer's location and time of request is dispatched. Once this match is made, everything else falls in place. The taxi turns up, the traveler is taken to her destination, the appropriate charge is transferred from the traveler's account, and the taxi driver is compensated. *All subsequent exchanges occur once the information exchange takes place successfully.* The information exchange has three key components:

1. The producer (taxi driver) creates a core value unit (information about availability, location)
2. The consumer (traveler) sets up a filter (location and time)
3. The value unit that best passes through the filter is served to the consumer

Accordingly, a cab shows up at the location of the traveler in the real world.

UNDERSTANDING CORE VALUE UNITS AND FILTERS

On platforms, units are produced and served to consumers based on how well they pass through certain filters.

If you haven't used Uber's taxi-booking platform, you've probably used Google's search engine at some point. Google's search engine acts in a very similar way.

Google's crawlers crawl the Web and create Web page indices. These serve as value units on top of Google's infrastructure. Unlike Uber's drivers, Google's crawlers are owned and managed by Google, but they perform a similar production role. This goes to show how many of the business design considerations discussed throughout this book apply equally well to all forms of information businesses.

Google's crawlers index the Web and create billions of units of value. When users type in a search query, they create a filter. Value units are passed through this filter, and the ones that are most relevant are served to the user. Google's algorithm includes many more inputs into the filter, including social signals and a user's previous search patterns, but this serves to illustrate how units and filters work together.

Instagram-wielding teens take selfies all day and create core value units on the platform. Users' connections and past consumption actions on Instagram create a consumption filter. These units are then served to users based on their respective filters.

The mechanics of Facebook's newsfeed illustrate this point further. One's entire network creates status updates, pictures, comments. All these are added as value units to the platform. The newsfeed serves updates based on units that pass through a user's consumption filter. This filter is built on signals that the user has provided in the past through actions (likes, comments) on the newsfeed. *Google's crawlers, Uber's drivers, and Instagram's selfie-clickers are the new producers in the platform economy.*

HOW FILTERS DRIVE CONSUMPTION

Successful platforms must ensure that the most relevant value units pass through filters. This involves two key factors:

1. *Overlap.* Ensuring that there is significant overlap between what producers produce and what consumers need. We explore this in greater detail in Section 4.
2. *Data.* Ensuring that the platform captures rich data about core value units as well as filters. We focus on understanding this further here.

Consider how a YouTube video is served to a consumer. The video (core value unit) has various forms of data associated with it. These include information on WHAT it is (title, description), HOW GOOD it is (indicated by votes), and WHO it can be served to. The video is served in various ways:

1. It may show up on a user's newsfeed. The newsfeed uses a filter that takes into account data on WHAT the user has consumed in the past.
2. It may show up in response to a search query. The search query acts as the filter. A user may slice and dice the search results further by adding parameters to the filter (video length).
3. It may be shown as a related video alongside a video that the user consumes. In this case, the similarity to the current video and to past consumption behavior work together to create the filter.

Value units carry data and are matched against the data in a consumer's filter. Units pass through filters when the data from the two match.

BUILDING FOR RELEVANCE IN THE ABUNDANCE ECONOMY

The role of filters cannot be overstated. Platforms, by their very nature, enable abundance. As open, plug-and-play systems, they allow a host of external participants to create value. This naturally results in abundance. An economy of abundance, instead of creating value with greater abundance, can actually lead to diminishing value as consumers find it harder to find what they are looking for and swim around in a sea of irrelevance. This is a problem that all platforms face as they achieve platform scale and invite greater participation. Filters ensure that consumers are served only the goods, services, and content that are most relevant to them.

A BRIEF TAXONOMY OF FILTERS

A good filter is representative of what a consumer would find most relevant. For a location-based application, the location may serve as a filter. For search engines, search queries act as filters. A newsfeed creates a filter based on a user's past actions and social signals. A Twitter feed's filter relies almost exclusively on recency.

Filters may *pull* units to themselves. That's what search queries do.

Units may also be *pushed* through filters. That's how a newsfeed works.

Filters may be *point-in-time* or *cumulative.*

If a search engine serves results to queries based only on search terms, it is employing a point-in-time filter. If, however, it also factors in the user's past search behavior, it is incorporating a cumulative filter as well.

As another example, a local commerce application that serves merchant deals based on a consumer's location may use one or both types of filters. If deals are served based purely on the consumer's location, the application uses a point-in-time filter. If the deals served also account for the types of deals that the consumer has taken advantage of in the past, a cumulative filter is also leveraged.

Filters may be based on active intent or passive context. A search query is an active intent filter. A newsfeed works on a passive context filter. Passive context filters are typically cumulative, though they may also be point-in-time. A user using a location-based app may not actively request deals but may be served them based on her passive context.

Context may be static or dynamic. Many Web 1.0 era filters were created based on long sign-up forms that the user filled out. Today, filters are created based on data captured on an ongoing basis through a user's actions.

Filters may be standalone or collaborative. Amazon's "People who purchased this product also purchased this product" feature is based on a collaborative filter. Many recommendation platforms allow users to filter results based on a "people like you" parameter. This, again, is a collaborative filter. The most important innovation in recent times that has led to the spread of collaborative filters is the implementation of Facebook's social graph. Through the social graph, third-party platforms like TripAdvisor serve reviews based on a collaborative filter of people who are close to you on the graph.

Finally, it is important to note that the network itself is a filter. Who you follow determines what you consume. On Twitter, who you follow is the critical filter. Relevance is almost entirely dictated by it. On Facebook, who you are connected to and how often you interact with them strengthen the newsfeed filter. On Quora, users may follow other users, topics, and even questions. All of these, in turn, act as filters. *The new economy runs on data. Platforms use data to match value units with filters.*

PLATFORM SCALE IMPERATIVE

The core value unit is the fuel that powers the platform. At any given point, a platform is only as useful as its ability to match these units to consumers' filters. In its steady state, a platform is an engine that works on the following heuristic, three things are required to make this happen:

1. Value units must be created
2. Filters need to be structured
3. The platform needs good data about units as well as filters to ensure that the right units pass through the right filters

Platform scale relies on the coordination of distributed production and personalized filtering.

THE CORE INTERACTION

How Flappy Bird And Super Mario Bros. Build Complex Experiences From Simple Actions

A good part of my childhood was spent glued to the television playing Super Mario Bros. A generation that never swiped screens spent its childhood wielding joysticks and clicking on handheld controls.

Try as she might, my aunt never understood the obsession. "All you do is click that one button all day. What do you get out of it?"

That one statement captures the brilliance of game design. A player may have the lofty goal of saving the princess. One may get a kick out of crossing multiple levels and collect points and lives on the way. But the player merely clicks a set of buttons that help the game character jump and stomp the evil turtles and fire cannonballs.

More recently, Flappy Bird had the whole world in outrage when its creator pulled the game from the App Store. As a set of actions that players take, Flappy Bird is quite similar to Super Mario Bros. One or two simple actions,

when repeated, deliver value, as long as they are performed well.
That's the brilliance of game design. A large goal can be broken down into a set of simple actions for users to perform repeatedly. These simple actions enable users to obtain value from the game and progress towards a larger goal.

GAME DESIGN AND PLATFORM SCALE

The most alluring aspect of game design is the possibility that simple actions could yield important consequences. What if platforms could break complex business and social interactions down into a set of simple actions?
Some of the best platforms today are designed in this fashion. A constantly evolving online encyclopedia is based on a set of repeated writing and editing actions that users perform. The world's largest accommodation marketplace may threaten to disrupt the traditional hotel industry, but it relies on a set of simple actions from hosts and travelers to guarantee a thriving marketplace.

THE CORE INTERACTION

Every platform has a core interaction, a set of actions that producers and consumers on the platform perform repeatedly to gain value from the platform. YouTube relies on the uploading, viewing, and voting of videos. It works as an engine where all three actions are required. If any of these breaks down, the platform may fail to continue creating and delivering value in the manner that it currently does.
Wikipedia's platform may seem complex, but it may be broken down into a set of actions involving the start of a new article stub, the creation and editing of content, the reversal and resolution of edits, and the consumption of content.
The core interaction is a set of actions that producers and consumers engage in repeatedly to derive value from the platform.
Users might perform other actions, but the actions constituting the core interaction are those without which the platform would cease to perform its function.

THE ANATOMY OF THE CORE INTERACTION

The core interaction follows a common template across platforms. Most platforms require very similar actions to be performed by producers and consumers.

Setting up a listing on a marketplace and adding content are examples of producer actions that occur repeatedly. Similarly, searching, consuming feeds, and purchasing items are consumer actions that may occur repeatedly. Additionally, both producers and consumers may also engage in other actions, such as voting, rating.

All actions in the core interaction fall into one of the following buckets:

1. *Creation.* In every interaction, there is at least one producer role that creates value. For any core interaction, this involves the creation of the core value unit. This increases the amount of supply on the platform. An Uber driver clicking on his availability over the app, a Medium writer creating a new article, and a smart refrigerator creating data about the level of stock within it are all examples of creation.
2. *Curation.* Curation is a necessary component of every interaction. Curation scales the quality of the supply on the platform. It encourages desirable behaviors and discourages undesirable behaviors. Rating and reviews help with curation. Upvoting and downvoting of content enable curation. Curation also has a more persistent impact throughout the system. A producer who regularly creates high-quality content may gain greater power to create in the future. A producer flagged for poor quality may find her task cut out on the platform. Curation also provides feedback to the producer that may encourage her to return and create often on the platform.
3. *Customization.* Customization refers to the platform's ability to create a highly relevant experience for the consumer. This is achieved through filters. Users should be encouraged to engage in small actions that increasingly improve the filter and the platform's ability to customize. New users signing up on Twitter or Facebook are encouraged to connect and follow certain recommended users, as this creates a filter for them to start receiving content. New users on platforms like Pinterest are

asked to indicate topics of interest and follow relevant boards to create a filter that serves them a customized experience. These actions are used to activate new consumers. Platforms that succeed in delivering a customized and relevant experience sustainably encourage users to participate in this action throughout the life cycle of the platform. Customization is an ongoing quest that parallels the quest for platform scale.

4. *Consumption.* In every interaction, there is at least one consumer role that consumes value.

The keys to platform scale lie in simplifying each constituent action in the core interaction.

A platform must enable all four actions - creation, curation, customization, and consumption - in order to enable value creation and exchange sustainably.

The core interaction connects individual user actions with the overall purpose of the platform.

INTERACTION FAILURE

If a platform fails at encouraging creation, it breaks down. Imagine Uber's drivers not showing up, Google's crawlers taking the day off, or Etsy's sellers abandoning the platform. The consumption side would have nothing to get out of the platform, and the whole business would break down.

If a platform fails at encouraging consumption, there's a different problem. A lot of value is created without anyone interested in consuming it. This, in turn, discourages further creation and destroys the activity on the platform.

A platform that fails to encourage curation becomes loaded with poor-quality content and fails to stay useful and engaging.

Finally, a platform that fails to encourage customization will increase search costs for the consumer. Consumers will find the experience irrelevant. This, in turn, may lead to a user exodus over time.

When running a platform business, one must ensure that all four actions are repeatedly performed across all interactions. Failure to encourage any one of these actions may lead to failure of the entire interaction.

VALUE UNITS AND INTERACTIONS

The actions of creation, consumption, and curation and, indeed, the overall core interaction are determined in relation to the core value unit. Customization actions help to build out the filter.

To design the core interaction, ask the following questions:

1. For a particular platform, what is the core value unit? What is the unit of supply on the platform that defines value for its users?
2. Who is the producer?
3. How does the producer create the core value unit?
4. Who is the consumer?
5. How does the consumer consume the unit?
6. How is the quality of the unit determined?
7. What is the filter used to serve the unit to the consumer?
8. What consumer actions help to create the filter?
9. How does the consumer consume relevant units?

The design of a platform should start with the core value unit. It should then determine the producer and consumer with reference to the unit. Finally, it should lay out the actions that are performed in the core interaction. The platform's role is to ensure the performance of these actions. *The core interaction is the repeatable formula for value creation and exchange on the platform.*

The cycle of value creation and consumption must be repeated for the platform to scale and repeatedly solve the problem it is meant to solve.

THE MINIMUM VIABLE PLATFORM AND IMPLEMENTATION ROADMAPS

A focus on the core interaction helps us define the requirements for a minimum viable platform. Unlike single-user products, platforms must cater to multiple user roles. The core interaction defines the minimum unit of value creation and exchange that caters to the key roles on the platform. The minimum viable platform should ensure that it designs all four actions in the core interaction sufficiently to enable the end-to-end interaction.

In the Lean Startup methodology, one often builds out a product by validating a set of hypotheses sequentially. Every iteration of the platform may validate a hypothesis related to one of the four actions, but it is important to ensure that all other actions are also designed into the platform. Without designing the entire interaction, it may be counterproductive to try to test a hypothesis related to an individual action.

When implementing large platform projects, teams should ensure that they plan the roadmap in a way that progressively enhances the repeatability and efficiency of the core interaction. Features, functionalities, and initiatives that do not directly affect the core interaction, especially in the early days of the platform, may distract the team from more important execution.

PLATFORM SCALE IMPERATIVE

All too often, we still view platform businesses as software businesses. But platforms are fundamentally different from traditional software businesses.

We are not in the business of building software!
We are in the business of enabling interactions!

If there is one shift that is required of both startup developers as well as CIOs at large enterprises, it is this. If you're building for network effects, you're not building mere software anymore. Platforms that shift the design process from a technology-first to an interaction-first approach will win.

PULL-FACILITATE-MATCH

A Framework For Managing Platform Scale

A traditional story with roots in the Indian sub-continent speaks of six blind men who try to understand what an elephant feels like by touching various parts of the animal. Each one feels a different part: the one feeling a leg concludes that it is like a pillar, while the one feeling a tusk concludes that it is like a snake. They get back to comparing notes and learn that they are all in complete disagreement.

Organizations that work on platform businesses often face the same challenge. Owing to the complex nature of platform businesses, employees working on different elements of the business find it difficult to zoom out and understand the overall business that they're building.

This is why our quest for platform scale starts with laying out the architecture of the platform business model. The overall architecture - as we frequently note - is organized around central principles: the focus on the core interaction, the choice of the interaction-first approach over the technology-first approach, and the priorities centered on the creation of core value and the strengthening of consumption filters.

This framework, centered on the core interaction, helps us understand a large, complex, emergent system like a platform in terms of simple and specific business goals. In turn, this helps individual teams always keep track of the overarching goals and align their efforts towards it.

In this chapter, we build out a framework for managing platform scale across the organization. Starting with the goal of powering the core interaction, we lay out the priorities that a platform organization should focus on to enable the core interaction.

ORGANIZING FOR PLATFORM SCALE

Every aspect of running a platform business centers on the platform stack. The design of the organization that runs a platform business should also stem from the platform stack.

The three layers of the platform stack are as follows:

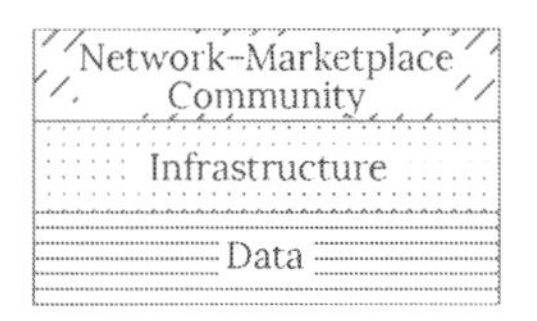

Platform Stack
Figure 13

A platform that creates value sustainably and repeatedly must ensure that it has a healthy network layer, a functioning infrastructure layer, and a data layer that ensures a relevant and compelling experience at all times.

To power the core interaction, a platform must be organized in a manner that leverages all three layers of the business model appropriately.

Data-dominant platforms, for example, must be organized differently from marketplace-dominant platforms. A data-dominant platform may need higher resourcing aligned to the data layer, whereas a marketplace-dominant platform may invest heavily in producer-relationship management, consumer acquisition, and overall community management.

Below, we explore a framework to craft an end-to-end platform strategy and design organizations that power a particular type of platform.

PLATFORM STRATEGY

Platform strategy involves three primary priorities, aligned with the three layers of the business model described above.

1. *Pull.* The platform must pull the producers and consumers to itself on an ongoing basis. This creates a healthy and active network and ensures that users are actively engaged on the platform.
2. *Facilitate.* The platform must ensure that the tools and services it provides to its users enable them to interact with each other. It also needs to set the rules of access and usage to ensure that desirable interactions are encouraged and undesirable ones are discouraged.
3. *Match.* The platform uses data to serve relevant items to consumers. Data about the core value units and consumption filters must be constantly acquired and enriched to deliver on the platform's matchmaking ability.

Pull, facilitate, and match: three roles that must be performed repeatedly to power platform scale.

A platform that fails to perform even one of these three roles will fail to achieve platform scale.

1. Platforms that fail to pull users fail to create the conditions for platform scale. Network effects and virality, two of the key forces that power platform scale, are created as a consequence of user participation. The failure to create ongoing pull leads to the failure to create network effects and virality.
2. Platforms that create unnecessary friction in access and usage may hinder user participation, leading to a loss of network effects and failure of the platform to enable interactions. However, platforms that make it too easy for users to participate may invite a rapid deterioration in quality. Users rapidly abandon such platforms.
3. Platforms that fail to match value to users with high relevance will fail to engage users.

A focus on all three priorities is required to manage platform scale. Below, we explore all three in further detail and lay out the key organizational elements to enable each. Subsequently, Section 3 is devoted to the various management decisions that are needed to plan for achieving these three priorities.

PULL: ATTRACTING AND ENGAGING ALL ROLES

Marketers find platform scale daunting. Traditional marketing has relied on identifying channels and optimizing for the lowest cost of customer acquisition. Platform scale, instead, requires the ongoing creation of pull to keep pulling both producers and consumers to the platform (*see Figure* 13).

Creating pull involves both inorganic and organic elements. In its initial days, a platform may have no pull. In fact, platforms often suffer from a chicken-and-egg problem. Producers won't participate without consumers and vice versa. Many platforms exhaust their resources through a traditional marketing approach, lacking a clear strategy for creating pull. The initial pull may need some form of inorganic effort. This is explored in detail in Section 4.

To generate pull on an ongoing basis, platforms must implement viral mechanics, which we explore in depth in Section 5. Platforms also need to ensure that they create some form of long-term investment for producers and consumers that keeps them loyal to the platform. Our traditional view of loyalty has often involved lock-in and other forms of schemes that are not in a consumer's best interest. On platforms, loyalty is created through designing new behaviors for users and by providing greater reputation and influence to producers over time. These mechanisms are explained in Section 3.

Creating pull also requires reactivating deactivated users. It involves creating off-platform notifications that drive users back to the platform. Likewise, the initiation of pull also involves activating users who first come on board. Given the abundance of choice on the Internet, getting a new user to download an app or sign up on a website is no longer an indicator of her continued participation. Activating a user involves onboarding her onto the platform

Pull

Figure 14

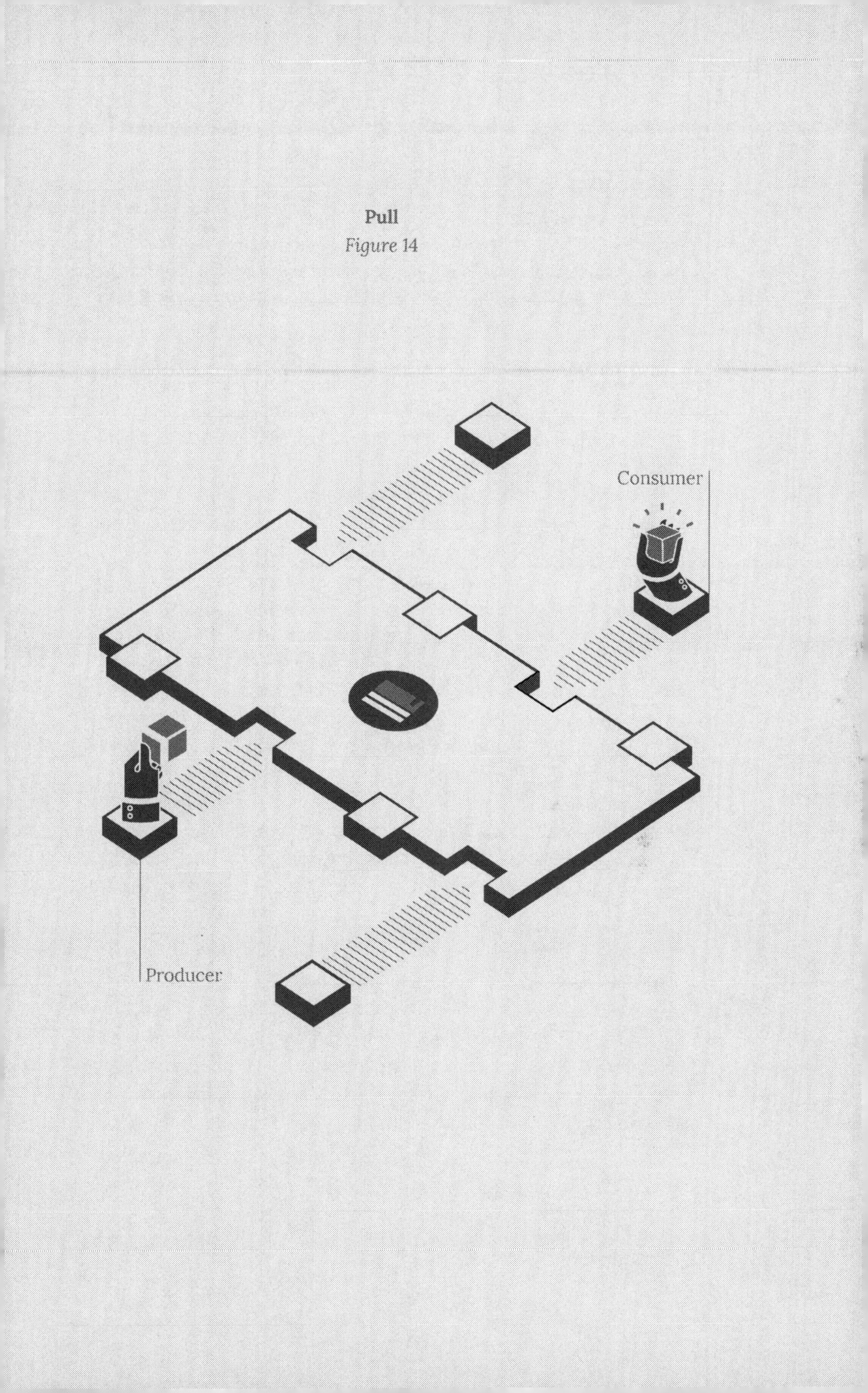

and demonstrating the platform's benefit with minimum investment from the user. Platforms must design reward schedules that constantly encourage the user to participate more. New users who start participating on Quora see their Quora Credits – virtual currency on Quora – grow as their participation is appreciated by other users.

These reward schedules shouldn't be limited to new users. In fact, they should continue to be in operation throughout the life cycle of any user on the platform. The blogging platform Medium keeps providing feedback to bloggers who write articles on it. Every time readers recommend these articles, the platform provides feedback to encourage producers to produce more.

Some platforms have a central feed of relevant content that keeps re-engaging users. Facebook's news feed is one such example. Social networks prior to Facebook would wait for users to return to the platform only when users actively wanted to interact and produce content. The newsfeed encourages users to keep returning in a more passive consumption mode.

The nuances of creating pull are often lost on traditional marketers. Creating pull may often work in a counterintuitive fashion. Because of the chicken-and-egg problem, many marketing channels may not work during the early stages of a platform. However, all of these channels need to be revisited as the platform scales, as those very channels may work for a thriving, active platform.

A final word on pull. To achieve platform scale, a platform must constantly monitor how it creates pull. It must constantly measure the split between organic and inorganic sources of pull. As the platform scales, it must ensure that the organic sources of pull start dominating and constantly growing.

FACILITATE: PROVIDING THE TOOLS AND RULES THAT ENABLE INTERACTIONS

Platforms must provide tools and services that enable producers and consumers to interact with each other *(see Figure 14)*.

On infrastructure-intensive platforms, these tools may involve content creation and management tools. Vimeo provides video hosting, streaming, and monetization capabilities to indie filmmakers. Viki, a platform that uses a community of translators to create subtitles for foreign language soaps

Facilitate
Figure 15

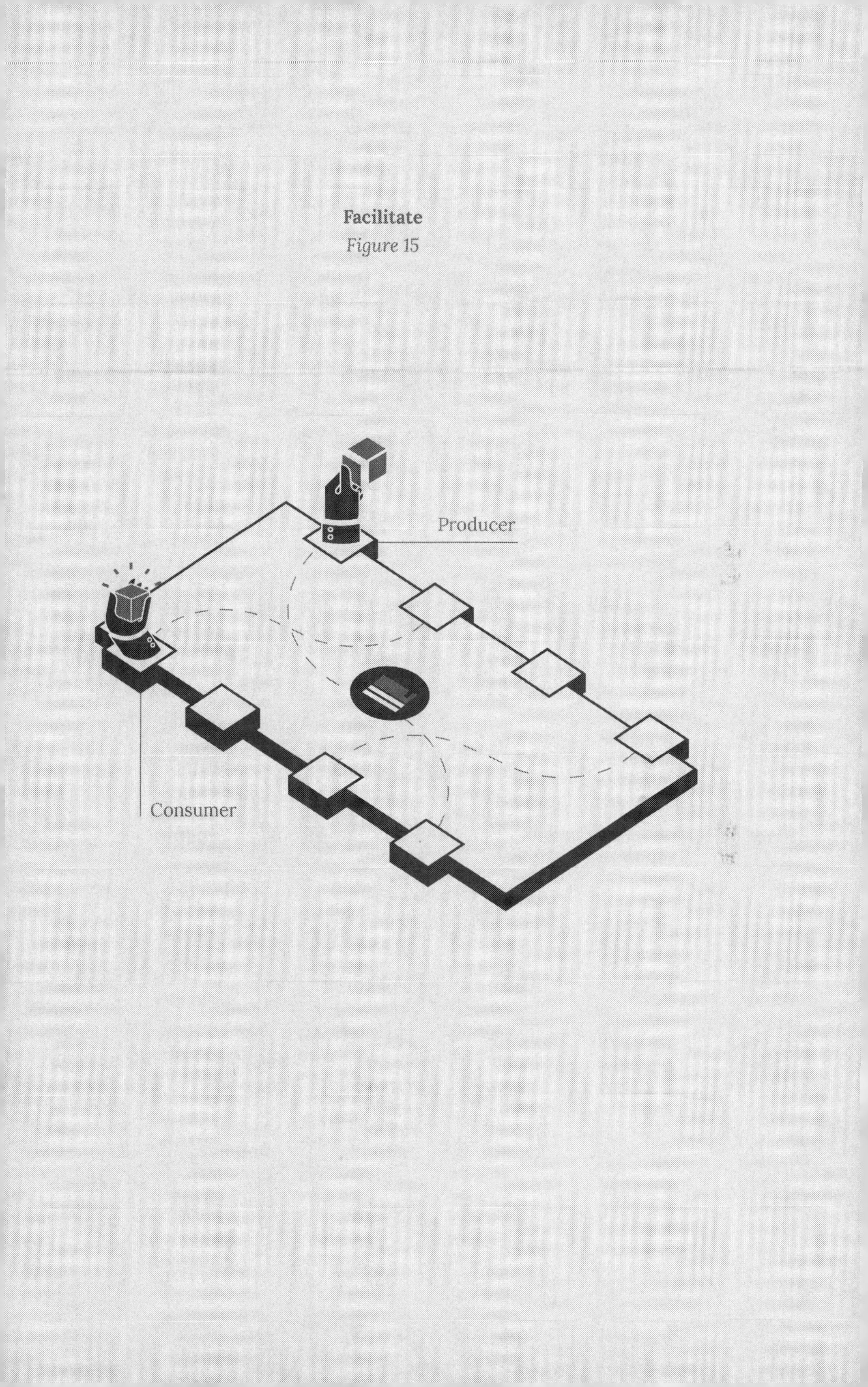

and movies, provides the tools needed to create and edit those subtitles and ensure accuracy. Users work together on Viki using tools of co-creation and collaboration.

Interactions on marketplace-dominant platforms may require centralized provision of tools and services to enable smooth interactions. An escrow payment service encourages buyers and sellers to participate without fear of losing money in a fraudulent transaction. Central insurance coverage encourages travelers and hosts to interact on Airbnb.

As we note in Section 3, platforms scale by removing the friction in these tools and services. Users often migrate from other substitutes that have more friction.

The platform must also set the rules of interaction. It must ensure that desirable behaviors are encouraged and undesirable ones are discouraged. Platforms achieve this through a variety of mechanisms. Social curation and community feedback are very explicit mechanisms of providing feedback. Some platforms may even have centralized moderators. Many rules of usage may be baked into the platform in the form of algorithms that prevent users from taking certain actions. In recent times, the importance of encouraging users towards specific actions has gained a lot of traction in the guise of gamification – an approach to make systems behave like games that encourage users to take certain actions and provide some form of reward in return.

MATCH: MATCHING THE TWO SIDES WITH EACH OTHER

The platform's role as a matchmaker is central to its ability to continue creating value as it scales. Traditional agents also connect producers to consumers. However, they can never operate at platform scale because their ability to match the two sides doesn't scale. A platform's ability to scale matchmaking helps it to achieve platform scale *(see Figure 15)*. Matchmaking is accomplished through data. As a result, data acquisition becomes an important priority for platforms. Designing the data model – specifications for what data are required for the value unit and the filter – is a critical step in platform design. This informs a platform's data acquisition strategy.

Match
Figure 16

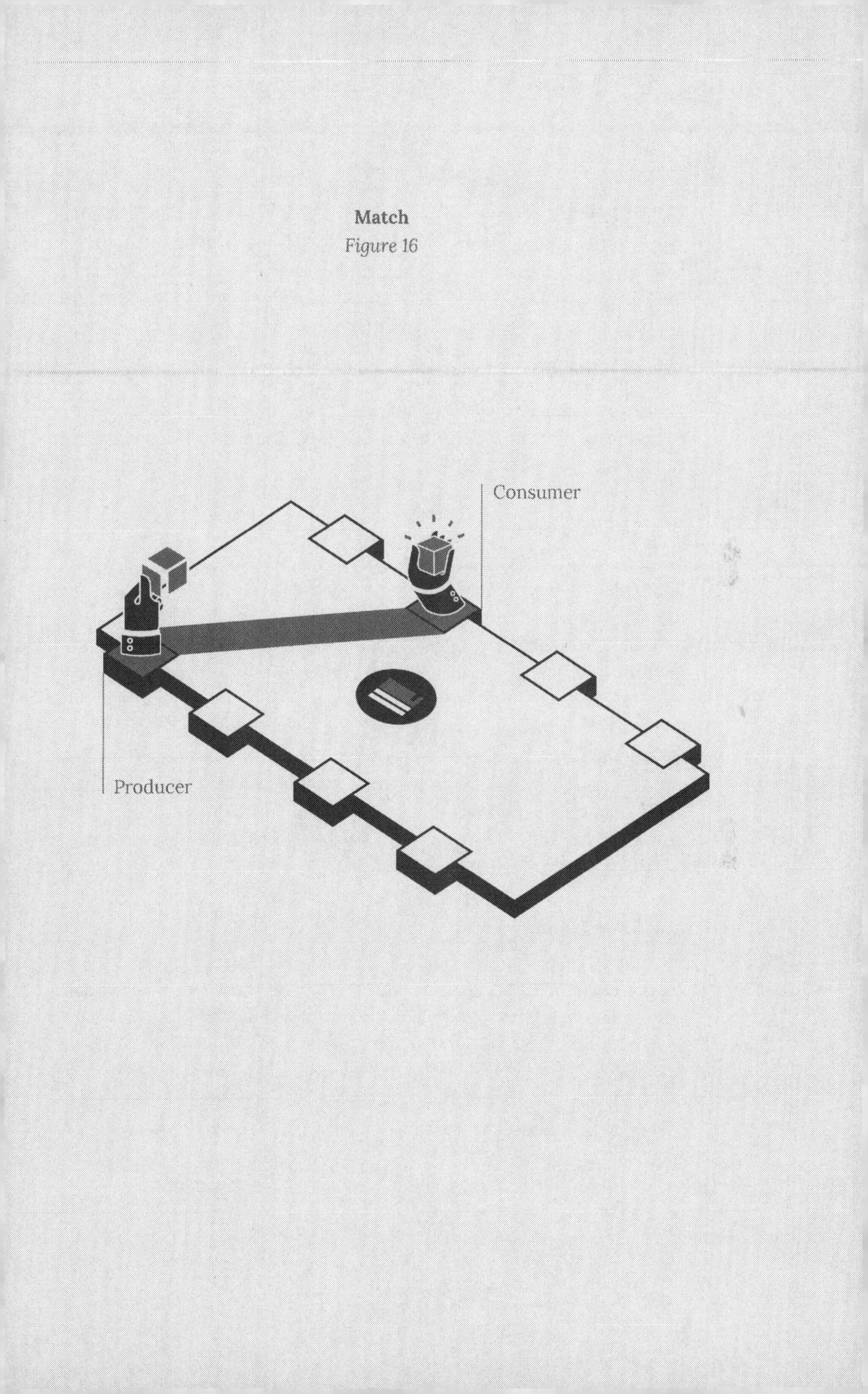

Data acquisition is subtle but critical. LinkedIn's progress bar encourages users to provide more data to the platform by showing them the completeness of their profiles and suggesting simple actions to enrich them further. Distracted users are often taken through an initial sign-up process on multiple platforms using similar progress bars. Data may also be acquired from third-party data providers, e.g., Facebook Connect.

Platforms need to capture implicit forms of data based on usage patterns. These data points strengthen the filters for serving value to consumers. As a user uses Facebook's newsfeed more often, the relevance of the newsfeed for the user increases.

THE PLATFORM LIFE CYCLE

The organizational focus of platform businesses may change over the course of their life cycle. Early on, a platform may invest heavily in creating pull. As a platform achieves scale, its ability to scale further increases. Hence, the need to invest in creating pull may drop. Conversely, a platform may not have a problem performing the matchmaking at a low scale. However, as more users get on board and abundance ensues, matchmaking may become the single most important focus of the platform.

Throughout the life cycle of the platform, it is important to keep re-evaluating organizational focus across these three priorities. As a platform scales, it is also important to ensure that an increasing chunk of these priorities is automated or moved out into the ecosystem in some form. We explore this in detail in the sections that follow.

PLATFORM SCALE IMPERATIVE

The importance of an interaction-first approach to building platforms cannot be emphasized enough. Focusing on the actions involved in an interaction helps us design the tools and services as well as the rules required to facilitate the interaction. Understanding the players participating in the interaction and their motivations helps us design the actions and rewards that create pull on the platform. Finally, only by focusing on the core interaction can a platform know what data it needs to capture.

THE PLATFORM CANVAS

A Tool For Makers To Build The Interaction-First Platform Business

The one theme that ties together all aspects of platform architecture is the plug-and-play nature of a platform business. At its very heart, a plug-and-play business is a participatory business, and it must be designed in a manner that encourages desirable and relevant participation. The plug-and-play nature of the platform enables it to perform its core goal of enabling interactions. This chapter, probably the most important one in this entire book, brings together all elements of a platform as a set of building blocks and arranges them in a central planning framework: the platform canvas. The canvas is a tool for makers to architect and build interaction-first platform businesses.

ESSENTIALS OF THE PLATFORM BUSINESS MODEL

Platforms allow producers to co-create value by plugging into the platform. A platform needs to be built as an open system so that external producers and consumers can easily plug in. As a business model, a platform should balance ease of plug-and-play with the ability to ensure quality and relevance. Open systems are also open to abuse, and a platform should ensure that it creates the right curation and filtering mechanisms to manage external participation. To lay out a framework for building the platform business model, let us revisit the key themes surrounding value creation on platforms:

1. The fundamental unit of value creation on platforms is the interaction between producers and consumers on the platform.
2. A platform may enable multiple interactions, but every platform has one core interaction. Edge interactions are built on the core interaction and often serve to reinforce the core interaction.
3. Platform architecture starts with structuring the interaction. The role of the platform business is structured as a consequence of structuring the interaction.

A business model is structured around the central mechanism of value creation and capture. *The platform business model is structured around the core interaction that it enables.* If a platform enables multiple interactions, the business model and architecture must be planned out one interaction at a time, starting with the core interaction.

The focus on the interaction is very important. In a traditional, linear, pipe business, analysis is focused on the customer or the user. In the case of a platform, focusing analysis on the user isn't useful enough. It is possible to engage and serve users without enabling the core interaction of the platform. When different types of users use the platform simultaneously, optimizing the experience for one user group may discourage the other user group from participating. The design of platforms needs to move away from user-centricity to interaction-centricity. In this context, the three essential elements of an interaction-centric platform business model are as follows:

1. The value-creating interaction
2. The platform that enables the interaction
3. A mechanism for value capture

The platform canvas, as we explore in the rest of this chapter, brings together all the building blocks of the platform and organizes them along the three principles shared above.

THE PLATFORM CANVAS – START WITH THE CORE INTERACTION

The starting point of the platform canvas is the interaction. As noted earlier, an interaction involves the creation of value by the producer. The platform provides an infrastructure for the creation of value and enables the transfer of value from producers to consumers.

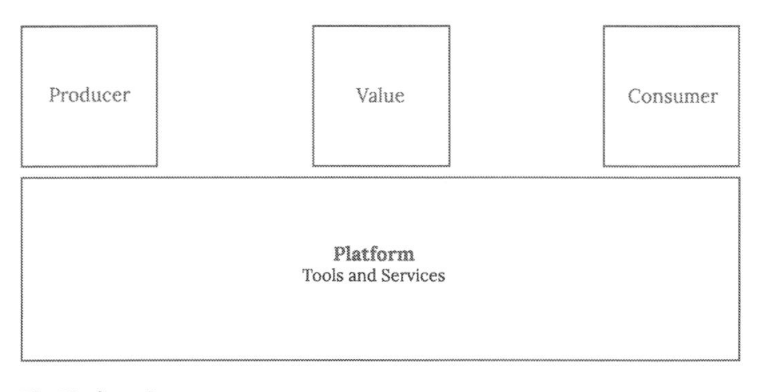

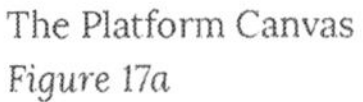
The Platform Canvas
Figure 17a

This brings together the first four building blocks for the platform canvas.
Producer, Consumer, And Platform. The platform acts as the infrastructure on which value is created and exchanged. The producer and consumer plug in to the platform to create and exchange value. As mentioned earlier, the terms "producer" and "consumer" refer to specific roles rather than specific user bases. The same person may act as a producer and consumer but will perform only one role in a particular interaction. Platform design should start with defining the roles of the producer and consumer and laying out their motivations for participating on the platform. This is explored in further detail in Section 3.
Value. The concept of value created on the platform is one of the most

important concepts. This value refers to what one would consider supply or inventory on the platform. These could be physical or digital goods, the availability of services, or the availability of service providers. In the case of data platforms, it could refer to data. On a platform like Facebook, the status updates and other content create value. On Etsy, the goods listings act as inventory. The supply of value on TaskRabbit refers to the availability of service providers. On a data platform like Nest, the data captured by the thermostat creates the supply of value. In addition to elaborating on the producer and consumer, the first step of platform design should also clearly lay out the atomic unit of value creation on the platform, as explained in Chapter 2 of this section.

THE PLATFORM CANVAS – BALANCE OPEN PARTICIPATION WITH QUALITY AND RELEVANCE

The second phase of building out the platform canvas requires the enablement of the plug-and-play business model. The platform must balance the creation of an open, participative system with the need for quality control and relevance.

Channels. To enable open participation, the platform must create channels by which producers and consumers can plug in to the platform. Channels may involve websites and apps, but they may also involve distributed access mechanisms like widgets, browser plug-ins, and share buttons or the provisioning of APIs and SDKs. More importantly, channels may even refer to other forms of access, including channel partners who help certain kinds of producers and consumers participate. The sales force is a channel that helps merchants plug in to Groupon.

Access Control And Filters. In addition to the provision of channels that encourage open participation, the platform must focus on two additional priorities in order to balance open access with the need for quality and relevance. This is achieved through the following mechanisms:

1. *Access Control For Producers.* The platform must create checks and balances that determine what kinds of producers are allowed and which types of production actions can be encouraged. It is important

to note that access control may be designed to apply to both platform access and post-access rights. Wikipedia allows platform access but controls access at the level of post-access rights. Access control mechanisms may be editorial, algorithmic, or even social. These models are explored in further detail in Sections 3 and 6.

2. *Filter Creation For Consumers.* The platform must invest in the creation of consumption filters that ensure that content served to the consumers is highly relevant to them. To create filters, the platform must acquire data on an ongoing basis. The choice of filters is covered in detail in Chapter 5 of this section.

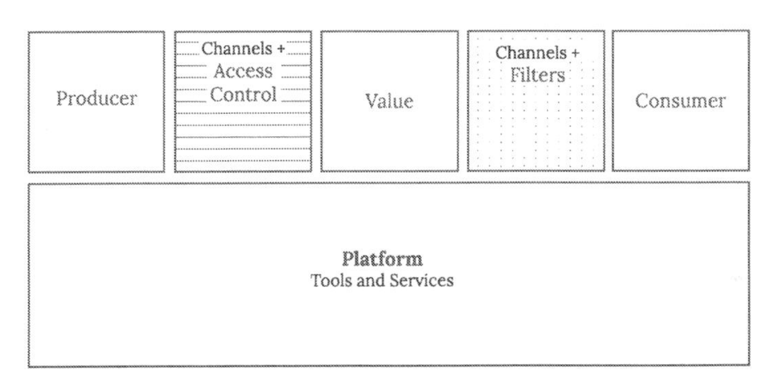

The Platform Canvas
Figure 17b

These two building blocks demonstrate the plug-and-play nature of the platform and balance open participation with the need for quality, abundance with the need for relevance

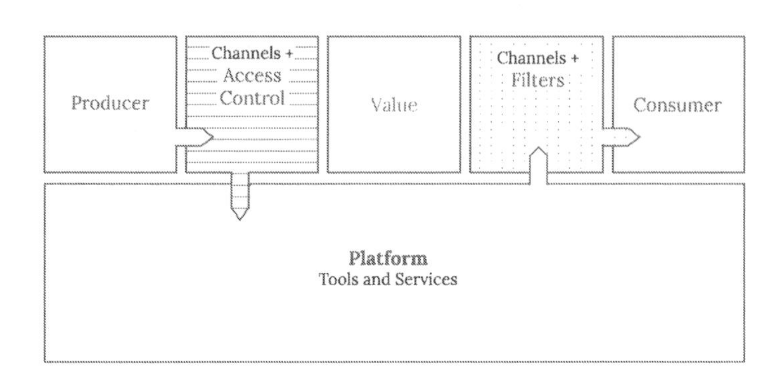

The Platform Canvas
Figure 17c

The relation of the platform tools, services, and channels to their ecosystem is demonstrated by how the building blocks of the canvas come together, as illustrated next:

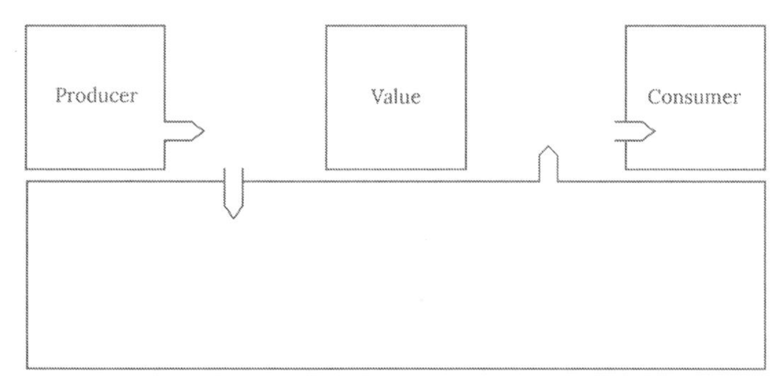

The Platform Canvas
Figure 17d

THE PLATFORM CANVAS – BUILD THE INFRASTRUCTURE TO ENABLE THE INTERACTION

Tools And Services: The platform enables the interaction. To do this, it must provide the right set of tools and services that producers and consumers can leverage. Across the interaction, the platform should provide the following:

1. *Tools And Services Of Creation.* This may constitute explicit specialized creation tools for producers, such as SDKs and content creation interfaces. Not all platforms require specialized creation tools. Platforms that enable the exchange of virtual goods (content) and remote services typically have the most sophisticated tools of creation.
2. *Tools And Services Of Curation And Customization.* This details the features, functionalities, and services that enable curation and customization on the platform. These may constitute in-house or partner-driven services as well as internal or external algorithms and social feedback mechanisms.
3. *Tools and services of consumption.* This may involve the set-up of consumption interfaces, newsfeeds, external widgets, and other such consumption tools, that serve value to consumers. It may even involve static interfaces. For example, an answer from Quora published in the Forbes magazine is an additional consumption outlet for value created on the platform.

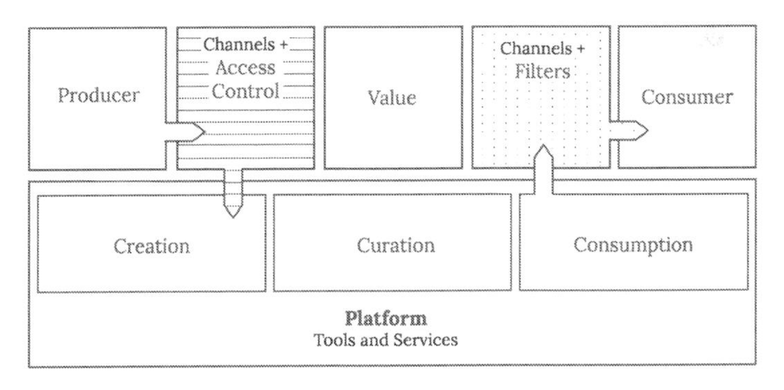

The Platform Canvas
Figure 17e

THE PLATFORM CANVAS – FOCUS ON VALUE CAPTURE

The last step of building out the platform canvas focuses on value capture by the platform. This involves two factors.

Currency. First, in every interaction, the consumer pays the producer using some form of currency. This currency may be money, but it may also be attention, reputation, influence, or some other form of non-monetary currency. This must be factored into the platform canvas. *(see Figure 17d)*

Capture. Finally, the platform must ensure that it captures value in some fashion. When actual money is exchanged through the platform, the platform may capture a cut of the transaction.

If not, the following are five other ways in which the platform may capture value:

1. Charging one side to access the other
2. Charging a third party for advertising
3. Charging producers and consumers for premium tools and services
4. Charging consumers for access to high-quality, curated producers
5. Charging producers for an ability to signal high quality

Regardless of the mechanism of value capture, the capture of value can always be traced back to the interactions that the platform enables.

It is also important to note that the platform captures some form of value from every interaction, though it may not be as money. The capture of attention or data through one interaction may facilitate the capture of money through another interaction. Similarly, the ability to increase network density (consumers following producers) through one interaction may lead to a greater ability to monetize through another interaction.

Accounting for currency and value capture, the following is the fully laid out platform canvas *(see Figure 17f)*.

PULL-FACILITATE-MATCH AND THE PLATFORM CANVAS

The design of tools and services should closely align with the three roles of the platform: pull, facilitate, and match. The platform must ensure that it pulls, facilitates, and matches users on an ongoing basis and designs its tools and services to do so.

The Platform Canvas

Figure 17f

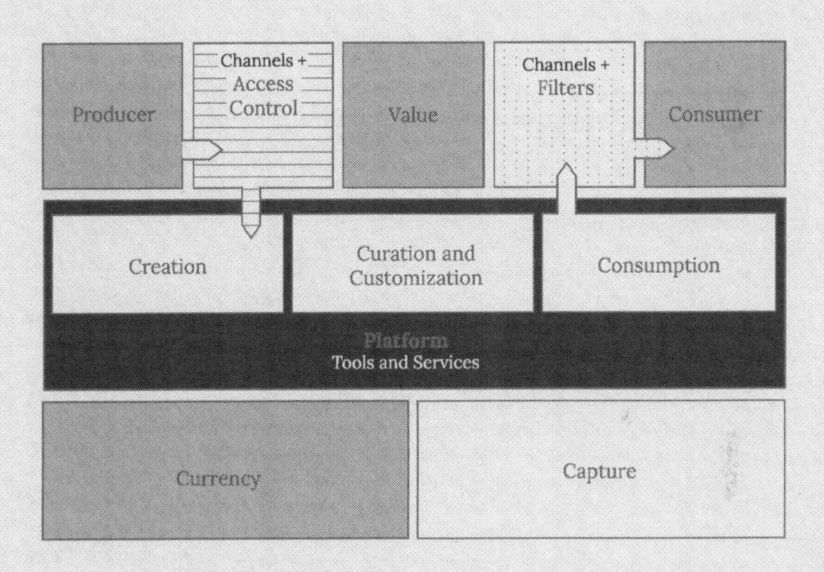

MULTI-SIDED PLATFORMS WITH MULTIPLE INTERACTIONS

Some platforms focus almost entirely on enabling one core interaction, but many platforms have more than one interaction. These platforms enable edge interactions around the central core interaction.

The architecture of these platforms must evolve one interaction at a time. Starting with the core interaction, the platform canvas may be used to lay out the architecture of the platform. Once the platform is architected to enable the core interaction, the canvas may now be leveraged to lay out an edge interaction. In all likelihood, the edge interaction leverages some part of the core interaction and thus benefits from platform elements that have already been laid out. In addition, the value captured in the core interaction may be leveraged in the edge interaction and vice versa.

LinkedIn's core interaction involves the connection and interaction of professionals with each other. An edge interaction allows recruiters to target professionals with jobs. The data captured in the core interaction may be used in the edge interaction. Many of the tools and services made available by the platform in the core interaction are leveraged in the edge interaction.

In general, designing the platform around the core interaction fleshes out most elements that the platform business must have. Additional elements may be designed on top of this by visiting each interaction in turn and building out the incremental components required to enable the same.

PLATFORM SCALE IMPERATIVE – THE MAKERS CHECKLIST

The creation of any platform starts with identifying the core interaction. The platform needs to be architected in relation to the core interaction. The business architecture of the platform *(see Figure 17a)* starts with the following questions:

1. What is the core interaction that the platform enables?
2. What is the unit of value created on the platform such that, without it, the platform has little or no value? What is the supply or inventory created on the platform?
3. Who are the producers of value? What motivates them to produce?

4. Who are the consumers of value? What motivates them to consume?

   Once the core interaction is laid out in relation to the platform, the plug-and-play nature of the platform needs to be designed (*see Figure 17c*):

5. What channels are used by producers to create value on the platform?
6. How does the platform manage access control for producers on these channels? What are the rules of access?
7. What channels are used by consumers to consume value from the platform?
8. What filters does the platform need to serve relevant content to consumers and to connect them with relevant producers?

   The third phase involves the definition of platform tools and services (*see Figure 17e*):

9. What tools and services should the platform provide to enable the interaction?
10. What creation tools and services should the platform provide?
11. What curation and customization tools and services should the platform provide?
12. What consumption tools and services should the platform provide?
13. How do these tools and services help the platform to 1) pull, 2) facilitate, and 3) match?

    The final phase of platform architecture involves value capture (*see Figure 17f*):

14. What currency does the consumer provide to the producer in exchange for value?
15. How does the platform capture some portion of this currency for itself?

The canvas should first be laid out for the core interaction and subsequently for all edge interactions.

Leveraging the 15 questions above, platform builders can design and architect a platform business centered around an interaction. For a platform with multiple interactions, the same process is repeated for the edge interactions after the core interaction has been designed.

EMERGENCE

The Philosophy Of Building Airbnb For X, Uber For Y, Or Twitter For Z

Moodswing started as a platform allowing users to express their moods. Its founder called it "Twitter for moods." It went nowhere for some time, until it found traction among a group of users who started using it to express depression and insecurity. The founder realized that the platform needed to move in a different direction and layered an edge interaction: allowing users to connect to psychology students and practitioners for help. The platform had shifted direction.

Here at the end of Section 2, one may be forgiven for believing that platforms can be carefully designed and architected. However, the true measure of a platform lies in the fact that users tend to take platforms in vastly different directions from what the founder and creators ever imagined. How does one balance the need for architecture with apparent randomness and luck?

EMERGENCE

The answer to this lies in a phenomenon that we often see in the behavior of ants and bees or in the rise of cities: emergence. A small set of micro-level rules gives rise to macro-level movements on emergent systems. Ants and bees do not work in hierarchical order but self-organize themselves towards larger goals by following micro-level interaction rules. Every food-seeking ant and honey-seeking bee knows what to do at a micro-level when it finds what it is looking for. The ant's trail and the bee's dance sparks a coordination of actions across the entire group. Larger outcomes emerge as a consequence of these seemingly insignificant actions.

Platforms can be designed based on a set of rules, but they emerge of their own accord. This does not take away the importance of business design and architecture. Platforms need structured business architecture, but they must allow for emergent behavior, some of which may redefine the architecture and lead the platform in an entirely new direction.

THE TRIE (TOOLS-RULES-INTERACTION-EXPERIENCE) FRAMEWORK

A platform provides the infrastructure for interactions. It determines the tools and rules of interaction.

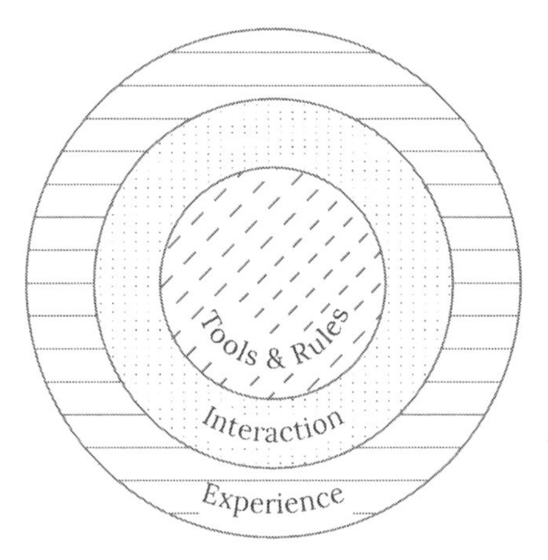

The TRIE
Figure 18a

The tools and rules define the kind of interaction allowed on the platform. This in turn creates a certain user experience for both producers and consumers. To understand the role of emergence in a carefully architected platform, one must understand the interplay of these three distinct layers. What appears on the surface is the result of emergent behavior. But as we peel away the various layers, we reach a core that must be carefully designed and architected. This core is the only portion over which the platform has any form of creative control.

Tools and Rules

The tools (and services) that a platform provides involve the infrastructure of the platform. The video uploading and hosting capabilities on YouTube are examples of tools.

The rules are baked into the platform and lay out the boundaries of user behavior. The 140-character limit on Twitter is an explicit rule. A more implicit rule is the search algorithm on Airbnb that determines which listings show up on the first results page for a query.

These are the boundaries of platform control. A platform may build out the technology (tools) and structure the constraints and algorithms that facilitate behavior (rules), but none of this guarantees success with the platform. Success can be planned for but not guaranteed.

This brings us to the next layer surrounding the core.

The Interaction

Unless users come on board and interact with each other, the platform will remain a ghost town. Consider an online education platform like Udemy. The teacher creating the course and the students learning from the course and rating the teacher/course together constitute the interaction. The interaction is determined by the tools and rules of the platform. The platform may specify what kinds of courses are accepted, what types of payment options are supported, or which countries/languages the platform supports. The actions that users take during interactions work together to determine the final experience.

The Experience

Producers and consumers participate on a platform repeatedly if they get value out of using it. While the interaction layer involves actions that users perform, the experience layer illustrates the value that users get out of using the platform.

While the interaction lays out the structure of value creation, there are various reasons that different users may use the same platform. The same interaction structure may yield different experiences. This is usually determined by the nature of the core value unit on the platform. Some users use YouTube for education, while others use it for entertainment. Some use Airbnb for travel, while others use it to find a roommate and split the rent for a short period. Different use cases may be powered by the same interaction structure.

The experience layer may solve diverse user problems, relying on the same mechanics in the interaction layer.

The three layers together provide a framework to understand the interplay between emergence and architecture.

TRIE: TOOLS-RULES-INTERACTION-EXPERIENCE

Interplay

The rules determine the boundaries of the interaction: what is and isn't allowed. The interaction, in turn, determines the experience for users.

Conversely, every desired outcome in the experience layer must be coded (in code or in principle) in the rules layer.

The interplay works out as follows. The platform provides the tools and rules. The users participate in the Interaction. The interaction is guided, facilitated, and governed by the tools and rules to deliver the experience. The role of technology in enabling interactions and eventual experience takes an inside-out view as described above.

Outside-In Vs. Inside-Out

An inside-out understanding, as described above, helps us understand how architectural and design decisions affect the overall experience. It also helps us appreciate how little control the platform architect has on the user experience. In an online marketplace, the marketplace owner only owns the tools and rules. In an online store, the store owner controls the inventory that is sold.

The inside-out perspective must be complemented with the outside-in

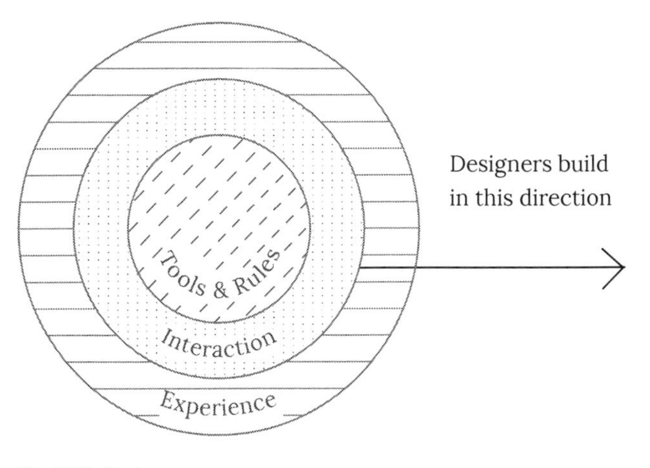

The TRIE: Designer
Figure 18b

perspective. The structure of tools and rules should be balanced with an understanding of producer and consumer motivations and the job to be done for both roles.

To understand, identify, and plan for emergence, the platform manager should lay out the job to be done for both the producer and the consumer, and should constantly monitor the platform for new behaviors and use cases emerging on it.

Understanding the jobs to be done helps to lay out the experience that users may derive from the platform.

Once the job to be done is understood from the producer's and the consumer's perspectives, it is far more intuitive to lay out the set of actions that these two roles perform to get that job done.

This set of actions constitutes the interaction.

With the interaction in place, the platform manager may determine the tools that will be needed for this interaction. At this point, one may also define which actions are allowed and which ones aren't. These are then baked into the rules of the platform.

This lays out the tools and rules.

All platform architecture should frequently flip from the inside-out view that has been discussed throughout this section to balance the outside-in perspective to ensure that the platform is designed in a way that encourages actual usage.

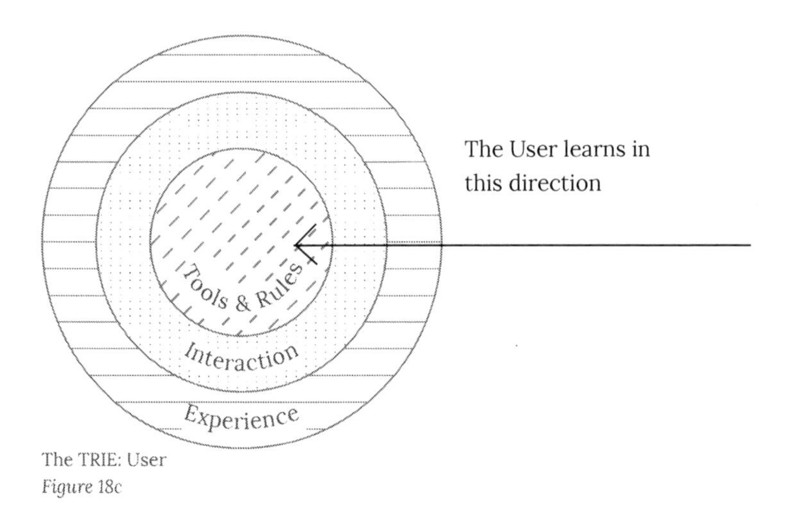

The TRIE: User
Figure 18c

WHY YOUR USERS WON'T SHOW THE WAY

Most platforms fail when they start with technology. They build out the inner core of the business (tools and rules) and stay stuck. Users don't use the platform to engage in interactions. Consequently, the platform doesn't get the job done for users.

At launch, every platform contains the center of tools and rules. In the world of platforms, the boulevard of broken dreams is strewn with well-engineered technology that no one wanted to use. To succeed, the platform must develop the next layer. The tools and rules layer should encourage interaction. One might argue that, in hindsight, Twitter's 140-character limit is a brilliant rule, as it enables more people to participate because of the much lower investment required to create content.

The TRIE: Tools & Rules
Figure 18d

WHEN USERS SHOW THE WAY

> "*You know you have a platform when the users can shape their own experience – not just accept the maker's ideas*" – Jeff Jarvis

A well-designed platform should, ironically, also work against its design to encourage emergence. Users should be provided guidelines but be allowed to take the platform in new directions. More often than not, a platform that succeeds in enabling interactions is taken in new directions as users figure out new ways of using the platform. Users tinker around in the interaction layer to create new experiences. Experiences that prove rewarding are repeated more often in the interaction layer. Over time, the platform notes how users are taking things in new directions and may make changes to the architecture – to the tools and rules – to enable users to move in that direction. This is one of the most common ways in which

successful platforms "pivot" after gaining initial adoption.
Twitter is a great example. Originally launched without a particularly specific use case, users started using it to discuss and share, and even break news. The hashtag (originally proposed by Chris Messina as a user) and the trending feature evolved over time to accommodate new use cases centered on real-time discovery. Changes in the interaction led to changes in the experience. Changes that were received well in the experience layer further spurred those interactions. Over time, the trending feature was instituted into the tools and rules to encourage these interactions further.

The TRIE: Interaction
Figure 18e

CASE STUDY: TWITTER

Twitter has a fairly simple set of tools and rules (in contrast to Wikipedia, Uber, or Quora, which have more complex rules).
Twitter's key rules involve the following:

1. Posts must have 140 characters or fewer.
2. Hashtags are clickable and reorganize the feed.
3. Users must be mentioned using @.
4. What you get is determined by who you follow.
5. The stream is reverse-chronological (though it now allows for threading).

6. Favorites, retweets, and mentions will drive notifications.

This is by no means a comprehensive list, but it gives an indication of the underlying rules at play.

The actions that make up the core interaction are also fairly simple. Users tweet, retweet, and favorite. But there are emergent actions. Hashtagging itself was an action that emerged from usage patterns and later fed back into the rules. $-tagging was another such action that gave birth to a whole new company: StockTwits.

Now, step back and look at the experience. The simplicity of the rules and interactions can barely predict the range of experiences, from the rise of the Arab Spring to the unbridled spread of selfies, from Justin Bieber fan-girling to Kevin Spacey photobombing, from breaking news to what I had for breakfast. Few platforms generate the range of experiences that Twitter does from such a simple set of core rules.

In the three circles of the TRIE framework, the outer circle is an explosion, despite the fact that the center is a small core. Twitter is probably the exception here rather than the rule, but it serves to demonstrate how architecture and emergence constantly interact to take the platform in new directions.

FEATURE CREEP SQUARED

The TRIE framework also demonstrates that the problem of feature creep has much larger implications in the case of platforms. On single-user software, feature creep may lead to poor usability. But on a platform, a slight tweak in the tools and rules layer may have a compounded impact on the experience layer.

PLATFORM SCALE IMPERATIVE

A robust business architecture is critical to building a scalable and sustainable platform business model. But the best-designed platforms are those that allow for emergence. An interaction-first mindset is best enabled when the interaction constantly guides the architecture, even as the architecture is aimed at enabling interactions.

The next section unpacks the management decisions that contribute to building a business with an interaction-first mindset toward achieving platform scale.

BUILDING INTERACTION-FIRST PLATFORMS

Platform scale is achieved by maximizing the repeatability and efficiency of the platform's core interaction.

INTRODUCTION

The Entrepreneur's Road To Execution

Execution toward platform scale works on two core principles discussed in the first two sections of this book:

1. The platform must build incentives and behaviors to encourage an ecosystem of producers and consumers to interact often.
2. The platform must increase the repeatability and efficiency of interactions over time.
3. Section 3 explores the design, engineering, and management choices that help achieve these objectives.

ECOSYSTEM INCENTIVES

User-producers scale value on platforms much like employees scale value in pipe businesses. In-house labor is organized around processes to achieve pipe scale. An entire body of management research is dedicated to helping businesses do this efficiently. Similarly, networked ecosystems of users and partners must be aligned so that they participate repeatedly in the value-creating core interaction on the platform. Users create value for platforms like YouTube, Medium, Quora, and Threadless. Users push the valuation of companies like WhatsApp and Instagram, both of which had a handful of employees while boasting valuations in excess of a billion dollars. Every time that users participate on these platforms, they contribute value in the form of content and data. As users participate more often, platforms scale faster. Airbnb and Uber fight employee-driven organizations with ecosystems. Apple and Android created ecosystems of developers around their respective platforms to disrupt an entire industry. Increasingly numbers of companies are turning to crowdsourcing to solve problems that they traditionally solved in-house.

The user-employee distinction is probably least stark in the case of a host of labor platforms that try to be Uber for X. Platforms like Homejoy, MyClean, and SpoonRocket create ecosystems of contract workers who might as well be employees. While some of these platforms are still negotiating the regulatory structures governing these new business models, many others have already demonstrated the power of producer ecosystems to drive value creation in a networked age.

INTERACTION REPEATABILITY AND EFFICIENCY

Producers and consumers should be encouraged to participate on the platform in a manner that maximizes the repeatability of the core interaction. The repeatability of the core interaction drives platform scale. To achieve platform scale, a platform must be managed such that the core interaction is repeated in a scalable and sustainable fashion. *Repeatable and efficient interactions hold the key to platform scale.* Repeatability involves ensuring that:

1. All actions in the interaction are executed smoothly.
2. The feedback loop in an interaction is executed so that it kick-starts the next interaction organically.

SIX ELEMENTS OF EXECUTION

To execute toward platform scale, the following elements must be in place:

1. *Choice of the overall interaction space.* The organization of producers

and consumers around an interaction determines their motivation to participate in these interactions.

2. *Production incentives.* Producers must be appropriately incentivized to participate repeatedly.
3. *Building long-term cumulative value.* Platforms must ensure that participants – particularly producers – find long-term value in participation, value that scales as producers participate repeatedly on the platform. A platform that becomes more valuable with usage will attract greater usage.
4. *Strong curation mechanisms and trust.* All participants must be encouraged to repeatedly participate by ensuring that the platform rewards quality and mitigates risk.
5. *Strong filters and relevance.* Consumers should be able to find items of relevance with minimal effort and risk.
6. *Ownable interactions.* The platform should be able to own interactions sustainably and create enough value to prevent off-platform collusion among producers and consumers.

The chapters in this section explore the six elements above, going into the management of platform business models. Chapter 1 lays a foundation for the construction of virtual interaction spaces that are essential to platform interactions. Chapters 2, 3, and 4 focus on interaction repeatability and efficiency from a quantity perspective. These chapters lay out strategies to maximize the number of interactions and make them more repeatable. Chapters 5 to 8 create a framework for understanding interaction repeatability from a quality perspective so that the platform encourages desirable interactions and discourages undesirable ones. Finally, Chapter 9 explores factors that determine a platform's ability to retain and sustain interactions between producers and consumers in the long run.

When building platforms, entrepreneurs and managers must ensure that they incorporate all six elements mentioned above. These elements work together to ensure the repeatability and efficiency of the core interaction.

3.1

INTERACTION DRIVERS

The Science Of Building Virtual Spaces

Cities and buildings are architected with a view to creating interaction spaces. Parks, malls, community clubs, and even traffic junctions are interaction spaces where residents of the city interact. Every individual participant is affected by the actions of others in the vicinity. Urban architects will readily concede that the construction of physical interaction spaces is a challenge for most cities. The construction of spaces that allow congregation and interaction of residents requires an interaction-first approach, similar to the one explored so far with regard to building platforms. Understanding how users interact in physical space helps in building out the physical space that helps such users interact most efficiently.

Platforms must build virtual interaction spaces. Unlike physical interaction spaces, virtual interaction spaces do not exist within inhabited cities. But the creation of virtual interaction spaces follows the same set of principles that guides the creation of physical interaction spaces.

INTERACTION DRIVERS

Interaction drivers form the basis for driving interactions among participants in any interaction space. The choice of interaction drivers determines how participants in that space interact. Six different forms of interaction drivers are commonly observed in physical and virtual interaction spaces:

- *Connection.* Participants in an interaction must have a pre-existing relationship before they can interact. Families are organized around this principle.
- *Content.* Participants in an interaction interact through the creation and consumption of content, without any prior relationship requirements. Shared interests rather than participant relationships drive interactions. Special-interest clubs and city walking tours work on this principle.
- *Clout.* The interaction space is structured such that certain participants – typically producers – drive interactions across multiple other participants because of their greater influence. Conferences are structured around this organizing principle.
- *Coordination.* Interactions arise from a set of instructed actions that coordinate participants toward an outcome rather than deriving from existing relationships, influence, or shared interests. Open workshops, especially those targeted at a mixed audience, work along these lines.
- *Competition.* Interactions may be dominated by competitive moves among participants. Racing events may seem like an obvious example, but long-term urges to keep up with one's neighbors are also governed by these principles.
- *Culture and code.* Certain interaction spaces may be structured entirely around a shared culture and code. The exchange of content, development of influence, coordination of work, and the creation of relationships are all subservient to the shared culture and code. Cults and movements organize themselves along these lines.

It is important to note that most interaction spaces evolve to leverage a combination of multiple interaction drivers even though they may start with a single dominant one. Shared interest groups may start organizing themselves around content and eventually lead to connection among participants, the emergence of clout for select participants, coordination toward common tasks, and, eventually, the development of a shared culture and code. Organizations and armies use a combination of all interaction principles to organize large groups of people toward a common outcome. Virtual interaction spaces are also organized around these interaction drivers. As with a physical interaction space, every virtual interaction space may leverage more than one driver. The choice of interaction driver significantly affects the type of platform that one builds. These choices are explored in detail in the context of virtual interaction spaces below.

CONNECTION

Virtual interaction spaces may be organized around relationships between participants. Social networks like Facebook and LinkedIn are organized in this manner. Users are required to connect before they may participate in any form of interaction. Certain marketplaces may also be organized under this model. Unlike eBay or Airbnb, where the listing to be transacted takes precedence, a connection-based marketplace is organized around user relationships. Users transact with people they already know.

CONTENT

Many interaction spaces online are structured around content. Platforms like Medium and YouTube as well as marketplaces like eBay and Etsy are structured around content. Consumers primarily explore content. Producers focus entirely on creating and promoting content. Even if the consumers and producers connect with each other, such connections center around some prior discovery of content. The participation may be scaled by scaling the quality and amount of the content on the platform. Discovery of content and the relevance of the content served determine the value created in these interaction spaces for consumers. Likewise, the ease of producing content determines the value created for producers.

CLOUT

Clout-based interaction spaces are organized around producer influence. A few producers with a high degree of influence determine the experience for a large number of consumers. Twitter works on a clout-based model, but so do producer-driven marketplaces like Udemy. The choice of producers is critical for such a platform. Clout-based interaction spaces also require the creation of a reputation system that assigns clout and influence to a specific producer based on the quality of his or her participation on the platform. Clout may be explicit, as in the form of a Twitter following or a StackOverflow badge. Clout may also be implicit, where highly reputed users may receive greater exposure on the platform algorithmically.

COORDINATION

Interaction spaces may also be structured around the coordination of tasks and workflows. Wikipedia, Viki, and Quirky are examples of platforms that are structured around the coordination of different types of producers toward a common goal. B2B supply networks are also structured around coordination mechanisms and will increasingly benefit from platforms with interaction spaces designed around coordination mechanisms. Coordination mechanisms organize users around small tasks that work together to create a whole. Every user's individual action in a coordinated workflow affects the experience and subsequent actions of every other user. An inflow of poor-quality contributors on Wikipedia may lead to greater coordination efforts and a poorer interaction experience for existing editors. As a result, coordination mechanisms invariably rely on a reputation management system to ensure that users are accorded rights and access on the basis of their reputation, derived from past activity on the platform.

COMPETITION

Certain interaction spaces may be structured around competitive dynamics. 99Designs is a platform that allows designers to bid competitively on design projects. Many crowdfunding platforms are organized under this model.

Competitive mechanisms choose one winner out of several participants. As a result, competitive mechanisms work best in scenarios where participants can compete with minimal investment to cap the losses incurred by those who do not win. If participation costs are high, participants who lose often may gradually become discouraged from participation, reducing the efficacy of such an interaction space.

CULTURE AND CODE

Certain interaction spaces may be centered entirely on a shared culture and code. Very few interaction spaces start centered on culture alone. Most are centered on content and shared interests, eventually giving rise to a shared culture. This is especially observed in the emergence of online gaming guilds. Certain platforms may seem to be organized around content but assume a unique culture over time. Reddit and HackerNews are functionally organized around content and clout but are well known for their strong, insular culture.

NETWORK STRUCTURES AND INTERACTION SUSTAINABILITY

On networked platforms, the network structure of the platform is directly determined by the choice of interaction driver.

The network structure of a connection-dominant interaction space is composed of explicit two-sided connections. Both sides need to connect with each other before any other forms of interaction can start. On such platforms, the sustainability of interactions depends entirely on users' connections and the nature and frequency of activity in their immediate network. The Facebook newsfeed remains lively and fresh as long as one's immediate network produces content often.

In contrast, the network structure of a clout-dominant interaction space is composed of explicit or implicit one-sided relationships. Consumers follow producers without explicit consent being required of producers. Certain nodes in the network develop a high connection density as a result. Less than 1% of users on Twitter have more than 10,000 followers. These interaction spaces scale by bringing high-quality producers on board and constantly nurturing and incentivizing them to increase their participation on the platform.

The network structures of content-dominant interaction spaces predominantly involve implicit relationships between users through the content exchanged. As an example, a writer and a reader on Medium may be related implicitly because of their interactions (views, favorites, and comments) centered on a unit of content. This may help Medium recommend more content from the writer to that reader in the future.

Coordination-dominant and competition-dominant interaction spaces may have more fluid network structures that reorganize themselves every time a new event occurs. For instance, a new competition on 99Designs positions a new set of designers against each other, while a new article on Wikipedia coordinates a new set of contributors toward an outcome.

Finally, culture-dominant interaction spaces function more through implicit beliefs than explicit network mechanics and may not exhibit discernible network structures until other forms of interaction drivers take hold.

PLATFORMS AS INTERACTION SPACES

Most platforms rely on multiple interaction drivers. For instance, Facebook started as a connection-dominant platform but has rapidly employed multiple other interaction drivers. The network has constantly layered new forms of content, from photos and embeddable links to apps, to enable new interactions. Fan pages and followings allow the creation of clout while Facebook Groups may be organized around culture and code.

Quora is another example of a platform based on a combination of interaction drivers. While the core interaction is centered on content (questions and answers), the mechanism of answers being upvoted and gaining greater exposure is based on competition. Its virtual currency (credits), combined with the ability to develop a user following, enables the development of clout on the platform. Users can collaboratively suggest edits to improve answers. Finally, it also allows some level of connection, allowing users to connect directly and exchange messages with each other.

PLATFORM SCALE IMPERATIVE

The same platform idea can yield vastly different business models when structured around different interaction drivers.

To leverage this fully, entrepreneurs and managers should revisit the platform canvas described in Section 2 and evaluate their ideas with a new interaction driver in mind every time. A connection-dominant platform may be strengthened when restructured as a clout-dominant platform. Adding competitive and collaborative mechanisms to a platform may engage users more often on a platform that is struggling to scale engagement.

Understanding interaction drivers also helps a late entrant enter a crowded space by choosing a different set of interaction drivers than those used by current players. For example, Twitter distinguished itself from all previous social networks by building a clout-dominant platform. Quora distinguished itself from traditional forums and question-and-answer platforms like Yahoo Answers by leveraging clout, collaboration, and content as interaction drivers in new ways.

Understanding these six interaction drivers helps entrepreneurs and managers give new strategic direction to the platform. Instead of competing on features, platform builders may use this framework to compete on a fundamentally different set of interaction drivers for their ecosystem of producers and consumers.

3.2

BUILDING USER CONTRIBUTION SYSTEMS

Designing For Production

Interaction-first platforms need an active ecosystem of producers to create value. A platform without producers is a ghost town, and there is little incentive for consumers to use it. Replicating the technology of Airbnb or YouTube is a considerably smaller challenge compared to replicating their respective communities of hosts or video creators.

Producers are active partners in creating (and delivering) the value proposition of the platform. Too often, they are bucketed under the term "users" without giving due importance to the production function on a platform. Understanding producer and consumer roles and catering to them individually is important for driving interactions on the platform. To execute toward platform scale, every platform needs to:

1. Understand the motivations of the producers.
2. Create enabling technology that caters to those motivations.
3. Have a clear strategy to maximize the number of producers on the platform and the frequency of their participation.

This chapter provides a checklist for planning and laying out incentives for producers on a platform.

DOES THE PLATFORM PROVIDE TOOLS, ACCESS, OR BOTH?

Platforms may provide producers with the tools to enable them to be creative. Alternately, platforms may provide them with channels to market their creations to an audience. Some platforms may provide both incentives.
Tools: Platforms may provide production and/or infrastructural tools. Vimeo gives anyone the ability to host a high-definition video online and delivers video streaming quality that is superior to those of all competitors. Instagram enables users to produce beautiful photos without being Photoshop experts. The provision of production tools goes beyond mere infrastructure. Instagram provides a production tool, but Flickr, in its original manifestation, provided only a hosting infrastructure.
Access. In some cases, platforms may provide access to a specific desired audience. Dribbble allows designers to upload their creations and gives them access to the right professional community. Airbnb provides global access in a way that enables anyone to be a host and run an accommodation and short-term rental business.
Tools + Access. Platforms that provide producers with both tools and access often beat platforms that provide only one of the two. That is what enabled Instagram, a late follower, to disrupt Hipstamatic, a far superior product. Hipstamatic allowed users to apply filters to pictures (initially), but Instagram created a thriving community around such photos, thereby providing tools as well as access. Facebook Photos similarly disrupted Flickr to become the largest storehouse of photos on the Internet. Facebook provided access to an audience while Flickr provided only hosting tools. WordPress provides superior tools to producers, but Medium provides tools as well as access. In a networked age, access constitutes much of the value proposition. Platforms that offer producers only tools may be disrupted by those that provide access as well.

DOES THE PLATFORM SIMPLIFY THE PRODUCTION PROCESS?

There is no dearth of choice on the Internet. Competing platforms are a click away. In such a scenario, platforms that make creation easy and allow users with lower skills to create high-quality creations may achieve higher traction.

The number of people who tweet is much higher than the number of people who blog. This is partly because Twitter provides channels to an audience in addition to tools. However, the more important factor is the lower skill level and investment required to tweet compared to writing a blog post. Similarly, Instagram lowers the level of skills required to create beautiful pictures, a factor that led to its widespread adoption.

DOES THE PLATFORM LEVERAGE A ROBUST CURATION MODEL TO SEPARATE THE BEST FROM THE REST?

Curation is critical on an open-access platform. The platform should have a robust model to separate the bathroom singers from the award winners. There are typically three broad models of curation, and a scalable platform usually leverages a combination of all three:

1. *Algorithmic curation.* The key ingredient of a scalable model of curation is the algorithmic detection of good versus bad, based on certain rules. While algorithmic curation is highly scalable, it may also lead to false positives and reject good creations, similar to a spam filter erroneously capturing legitimate email and classifying it as spam. Hence, it should be scaled carefully and constantly "teach" and optimize itself with social and editorial inputs.
2. *Social curation.* Social curation leverages the networked and distributed nature of platforms. The community of consumers is provided with tools (such as voting, rating, and flagging tools) to offer inputs and signals regarding the quality of the creation, and the aggregation of these inputs is used to sort and rank creations on the platform. Beyond being a source of curation and quality control, it also ensures that producers constantly receive feedback from consumers. For all its benefits, social curation may not apply in certain scenarios, as illustrated later in this section.
3. *Editorial curation.* While tech entrepreneurs would want everything to be automated, manual curation holds a place on every platform, especially in its early days. Editorial curation helps in understanding patterns that can then be automated and scaled. In some cases, editorial curation can even be used to kick-start the platform when there aren't enough producers

on the platform. Quora, the popular community-driven Q&A platform, has employed editorial resources in both forms. In the early days of the platform, editors would ask and answer questions to generate activity. Editorial inputs would hold sway over a regular user's judgment in curating. Over time, editorial control over the platform was gradually relaxed as the users started driving curation.

DOES THE PLATFORM CREATE A CLEAR, DEMOCRATIC, EQUAL-ACCESS PATH TO THE TOP?

Platforms like Etsy and Airbnb allow producers to run entire businesses on them. Producers wouldn't participate unless they were assured of the democratic nature of such platforms.

Platforms need a curation model to separate signal from noise reliably. Content and listings that are ranked higher are also consumed more often. As a result, producers should understand the mechanisms by which curation and the ensuing exposure on the platform work.

In a manner similar to how website publishers invest in SEO to score high on Google's "curation" of the Web, producers on a platform need an understanding of what it takes to "rank high" on a platform. If the mechanism of ranking high and gaining visibility is unclear, producers may not be motivated to participate on the platform.

Platforms often struggle to ensure democratic exposure for all producers. Those who join early get to the top faster. Early Twitter and Pinterest users succeeded in building massive followings. Producers who come in later have a greater problem being discovered. The platform must ensure that all users, regardless of when they join, find equal opportunity.

DOES THE PLATFORM USE INORGANIC INCENTIVES TO MOTIVATE PRODUCERS?

While marketplace platforms allow producers to earn money and run businesses, most other platforms do not provide content creators with monetary benefits. Platforms may use inorganic incentives to encourage producers to stay engaged.

Threadless is a platform where designers can upload new T-shirt art, and the best-curated creations are printed on T-shirts and sold, with monetary incentives offered to the design creator. Inorganic incentives complement the organic incentives of community recognition and reputation. Similarly, designers who are ranked high on Dribbble have a greater chance of being selected for a design job on the Dribbble job board. Chictopia, a platform that allows fashion bloggers and enthusiasts to build influence, gives its top producers exclusive access to events like Paris Fashion Week. On a different note, writers on Quora and Medium have been known to land book deals, though not directly through their involvement with the platform.

DOES THE PLATFORM CONVERT CONSUMERS INTO PRODUCERS?

User-generated content has come a long way on the Internet. At one point, the 90-9-1 rule was often quoted to explain the low levels of contribution in online communities. Online communities were supposed to have 90% of users performing only consumption actions, 9% performing curation, and only 1% performing creation actions. Over the last few years, platforms have emerged with much higher percentages of producers, especially owing to the rise of smartphones, which allow a larger user base to create more often.

The success of a platform still hinges on its ability to maximize the percentage of producers. In its initial days, a platform must focus on attracting producers. But once a minimum number of producers are on board, a second cycle must be started: the platform needs to convert consumers into producers. Two mutually reinforcing mechanisms must work together. Producers coming on board attract consumers, and consumers, in turn, are converted to producers. This ensures that the platform constantly scales the number of producers on board.

HOW DOES THE PLATFORM COMMUNICATE FEEDBACK FROM CONSUMERS BACK TO PRODUCERS?

Producers participate repeatedly on a platform only if they are repeatedly encouraged and motivated. This is achieved through feedback. Every action taken by a producer involves effort. Producers are encouraged to participate repeatedly on a platform when they receive appropriate feedback for their effort. Feedback may take various forms. Producers on Twitter get explicit feedback in the form of retweets and favorites. Sellers on marketplaces may receive ratings and reviews that help them stand out for future transactions. Communicating feedback from consumers to producers is the single most important driver of sustainable and repeatable interactions on the platform.

PLATFORM SCALE IMPERATIVE

Producers power the platform engine by creating value on the platform. The platform must ensure that it bakes in incentives that encourage frequent participation, reward desirable behavior, and discourage undesirable actions. The effectiveness of an incentive should be measured by its ability to power the core interaction and drive higher value creation on the platform.

FRICTIONLESS LIKE INSTAGRAM

Removing Barriers For Producers

Platforms are often built with a feature-centric approach. Different platforms try to compete on features. The need to provide tools and access to producers is often misconstrued as a call to focus on features that enable producers to produce and distribute their creations. Production interfaces and technologies should be built not with a feature-centric approach but with the intent to lower the barriers to participation in the core interaction. To ensure repeatability of the core interaction, producers should be able to participate in it with minimum effort. Platform interfaces that lower – or completely remove – such barriers create entirely new markets that had never existed before.

THE SKILL BARRIER

Lack of skills is a barrier to getting something done. Tools help "unskilled" producers do something they couldn't have done before, break the skill barrier, and open up a new segment of producers.

Instagram lowers the skill barrier required to create beautiful photographs that once required Photoshop prowess. A Photoshop competitor, even if it were free, would never have gained the level of adoption that Instagram did.

THE TIME/EFFORT BARRIER

Bloggers must invest time and effort to write posts and build a following. Twitter lowers that barrier and enables publishing with a very low investment of time and effort. The 140-character limit, combined with the democratic nature of the real-time feed, encourages users with small followings to participate as well. Medium helps more serious writers build an audience while simplifying the writing interface and the act of finding an audience. Platforms that abstract all non-core activities for producers and act as true plug-and-play infrastructures succeed in attracting more production activity.

Overcoming the time/effort barrier may be equally useful for the consumer. Platforms achieve this through efficient aggregation and by lowering search costs for consumers. In the early days of the Web, Yahoo provided value as the home page of the Web. As the Web grew, and portal-based navigation grew more inefficient, Google's pull-based search helped consumers navigate the Web. In recent times, a variety of content consumption tools, ranging from Flipboard to Pocket, have attacked different content consumption problems with the sole purpose of reducing the time or effort barriers involved in the act of consumption.

THE INVESTMENT BARRIER

Platforms may help producers overcome the investment barrier. Marketing and promotion require investment, but all platforms allow an organic path to the top. Google allows users to rank high organically. Yelp enables merchants to be ranked high if they are rated favorably by consumers. In general, platforms allow producers to obtain market access without commensurate investment.

Platforms may also provide access to tools for free that may have been expensive to access in the past. Such platforms shift monetization from providing tools to enabling interactions. Platforms may often rely on complementary production technologies. Dribbble, Behance, and other designer-focused platforms gained traction with the democratization of design software and the associated rise in freelancing among designers. Some platforms may invest in providing monetary incentives to producers. Uber offers benefits and vehicle purchase schemes to drivers who want to buy a new car and start participating on Uber.

THE RESOURCE BARRIER

It is much easier to start a business in 2015 than it was in 1995. One of the most important reasons is the significant reduction in the amount of resources required to get a business up and running. An important contributor to this change is the rise of Amazon Web Services, which lowers the amount of resources required at the outset to start up. A startup that would have needed to procure a minimum level of infrastructure in 1995 may leverage Amazon's resources on demand in 2015.

THE ACCESS BARRIER

Platforms often disrupt gatekeepers by giving producers direct access to potential consumers. Most media businesses (publishing, performing arts) are industries with gatekeepers that determine which producers get market access. Platforms like Amazon Kindle Publishing, YouTube, and CDBaby reintermediated these industries to varying degrees by giving producers direct access to a market of consumers.

The long tail of sellers on online marketplaces wouldn't exist if not for the targeted access that online marketplaces provide. eBay created a large segment of sellers that never existed previously by lowering the access barrier, much like Airbnb unlocked apartments that would never have welcomed guests before.

The investment community (angel investors, VCs) is not necessarily an equal-access community, and the right connections and introductions can open many doors that would otherwise remain shut. Kickstarter and other crowdfunding platforms seek to democratize access to investment by allowing anyone to set up a project, state funding requirements, and raise money online.

PLATFORM SCALE IMPERATIVE

Platforms must reduce friction in usage and lower the barriers to participation. Platform managers should seek to maximize the return on investment for producers. Lowering investment ensures higher ROI and greater participation from producers, which ensures that the platform's core interaction is highly repeatable.

THE CREATION OF CUMULATIVE VALUE

Lock-In For An Opt-In World

The power of network effects cannot be disputed. As platforms gather more value through external production, they attract more consumption, which in turn attracts even more production. Network effects guarantee repeatable interactions. Both producers and consumers repeatedly participate on a platform that has strong network effects. Network effects hold the keys to the long-term retention of producers and consumers, which increases the repeatability of the core interaction.

But today, the power of the network effect is fading. The network effect isn't the one-stop solution for repeatable interactions that it once was.

SUFFICIENT NETWORK EFFECT

Platforms with network effects often benefit from a winner-takes-all dynamic. The winner usually aggregates all producers and consumers onto one platform because of ever-strengthening network effects. This results in the creation of virtual monopolies. There is, however, a small caveat: the consideration of multihoming costs.

In computer networking parlance, multihoming occurs when a computer or device is connected to more than one computer network. In the world of platforms, this notion is an important one. If producers and/or consumers can co-exist on multiple platforms, the platform faces a constant competitive threat. Eventually, it may be difficult for clear winners to emerge. Multihoming can prevent the onset of winner-takes-all scenarios. The defensibility and competitive advantage of a platform business are very closely related to the multihoming costs that its producers and consumers incur. High multihoming costs result in the strengthening of network effects around a dominant platform, leading to a winner-takes-all outcome. Multihoming costs are rapidly falling on today's platforms. In the age of the fax machine, users paid through their upfront investment in hardware. These upfront costs created lock-in, thereby creating barriers to entry for would-be competitors. Multihoming costs were high. In the age of the Internet, users no longer need to invest in physical hardware and upfront costs to join new networks. Multihoming is discouraged on online networks, allowing users to create their personal networks of connections. Switching between instant messaging services or between social networks is a non-trivial task. Users stick to Facebook or LinkedIn because they've invested in creating their personal network of connections. Multihoming costs are now associated with the creation of networks of people. However, these multihoming costs are not as strong as they used to be.

INSUFFICIENT NETWORK EFFECT

Two shifts have brought about a rapid decline in multihoming costs. First, the rise of the social graph allows users to port their personal networks between different platforms. A new platform, like Instagram, can leverage the single sign-on enabled by the social graph to build an alternate network of users rapidly. Second, mobile-based access allows users to switch easily and rapidly between different apps multiple times a day. This allows multihoming at a scale that was once unimaginable. Drivers today use Uber, Lyft, and a host of other apps simultaneously and switch between them several times a day. The convenience of the social graph, coupled with the ease of switching between platforms, has eroded the lock-in that once kept users bound to a network.

THINKING BEYOND THE NETWORK EFFECT

The network effect isn't quite as effective at retaining producers and consumers as it once was. Today, platforms need additional mechanisms to ensure that their best producers and consumers stick with them and continue to participate.

Platforms achieve this today by creating "cumulative value": value that scales as the producer/consumer uses the platform more often. Traditional lock-in was often predatory and contrary to the user's best interests. Cumulative value ensures that value for the user accelerates with greater usage. Traditional lock-in was achieved through levying high upfront costs for the user, as with a two-year mobile phone contract. Cumulative value is achieved through small actions that the user is encouraged to take over time. Cumulative value leads to higher value with higher invested effort, which in turn encourages the user to invest even more. In the long run, the creation of cumulative value ensures that the producers and consumers remain loyal to the platform.

CUMULATIVE VALUE

Platforms leverage cumulative value to encourage repeat participation by the best producers and consumers. Cumulative value doesn't merely encourage repeatable interactions; it increases the repeatability of desirable interactions. By design, it scales the participation of the best producers and consumers on the platform.Cumulative value takes four forms.

1. *Reputation*

Platforms like TaskRabbit may create greater stickiness for producers by allowing them to gather reputation. Reputation may take the form of explicit reputation, based on ratings and reviews, or implicit reputation, which does not have an explicit manifestation but is leveraged by a platform's algorithms to promote or demote a producer based on past actions. Reputation built on the platform contributes to better future opportunities and greater value for producers. To build reputation on a platform, producers must deliver highly rated goods and services consistently. Some platforms, like Airbnb, may have both sides explicitly rated. Some platforms may even create reputation based on editorial curation and vetting at the time of sign-up.

Reputation increases multihoming costs because it's difficult for producers to build reputation on multiple platforms. If a platform succeeds in helping a producer build reputation through a set of initial engagements, it succeeds in creating repeat participation for that particular producer.

2. *Influence*

Influence is created through two mechanisms. First, platforms that utilize a one-sided follow model enable producers to gain influence by building a loyal and engaged following of consumers. YouTube channel subscribers and Twitter followers are measures of influence on the respective platforms. In general, building a large, credible, and engaged following is possible only through repeated, engaged production on the platform. As the producer's follower count grows, so does the cumulative value.

Influence may also be created through a second mechanism. Platforms like Wikipedia and StackOverflow give producers access to new rights on the platform as they participate more. The best producers acquire higher creation and moderation rights on these platforms. In both cases, the creation of influence increases multihoming costs because producers find it difficult to invest efforts toward influence creation on multiple platforms. As a result, producers with greater influence tend to participate repeatedly on one platform.

3. *Collections*

A third source of cumulative value comes through allowing producers to create a collection. Photographers and designers use platforms like 500px and Dribbble to showcase their portfolios. Writers may use Medium to showcase theirs someday. A larger collection creates increasingly higher feedback for a producer. The more content a producer creates in her collection, the more social feedback she receives over time. Higher social feedback also leads to greater reputation and influence. In general, producers who invest in creating collections tend to invest more in a platform where they see more activity around their collection.

4. Learning filters

Consumers may also benefit from cumulative value. Consumers find that a platform becomes more useful with usage. The Facebook newsfeed understands a consumer better over time and becomes more relevant. These feeds are based on learning filters that constantly seek input from the user's explicit and implicit actions and refine themselves. The more a user consumes information, the more intelligent the algorithm becomes in recommending pertinent content, thereby retaining the user over time.

PLATFORM SCALE IMPERATIVE

The creation of cumulative value is one of the most effective ways for platforms to increase the repeatability of desirable interactions. It ensures that the best producers and consumers continue to participate and increase their participation over time. In tandem with other strategies mentioned in this section, every platform should carefully consider the most appropriate implementation of cumulative value for its producers and consumers.

THE TRACTION-FRICTION MATRIX

Experiments With Open Participation

Friction is often considered undesirable. This section devotes a whole chapter to the removal of barriers in order to encourage repeatable interactions. However, friction can also serve as a source of value by discouraging the repeatability of undesirable interactions.

Traction and friction are at odds with each other. Friction, arising from intentional and unintentional barriers to participation on the platform, gets in the way of traction – large-scale participation – on the platform.

Friction may be created by design (for instance, producers may have to go through background checks before they get access to the platform) or by accident (for example, the interface may have poor navigability or usability). Well-designed friction can lead to healthy and desirable interactions on the platform. Accidental and unintentional friction only gets in the way of traction, without creating additional value. Getting friction right is critical to the success of any plug-and-play architecture. This chapter explores some of the key design considerations when designing friction into the platform.

Platforms must be designed in a manner that optimally balances the quality and quantity of interactions by balancing traction and friction.

As with all design considerations, the ultimate goal of a platform is to enable repeatable interactions. Hence, as a rule of thumb:

Friction is a good thing only if it increases the repeatability of desirable interactions and decreases the repeatability of undesirable ones.

THE TRACTION-FRICTION MATRIX

The trade-off between traction and friction is best visualized through the traction-friction matrix.

- *High friction–low traction*: A platform may lie in this quadrant for one of two reasons: by design or by accident. Platforms that need high curation in their initial days fall into this quadrant. Alternately, poor interface design and navigability may throw a platform into this quadrant.
- *Low friction–high traction*: A platform falls into this quadrant for one of two reasons: frictionless experiences by design or a general lack of checks and balances.
- *High friction–high traction*: This is a great place to be, and successful platforms eventually migrate to this quadrant after starting off in one of the two quadrants described above.
- *Low friction–low traction*: This is the worst quadrant to get stuck in for too long. Platforms experiencing the chicken-and-egg problem fall into this quadrant.

MOVEMENTS IN THE MATRIX

The matrix helps to lay out the various strategic choices that a platform may take to balance the contrasting goals of open participation and curation that were explored in Section 2. This matrix provides a framework for understanding how different platforms achieve these divergent and conflicting goals.

1. *Pivoting around friction*

A platform may constantly need to juggle the quality of interactions with the number of interactions. Too much friction may lead to low participation and fewer interactions. Too little friction may lead to a poor-quality culture on the platform and discourage quality producers in the long run. The platform must ensure that it achieves the right balance between friction and traction at every point in its journey to platform scale.

2. *Avoiding friction altogether*
Some platforms may avoid friction entirely. This is especially true for platforms with low interaction risks. For instance, Instagram's adoption was driven by low friction in usage.
In contrast, platforms with high interaction risks may not benefit from avoiding friction. Craigslist enjoys strong network effects because it extends across categories with low as well as high interaction risks. The platform allows anyone to post a listing, without appropriate checks and balances. While the lack of friction may work very well for low-risk categories and encourage interactions there, it may lead to undesirable and dangerous interactions in high-risk categories.

3. *Embracing friction with scale*
Quora has been increasing participation friction as it scales in a way that encourages quality on the platform. Anyone could ask a question in its early days, but asking a question on the platform now requires the user to pay in Quora credits. Promoting a question or answer on Quora may also be accomplished using Quora credits. As the platform has gained further traction, it has gradually embraced a higher level of friction. Content promotion increasingly requires more credits than it once did.

4. *Relaxation of norms*
App.net started with high friction, instituted through a $50 subscription fee. However, it has gradually reduced friction to allow for traction and eventually moved away from its original goal of offering an alternative to Twitter. In contrast, other platforms, like Sittercity, have succeeded despite high friction and never had to relax their norms.

5. Scaling the country club
Some invite-only platforms scale well in spite of high-friction. They start small but preserve high quality as they scale. Participants value quality, and the higher friction encourages the repeat participation of a curated set of participants while discouraging that of others.

DESIGN CONSIDERATIONS FOR FRICTION

Two platforms in the same vertical and category may compete and co-exist by staying in two different boxes in the traction-friction matrix, as the examples below demonstrate.

1. Friction as a source of quality
Undesirable interactions on a platform hinder the repeatability of desirable interactions. Women tend to avoid dating platforms that attract stalkers. As the proportion of undesirable interactions increases, the repeatability of desirable interactions decreases further as high-quality producers and consumers rapidly abandon the platform.
Choosing a babysitter also benefits from high quality. False positives may lead to risky interactions. Friction, in the form of background checks on babysitters, provides a valuable source of information on quality. In contrast, the lack of friction on Craigslist makes it unsuitable for hiring babysitters online.

2. Friction as a source of superior signaling
Friction may also lead to better signaling. Background checks on babysitters yield exact parameters for parents to make a decision. Hence, the friction of curation helps with market signaling.
Employment markets also rely on signaling. The process of profile creation on LinkedIn is onerous and involves high friction. However, it helps the platform gather the requisite data required to signal candidate quality to recruiters. By breaking a high-friction and high-investment task into manageable chunks, LinkedIn successfully gathers rich data on every individual professional.

3. *Friction as a barrier*

For all the hype and fanfare surrounding App.net's launch, the platform never quite lived up to its initial intent of providing an alternative to Twitter. Two design considerations were flawed to begin with:

a) Applying friction to both producer and consumer roles: By requiring users to pay to access the platform, App.net added friction to both production and consumption. Twitter allows its producers to build a following. By restricting overall access to App.net, the platform limited its ability to enable producers to gain a strong following.

b) Friction without a guarantee of quality or signal: While an access fee introduces friction on App.net, that friction doesn't serve as a guarantee of quality or as a signaling mechanism. It doesn't help to improve interactions on the platform. App.net realized that friction wasn't helping and subsequently lowered the access fee, through a series of revisions, by more than 90%.

PLATFORM SCALE IMPERATIVE

In the relentless quest for platform scale, one may often see frictionless interfaces as a necessary design principle. However, friction may serve to encourage the repeatability of desirable interactions by encouraging high-quality interactions. The following is a non-exhaustive list of design questions to consider while introducing friction onto a platform.

a. Does the friction affect one side or both? Does friction on either side add value to the other side? Does friction on either side deplete value for the other side?
b. What are the sources of friction? Do they improve quality and help with signaling?
c. Does friction increase the repeatability of desirable interactions?
d. Is the interaction high-value or high-risk?

SAMPLING COSTS

The Failure Of Social Curation Systems

Platforms scale the curation of quality by leveraging social curation. Unlike centralized, editorial moderation, which scales linearly, social curation scales at the rate of platform scale. YouTube and Quora enable the community to curate content through upvotes/downvotes and the ability to report abuse. Airbnb and Uber leverage social curation to determine the quality of participants on the platform. Platforms like TripAdvisor and Yelp create industry-wide standards of quality by leveraging social curation. The ability of a platform to scale high-quality interactions is often determined by its ability to implement a strong social curation mechanism.

For all its benefits, social curation has its limitations. Social curation requires effort on the part of users. Platforms may fail when users either refuse to curate or are unable to judge quality well. Both these scenarios arise as a result of high sampling costs.

SAMPLING COSTS AND SOCIAL CURATION SYSTEMS

New product introductions at retail stores often start with sample packages being distributed for free. Enabling users to sample and experience value at low cost encourages them to purchase in the future.

The importance of sampling before making a decision applies equally well to every consumer decision. Sampling helps consumers make a decision regarding quality. A consumer may signal this decision to other consumers to help them in making decisions. Similarly, a consumer may provide feedback about quality to the producer.

All these actions are aggregated and internalized on social curation systems. Consumers sample content, a physical good, or a service and make a quality judgment on the basis of sampling. Unlike retail sampling, social curation goes a step further and aggregates these inputs to create:

1. *Social proof for new consumers to base their decisions on:* The number of upvotes may help a user decide which answer to read first for a question on Quora. Higher ratings invite more business on TripAdvisor;
2. *Quality scores for ranking algorithms:* Votes on an article determine where it shows up on the Reddit home page;
3. *Feedback loop for the producer:* Social curation allows producers to gather feedback. Photographers use 500px and designers use Dribbble to gather peer feedback.

A social curation system provides the weighted sum of all sampling decisions across a user base.

SOCIAL CURATION FAILURE

Every sampling decision has costs associated with it. Finding new artists to listen to by sampling a random assortment of artists is time-consuming. Rummaging through YouTube is equally time-consuming.

The act of sampling becomes increasingly inefficient as the costs increase. Choosing a course to study by sampling twenty different courses can be a very inefficient exercise. Instead, choosing whom to follow on Instagram by sampling twenty photos in the feed is much more efficient. The cost of sampling an online course is much higher than the cost of sampling photos.

SAMPLING COSTS AND INTERACTION RISKS

When sampling services, the risks of participating in an interaction determine the sampling costs. Interactions with high risks of participation tend to rely more on editorial control than on social curation. A platform enabling the discovery of plumbers is likely to need much less editorial control than one enabling the discovery of healthcare professionals. The risks of participating in an undesirable interaction are much higher in healthcare. As interaction risks increase, editorial control becomes increasingly important. When hosting content and services with high sampling costs, platforms often introduce additional friction to ensure quality through editorial checks.

There are scenarios where sampling costs may be so high as to discourage sampling entirely. Healthcare and banking/lending have very high sampling costs and rely on editorial control to a greater degree. A default on a loan is much more damaging than an irrelevant search result on a content platform. The advantage of social curation is that, at scale, it will likely be less biased than editorial judgment. The more expensive it is to sample some form of content or service, the more time it will take to achieve a scale where social curation works well. That's why social curation tends to be more inefficient on platforms with higher sampling costs.

CURATING SERVICES

Services marketplaces like oDesk, Fiverr, Airbnb, and TaskRabbit rely on social curation. In these instances, two additional factors need to be considered to determine the effectiveness of social curation:

1. The ability of the platform to own the end-to-end interaction
2. The service cycle

A platform that can own the end-to-end interaction is more likely to succeed in capturing user inputs on quality. For example, Upwork and Clarity enable the exchange of services on-platform, whereas Airbnb and TaskRabbit require the exchange of services to be conducted off-platform. When the actual exchange occurs on-platform, the consumer of services (and, in some cases, even the producer) may be asked to rate the other

party within the context of the exchange.
When the exchange occurs off-platform, the length of the service cycle determines the sampling cost. Uber benefits from a small service cycle and asks passengers to rate drivers right after the ride. The longer the service cycle is, the more difficult it may be for the platform to draw the users back in and rate the other party. The platform may have to rely on inorganic incentives to encourage curation in the case of long cycles.

MANAGING RIGHTS TO CURATE

Not all user feedback is useful. A platform may often benefit more from the opinions of a few users than from that of the entire user base. Agoda allows only users who have already booked and stayed at hotels through them to rate those particular hotels. This prevents users from entering false reviews, a problem that is often associated with TripAdvisor. Agoda's social curation system is designed to manage curation rights.

KICK-STARTING SOCIAL CURATION SYSTEMS

Social curation doesn't kick-start on its own. Many social curation systems are built on editorial curation efforts. Platforms like Quora and Medium have succeeded in building highly effective social curation systems by starting editorially and building a culture of quality on the platform. The creation of culture is especially important when sampling judgment is subjective. Decisions to downvote answers on Quora can be subjective. To avoid rampant downvoting or the lack of it when needed, users need to be made aware of the do's and don'ts of down-voting. They need to be invited into a culture that encourages or discourages certain types of downvoting. In its early days, Quora editors and administrators handled a lot of curation. As the community grew and took over the curation, the editors scaled down. In all such transitions, building reputation systems to differentiate good curators from bad ones helps to scale curation. Wikipedia built out a virtual hierarchy of editors in a similar fashion. Medium started as an editorially managed platform and today has a large distributed editorial workforce built across its user base. These user-editors own and manage collections of articles across the platform and manage the writers' access to readers.

PLATFORM SCALE IMPERATIVE

Social curation is not a feature. New platforms often copy features from successful ones. Copying features doesn't help in simulating the mechanics that make a certain platform work. Some platforms put in a voting system just because it seems to work for others. An understanding of sampling costs helps in identifying scenarios where social curation works well and those in which it doesn't.

TRUST DRIVES INTERACTIONS

The 7C Framework For Trust

Trust is a critical factor in enabling interactions on platforms. It is especially important in enabling peer-to-peer interactions in hitherto fragmented and unorganized markets. Trust creates an environment that fosters the repeatability and long-term sustainability of interactions. Travelers on a ride-sharing platform like BlaBlaCar must be assured of a safe ride. Peer-to-peer marketplaces for used goods must ensure that buyers are assured of a minimum level of quality in the transactions they engage in. Airbnb hosts must be assured of a solution if their apartments are ransacked. Dating platforms must ensure that everyone feels safe in the interactions that ensue. All these examples demonstrate the challenges of participating in fragmented and unorganized markets. Building trust among participants encourages the repeatability of interactions in such markets.

To understand trust, it is helpful to understand the evolution of trust as a driver of market interactions.

A TRYST WITH TRUST IN MEDIEVAL TIMES

Prior to the Industrial Revolution, much of Western society was organized in the form of small towns and rural communities. With most of the community members dependent on each other, everyone prospered by treating everyone else well. Moreover, a shared set of beliefs and culture helped cement strong relationships and create a sense of community. These relationships established trust and served as insurance coverage for social and economic interactions. In some cases, craftsmen organized themselves around guilds to signal quality and create an implicit code of conduct for new craftsmen. These communities were largely homogeneous, subscribing to the same set of beliefs, thus encouraging interactions within the various communities.

THE INDUSTRIAL REVOLUTION

With the onset of the Industrial Revolution, there was large-scale migration from small towns to big cities as the forces of production became concentrated. Large corporations aggregated business interactions, and national distributors reorganized consumption away from local markets. Interpersonal relationships or cultural norms could no longer serve as a safeguard to encourage interactions. Signaling trust to a larger base of unknown consumers became important. Near the turn of the twentieth century, formal systems emerged to solve trust problems. Industries like banking, insurance, and legal services evolved to establish rules and regulations to standardize business interactions in this new environment. Government regulators stepped in to establish rules for managing business interactions. Firms began to invest in market signaling through branding and advertising to build trust with their customers. The mechanisms of trust creation began to consolidate around formal systems.

THE REDEFINITION OF TRUST

Institutionalized and consolidated trust mechanisms introduced friction into interactions. Participants must subscribe to stringent norms and undertake significant due diligence before interactions can ensue. The risks of participating in a low-friction, low-trust environment are high

enough to discourage participants from exploring alternatives.
However, the platform economy requires the creation of alternate trust mechanisms. Peer-to-peer interactions require a low-friction environment. To enable interactions, platforms must innovate a whole new range of trust mechanisms. The 7c's of trust - Confirmed Identity, Centralized Moderation, Community Feedback, Codified Behavior, Culture, Completeness, Cover - explored in this chapter, are a set of themes that platform creators may use to build trust on platforms.

CONFIRMED IDENTITY

Identity can be used to help build trust. The rise of Facebook's social graph helped create real identity on the Internet, at least compared to the anonymity that was involved in much Internet participation prior to that. Today, Lyft riders link their accounts to their Facebook profiles. Tinder and a whole range of other social platforms require users to sign up through Facebook Connect.
The social graph isn't foolproof, and confirmation of identity may require more for different types of interactions. Airbnb confirms a listing by sending out photographers to a specific apartment. Sittercity babysitters must go through a stringent vetting process before being allowed onboard. The higher the interaction risks are, the more important is it to confirm the participants' identity to encourage interactions.

CENTRALIZED MODERATION

Centralized moderation is the first line of defense for building trust. In its early days, every platform uses centralized moderation in some form. Many platforms continue to use some elements of centralized moderation as they scale. Moderators scan Airbnb regularly for potentially illegitimate listings. Moderators also reach out to guests who are flagged as posing the greatest property-damage risk. The platform looks for signals for guests that potentially pose a risk, such as first-time renters booking high-end listings. Instagram, Twitter, and other social content platforms have community managers to help moderate the content.

Centralized moderation is the simplest method to implement trust in the early days of the platform, but it is also the least scalable source of trust creation. As the community scales, the platform must decentralize trust creation mechanisms. As a result, community feedback plays an important role in building trust.

COMMUNITY FEEDBACK

Community feedback is by far the most scalable mechanism for creating trust. Community feedback may take several forms, such as comments, votes, ratings, reviews, or replies. On Airbnb, hosts and travelers rate each other. Quora creates high-quality feedback in the form of votes and the reporting of abuse. On Fiverr, where all prices are standardized to $5, community feedback is the single most important decision-making factor for a buyer. Community feedback is also the most scalable approach since it allows the community to regulate itself while reducing overhead for the platform.

CODIFIED BEHAVIOR

Codified behavior involves the implementation of implicit rules in the workings of the platform. This enables the platform to nudge producers and consumers toward desirable actions and away from undesirable ones. These rules may be baked into the platform in the form of algorithms that implement checks and balances on user actions. They may also manifest themselves as small cues on the user interface that encourage a user to take certain kinds of actions.

Airbnb algorithmically blocks messages between hosts and guests that include the words "Western Union." If a certain host and guest repeatedly book rooms with one another, they may be identified as a scam to build a reputation based on fake reviews. The platform leverages different forms of signals to manage interactions algorithmically.

CULTURE

Culture, often overlooked by developers, can have a significant impact in building trust. Reddit, Threadless, and Dribbble show the importance of a good community culture and its role in building a high-trust environment. Culture directly influences community feedback and its quality.
Most platforms try to improve the culture by fostering interpersonal connection. Lyft's motto – "Your friend with a car" – encourages riders to converse with drivers and sit in the front seat as a friend would. Airbnb hosts do not simply provide accommodations; they also create a local experience when hosting the guests in person. An interpersonal connection can improve the culture significantly and build trust for future interactions.

COMPLETENESS

Completeness of information may sound tactical, but it plays an important role in building trust. Users trust platforms that have complete user profiles and detailed information. Many interaction decisions involve multiple decision points, and complete information helps one participate in an interaction without any nagging doubts.
LinkedIn builds trust by encouraging professionals to complete and frequently update their resumes and the world's largest professional database. The more information that LinkedIn has on professionals, the better it can build trust and encourage interactions. To achieve complete profiles, LinkedIn famously implemented the progress bar, showing users how much more information they needed to fill in to complete their profiles.

COVER

Cover, or insurance, is the final contributor to trust on the platform. Cover protects participants from extreme loss. It provides the producers and consumers with the assurance that they will be protected financially if they were to participate in a risky interaction. Cover works similar to a product guarantee: if the interaction does not work as expected, the platform covers the loss. Uber and Airbnb encourage producers to participate by offering them cover against undesirable situations.

PLATFORM SCALE IMPERATIVE

Trust isn't merely a set of features; it is the minimum set of requirements needed to ensure the repeatability of interactions. It must be built over time and may diminish rapidly once violated. Platforms must ensure that they use a combination of the seven mechanisms listed here to build trust and encourage interactions.

UBER VS. LYFT AND INTERACTION FAILURE

How Interaction Failure Kills Platforms

The on-demand economy is bringing together technology and freelance workers to deliver services in exciting new ways. We are increasingly using our cell phones as remote controls for the real world. In the past, one could sit on a sofa and flip through TV channels using a remote control device. Today, the phone works as a remote control for the real world, and one can request a taxi, get a home cleaned, or order a bite to eat at the click of a button. On-demand experiences are delivered by platforms – like Shyp, Uber, Washio, and DoorDash – that connect consumers with freelance labor or spare service capacity. *Two critical factors will determine the success of a company in the on-demand economy: multihoming costs and interaction failure.*

MULTIHOMING COSTS AND WINNER-TAKES-ALL

As explored earlier in this section, multihoming costs determine a platform's ability to develop strong network effects and achieve a winner-takes-all position in the market. The defensibility and competitive advantage of a platform business are very closely related to the multihoming costs that its producers and consumers incur. Multihoming costs vary for different platforms. When developers co-develop for the Android and iOS platforms, they incur high multihoming costs. Multihoming costs are high for consumers as well because of the cost of mobile phones. Most consumers will own only one phone. However, multihoming costs for drivers to co-exist on Uber and Lyft are relatively low. Many drivers participate on both platforms. Given the ease of booking rides, multi-homing costs are very low for travelers/riders on these platforms as well.

This is an important consideration for on-demand platforms. With a limited supply of service providers available, multihoming may lead to a strong, ongoing competition between platforms for access to service providers. Producers can easily switch between platforms without allowing any single platform to develop a long-term competitive advantage and a strong network effect. Multihoming can be a contributor to the eventual loss of platform scale when it leads to interaction failure on the platform.

INTERACTION FAILURE

Interaction failure occurs when a producer or consumer participates in an interaction, but the interaction fails to reach its logical, desired conclusion. Imagine a merchant setting up a listing on eBay that never gets any traction or a video enthusiast uploading a video on YouTube that fails to get a minimum number of views. These producers experience interaction failure. Often, these outcomes could be the result of poor-quality listings or videos, but they could also result from the platform's inability to match supply with relevant demand. Producers and consumers who experience interaction failure become discouraged from participating further and eventually abandon the platform.

THE UBER–LYFT WAR

Interaction failure is especially important for on-demand platforms. Imagine a consumer requesting a service and never being served with a solution.

Imagine, in turn, a producer receiving a request and preparing to fulfill that request, only to find that the request is canceled. In both cases, the respective consumer or producer may become discouraged and decide to abandon the platform.

In some of the largest cities, drivers drive for both Uber and Lyft, as well as other competitors. It's not uncommon for these drivers to switch between the two platforms multiple times a day. With a limited supply of drivers in a city and the cost for a driver to connect to an additional platform being so small, drivers multihome on both Uber and Lyft. This has naturally led to intense competition between the two companies, and Uber infamously resorted to a playbook to create interaction failure on Lyft using questionable tactics.

Uber decided to target interaction failure on Lyft by contracting third-party agents to use disposable phones to hail Lyft taxies. Before the Lyft taxi arrived at its pickup location, the Uber-contracted agent would cancel the ride. With so many cancelations on the Lyft platform, drivers would become frustrated driving for Lyft and, in some cases, switch to Uber. A smaller number of drivers on the Lyft platform meant longer waiting times for traveler. This would, in turn, frustrate travelers, eventually spurring them to abandon the platform.

When multihoming costs are low, producers and consumers may easily participate on multiple platforms. With multiple platforms sharing the same producers and consumers, it is difficult for a business to build defensible network effects. Thus, it is difficult for a clear winner to emerge in the market. With many platforms operating and defensibility low, interaction failure becomes a key factor in determining long-term winners.

PLATFORM SCALE IMPERATIVE

Platforms must define interaction failure scenarios and track metrics that help to determine the degree of interaction failure on a platform. Freelancers who don't get business within X days, requests that don't get satisfied within Y minutes, and products that aren't liquidated within a certain period may all be indicative of interaction failure. The exact measure of interaction failure will vary by platform, and the importance of tracking interaction failure will, in turn, depend on the multihoming costs. Tracking and avoiding interaction failure is an ongoing discipline that all platform-scale businesses must embrace.

INTERACTION OWNERSHIP AND THE TASKRABBIT PROBLEM

When The Ecosystem Avoids The Platform

Platforms that connect non-standardized service providers with clients (such as TaskRabbit and Upwork) are faced with a unique challenge. Most such platforms cannot facilitate a transaction before the buyer and seller meet and discuss the scope and terms of service. However, connecting the buyer and seller often encourages off-platform collusion, in which the buyer and seller take the transaction off-platform to avoid the transaction cut that the platform charges. In such a scenario, interaction ownership is a critical priority to create a sustainable platform business. Encouraging repeatable interactions isn't useful unless the platform can own the interaction and prevent off-platform collusion.

THE CHALLENGE OF ENABLING NON-STANDARDIZED SERVICES

Platforms that enable the sale of products (such as eBay and Etsy) or standardized services (such as Uber and Airbnb) do not require the buyers and sellers to discuss before transacting. These products and services are highly standardized, and the buyer can make a purchase decision based on the information available in the listing.

Platforms that allow service providers to offer customized services to clients work in a different manner. Buyers and sellers must interact and discuss the scope and terms of service before transacting. The actual exchange of money often follows the delivery of the service, and the delivery of the service itself requires the buyer and seller to interact directly with each other. When hiring a freelancer on a freelancer platform, the client must define requirements and potentially interview freelancers. Once the end users know each other, they can potentially connect directly on LinkedIn or other networks, thus avoiding the platform cut. Connecting buyers and sellers directly before charging the transaction cut weakens the platform's ability to capture value. The party that is charged the transaction cut is motivated to abandon the platform and conduct the transaction off-platform.

This problem is further enhanced when the delivery of the service requires the buyer and seller to meet in person. A platform like TaskRabbit enables users to find service providers locally. Since the delivery of service may often involve an in-person meeting, the payments may also be executed in person. This prevents the platform from extracting the transaction cut.

Finally, on platforms like TaskRabbit, a client may want to continue using the same plumber for subsequent interactions once he finds a good one. Every time the platform enables a successful interaction, it is reducing its repeatability, as the client and the service provider can connect off-platform for subsequent interactions. This is a challenge that is not necessarily faced by Airbnb, as most travelers are unlikely to travel to the same city every time and will need to discover new accommodations. This is not a problem for a platform like Uber, either, as travelers care more about waiting time than about riding with a specific driver. Uber helps to optimize for the former criterion, and travelers repeatedly return to the platform.

Platforms that fail to extract the transaction cut often resort to a lead-generation, paid placement, or subscription-based revenue model. The classifieds model has traditionally worked on paid placement. Dating websites and B2B platforms work on a subscription-based model while several financial comparison engines work on a lead-generation model. However, lead-generation models are attractive only at very high levels of activity, and subscription-based revenue models make the chicken-and-egg problem worse than it already is. A *monetization model that involves extracting a cut from the buyer–seller transaction requires a mechanism for owning the end-to-end interaction.*

Some platforms may charge the buyer ahead of the transaction and remit money to the service provider only after the provision of services, thus providing some insurance to the buyer, encouraging her to transact. However, service providers who would normally pay a transaction fee to the platform may often offer a discount to the buyer to encourage off-platform payment. Professional services platforms also require discussions, exchanges, and workflow management during the provision of services before the actual charge can be levied. As a result, charging the buyer ahead of the transaction is all the more complicated.

SOLVING FOR INTERACTION OWNERSHIP

To own the interaction, platforms must create more value than they capture. While the principle sounds simple, its implementation is fairly nuanced. There are several mechanisms by which interactions may be owned by the platform.

1. *Exchange tracking tools*

Clarity's early success illustrates that a platform's role may involve a lot more than merely connecting buyers and sellers. Clarity connects advice seekers with experts. Traditionally, such platforms would connect the two sides, charge a lead-generation fee, and allow them to transact off-platform. Clarity provides additional call management and invoicing capabilities that help to capture the transaction on the platform. Since the call management software manages per-minute billing, advice seekers have the option to opt out of a call that isn't proving useful. For the experts, the integrated payments and invoicing provide additional value. There is enough value for both sides to prevent them from colluding off-platform.

2. *Workflow management tools*

Upwork allows clients to manage the work being done by freelancers. Since most freelancers charge by the hour, Upwork provides time-tracking software and constantly monitors freelancers' work by taking regular screenshots of their screen to ensure that they are working as required. Clients benefit from the additional monitoring. Moreover, the platform charges a reasonable 10% transaction fee. It can afford to do this since it retains all ongoing interactions and makes up for the lower margin through volume. Workflow and interaction management tools help to strengthen network effects on the platform in two ways:

1. They help to capture repeat interaction between the same service provider and client. If the platform served only to match a service provider to the client, it would lose all subsequent interactions.
2. Workflow management tools involve a learning curve and increase multihoming costs. Service providers find it difficult to learn the usage of workflow management tools on multiple platforms and may eventually stick to the one where they see most business, thereby strengthening network effects on that platform.

3. *Reputation as a source of value*

Some platforms may not allow service providers to gather a rating unless the transaction is executed on the platform. Since ratings help the service provider build a reputation and garner further business, service providers may be incentivized, at least initially, to participate in the transaction through the platform.

DESIGN PRINCIPLES

When platforms offer additional tools and services to retain the interaction, the following design principles are commonly observed:

1. The workflow tools should create additional value for both sides, not just for one. This prevents either side from abandoning the platform for the transaction.
2. The tools should reduce friction in the interaction.

3. The interaction management tools should feed back into some form of on-platform reputation. Reputation is an added source of value that ensures stickiness on the platform. Clarity calls are followed by a request to rate the other side. Over time, the rating increases the discoverability of an expert on the platform and acts as social proof for future interactions.

PLATFORM SCALE IMPERATIVE

Platforms may encourage repeatable interactions but fail to capture them. Large platforms with millions of users have failed to monetize because of their inability to own interactions. When platforms monetize by charging a transaction cut, it is important to ensure that all factors that contribute to retaining and owning the interaction on the platform are architected into the platform.

Section
4

SOLVING CHICKEN-AND-EGG PROBLEMS

The solution to the chicken and egg problem requires a bait that can break the vicious cycle of no activity.

INTRODUCTION

Breakfast For Startups

The network effect, while attractive in scale, is very difficult to kick-start. Most platforms and networks starting from scratch have no value in and of themselves. Value is created through the presence and activity of users. When these platforms start out, they do not have enough intrinsic value to attract an initial set of users. Conversely, unless they get some users on board, they will never get out of this problem. Producers of value will not come on board unless there are consumers, and consumers will not find the platform useful without any production. There is a chicken-and-egg problem involved. Who does one get first: the producers or the consumers? The chicken-and-egg problem is a vicious cycle, without an obvious starting point. Most new ventures starting out on this journey never fail to get past the chicken-and-egg problem. As a result, the first and most important step in the creation of network effects is crafting a sustainable solution to the chicken-and-egg problem.

This chicken-and-egg problem persists till a point where the platform gains critical mass – the minimum network size at which there are enough producers and consumers of value on the platform to ensure that interactions spark off reliably.

Facebook, Twitter, Airbnb, eBay, PayPal, Uber, and others – seemingly invincible platforms – all started out by finding creative solutions to this problem. Through this section, we explore repeatable patterns and design principles in crafting solutions to the chicken-and-egg problem.

A DESIGN PATTERN FOR SPARKING INTERACTIONS

Solving The Chicken-And-Egg Problem

Solving the chicken-and-egg problem starts with understanding the general pattern of the problem. In terms of the producer-consumer parlance that we used to explain network effects in Section 1, the problem can be reduced to the following pattern:

Problem. How do I get producers and consumers, given that

Condition 1. I need producers to get consumers, and

Condition 2. I need consumers to get producers?

If the two roles are not too distinct (e.g. Skype), the pattern may simply be stated as:

Problem: How do I get users, given that:

Condition 1: Users will not come unless there is value in the platform, and

Condition 2: There is no value in the platform without having users on it?

The chicken-and-egg problem continues to persist till a certain point at which there is enough overlap between supply and demand to sustainably enable interactions. The size of the user base at this point is referred to as the critical mass.

SOLVING CHICKEN-AND-EGG PROBLEMS

Solutions to chicken and egg problems have a few defining characteristics:

1. *Breaking The Vicious Cycle.* Like most vicious cycles, the chicken-and-egg problem is a conceptual loop with no predefined place to start. The platform needs to figure out a way to break into that loop.
2. *Positive Feedback.* Once a starting point to the loop is created, it is set in motion through a positive feedback loop. As one side grows, it attracts more of the other side, which in turn, attracts more of the first side, and so on.
3. *Maximizing Overlap.* The chicken-and-egg problem exists before a network reaches critical mass. Hence, the longer a network takes to reach critical mass, the longer it has to grapple with this problem. As mentioned, critical mass is a measure of the overlap between production and consumption. Hence, conditions that help maximize this overlap are likely to yield simpler solutions to the chicken-and-egg problem.
4. *Getting The Harder Side In First.* Some markets are asymmetrical, and it is usually more difficult to get one side than the other. For example, dating websites find it harder to attract women, than they do men. Content platforms find it harder to attract content creators, compared to consumers. Hence, the platform needs to figure out a model that incentivizes the harder side to join in.
5. *On-Boarding Of Two Distinct Markets.* On many platforms, producers and consumers may be two distinct markets. The same user may upload and view videos on YouTube but the traveler and driver markets, on Uber, are largely distinct. The typical user, on these platforms, plays only one of the two roles. Serving two-sided markets requires reaching minimum traction on both sides. Hence, two-sided markets require building two companies, often with completely different challenges, not just building two forms of behaviors among users.

FIVE DESIGN PRINCIPLES FOR SOLVING CHICKEN-AND-EGG PROBLEMS

With the above characteristics in mind, a solution to any chicken-and-egg problem relies on five key design principles:

1. *Finding A Compelling Bait To Start The Loop.*
   The first step in breaking a vicious cycle is to find an inorganic bait that attracts and hooks one of the two roles without the need for the other role being present. In many of the strategies that follow through the rest of the section, we look at different types of baits that are used by platforms when starting off.
2. *Ensuring There Is No Friction In The Feedback Loop.* Once one role comes on board, it is important to ensure that there are no barriers to getting the other roles on board. If producers come in first, the platform should make it easier for the consumers to follow suit, and vice versa. This works best when the first role is organically incentivized to bring the second role on board. As an example, project creators host their projects on Kickstarter and subsequently spread the word about their project among their followers and friends. A virtuous cycle of producers bringing in consumers – some of whom then become producers – is set into motion.
3. *Minimizing The Time It Takes For The Startup To Reach Critical Mass.* As we note subsequently with the case studies of Facebook, Tinder, and others, a platform reaches critical mass faster when it is launched in a hotbed of existing activity. In such cases, the platform enters a market that already has a high overlap of supply and demand, and is well-positioned to exploit it to gain traction. Facebook's launch at Harvard University, and subsequently in similar closed markets, ensured that critical mass was reached a lot faster than the many Myspace copycats that were launching globally around that time.
4. *Incentivizing The Role That Is More Difficult To Attract.*Some user types may require more incentive to be pulled in. Acknowledging this is important, and is counterintuitive to the principles of traditional marketing.
   And finally,
5. *Staging The Creation Of Two-Sided Markets.*In general, the nature of two-sidedness only allows us to capture such markets one side at a

> time. However, we do observe exceptions in the strategies that follow. Finding the bait or incentive that brings in one role and enables them to remain while we get in the other role holds the key to succeeding with this model. OpenTable used this strategy to get restaurants on board by providing restaurant management software (the bait) before any consumers signed up. Conversely, Megaupload seeded content (the bait) on its site to attract consumers on board, and subsequently, converted some consumers to producers of content.

Through this section, we look at several strategies that apply the above design principles to solve the chicken-and-egg problem.

ACTIVATING THE STANDALONE MODE

Starting Without Interactions

How do I get initial users to start using my platform when there is no activity on it?

One of the ways of solving this problem is to ensure that the first launch of the platform has a 'standalone mode'. Essentially, a user should be able to derive value out of it even when other users are not on it. The offering is launched as a standalone service with an intention to open out into a platform over time. A platform, that has standalone value before network effects set in, is more likely to get traction from at least one set of users. In most cases, the user signs up purely for the standalone value and not on the promise of the added benefit when the network effect kicks in. The network can then be turned on once enough users are acquired through this hook. The network, then, complements the standalone value powered by the initial product/service offering.

OPENING IT UP LIKE OPENTABLE

OpenTable (and subsequently, other service booking systems) was one of the first platforms to execute this successfully. Entering a highly fragmented market (restaurant), the company distributed booking management systems, which the restaurant could use as standalone software for managing table reservations. This enabled OpenTable to aggregate table inventory, and real-time data on table availability, across restaurants. Once it had enough restaurants on board – and, hence, access to their seating inventory, as well – it opened out the network to allow consumers to start booking tables at participating restaurants. By staging the network creation in this manner, OpenTable succeeded in aggregating a fragmented, technology-laggard vertical, like restaurants, on one central platform, something that may not have been possible if it had started by launching the entire platform and hoping for network effects to kick in. In OpenTable's case, the standalone model also provides additional revenue streams for the business, in addition to the lead generation fee that it charges for customer reservations. This model has been successfully replicated across multiple industries, which exhibit the same characteristics of inefficiencies created due to fragmentation. The standalone mode helps aggregate the players onto a central platform, and consumer access is subsequently enabled to create network effects. The standalone mode serves to create a central creation infrastructure for participants to create and manage inventory, e.g. the inventory of seating availability, in the case of restaurants on OpenTable. Referring to the architectural discussions in Section 2, the standalone mode allows the creation and accumulation of core value units. The real-time seating availability, created and managed on OpenTable, is the core value on the platform that consumers consume.

RedBus, an Indian bus-booking platform, and one of the biggest success stories from South Asia, used a similar approach to create a comprehensive database of real-time seating inventory across buses. Bus operators would use the standalone reservation management systems to manage their business. With enough operators on board, redBus opened its ticketing solution to consumers and created a thriving platform to aggregate a highly fragmented and inefficient industry.

Event-ticketing and venue-management platforms have taken a similar approach, in recent times, to aggregate another fragmented industry.

This strategy helps platforms to get over the chicken-and-egg problem by converting the vicious cycle of the chicken-and-egg problem into a sequential staging process.

A DELICIOUS APPROACH TO CURATION

This model applies equally well to the new breed of consumer Internet startups, billed as 'curation-as-creation' tools. Users use standalone tools, like a browser plugin, to curate content from around the Web and reorganize this content in new formats. Tools like ScoopIt and PaperLi allow users to reorganize existing content into new consumption formats, like magazines, newspapers, and boards. The subsequent goal for many such 'tools' is to enable a thriving community on top of the content that is created and develop competitive advantage through network effects so that a subsequent and better designed tool does not gain the same traction. These startups begin with the curation-as-creation 'tool' to enable a standalone mode and deliver value to the lone user. One of the first curation tools to adopt this approach, and establish a template of sorts for others to follow, was Delicious. Early adopters used Delicious to store browser bookmarks in the cloud and it delivered standalone value. Once the user base hit critical mass, the social bookmarking features started getting used and the value of the network grew with more users.

In recent times, Flipboard has adopted a similar approach by creating a service for consumers before enabling them to start producing as well, thereby building network effects. Flipboard provided a compelling consumption interface for consuming content on the iPad. It delivered this through a unique magazine format for the tablet interface. Once it gained enough traction, it allowed users to start creating their own 'magazines' on Flipboard, simply by 'flipping' content from another magazine. Unlike the other curation-as-creation platforms above, Flipboard's content universe is closed within the Flipboard platform, and users cannot (yet) flip content in from outside Flipboard, but the principle of launching a network on top of a standalone tool remains the same.

PERSONAL ANALYTICS AS STANDALONE MODE

Mint.com is a platform that enables users to gain insights into their finances, helps them benchmark themselves against peers and connects them with relevant financial products, based on their individual financial profiles. Mint offers a unique lesson in the provision of the standalone mode for platforms. Users utilize Mint in standalone mode to analyze their personal finances. Mint aggregates users' financial data and serves them analytics in return. In aggregating financial data, Mint is bringing value units onto the platform, that can then be served to external consumers. Leveraging this financial data, the platform generates individual financial profiles for every user. Based on the specific financial profile of a user, it then allows financial institutions to target relevant financial products to users. A user who regularly defaults on payment of credit card fees would be served an alternate credit card with lower late payment fees.

Mint's standalone mode allows the acquisition of data (creation of value units), which is subsequently used to bring financial institutions onto the platform. The provision of analytics to users provides standalone value, before the platform play kicks in. Much like OpenTable, the standalone mode itself offers enough of a value proposition for users to remain interested. The platform approach allows Mint to offer its standalone value for free, thereby disrupting earlier competitors that required users to pay for the standalone value of personal finance management.

FROM SOCIAL GRAPHS TO COMMERCIAL GRAPHS - POWERED BY THE STANDALONE MODE

A more complex, but rapidly emerging, use case of the standalone mode may be seen in enterprise SAAS plays today. Several startups, providing invoicing, payments, procurement management, and accounting tools to small businesses, are trying to take a similar approach to go beyond the tools and build out a 'commercial graph'. Much like Facebook's social graph, which maps out the social relationships between its users, a commercial graph would map out the nature of commercial relationships between businesses. Software as a service (SAAS) providers like Tradeshift, SPS Commerce, and Procurify are powering the first few instances of the commercial graph today. These providers follow a four-step strategy to build out the commercial graph.

1. *Provision Of Tools.* At the outset, they provide invoicing and procurement software to enable companies to manage their network interactions better. As the companies interact through the software, interaction data is captured. This may include explicit data about interaction between companies, but it is more likely that this will include implicit indicators like the turnaround time on a request. Such implicit performance indicators are likely to be more important, where tracking explicit data may discourage businesses from using the software.
2. *Provision Of The Standalone Mode.* Data is aggregated and packaged as analytics for every individual company. Every business can track suppliers that regularly default or buyers who fail to meet contractual requirements. This powers the standalone value for participating companies.
3. *Provision Of Implicit Network Benefits.* Commercial graphs use interaction data between companies to create a reputation score for every company. This helps every individual company benchmark itself against peers. It also helps every company determine the relative health of its supplier network.
4. *Creation Of A Platform With Explicit Network Effects.* Finally, the reputation layer provides visibility into the reputation of suppliers and customers outside one's network. This enables companies to find new partners and suppliers that outperform their existing partners and suppliers on certain parameters.

These would-be platforms are, again, taking the approach of gaining traction through a standalone mode and using the creation of value units in the standalone mode to open the platform and build network effects.

PLATFORM SCALE IMPERATIVE

It may not always be possible to create a standalone mode for every platform. A better way of leveraging this is to think of your value proposition as a combination of standalone computing and network effects. In general, the greater the standalone value in the offering, the easier it is for the platform to create subsequent network effects. Hence, even if a platform does not have a complete standalone mode, creating standalone value in some form may help simplify the traction problem in its initial days. A general rule of thumb while creating a standalone mode is the following: The standalone mode, for producers, should encourage the creation of value units on the platform, which can then be used to pull in the consumption side.

HOW PAYPAL AND REDDIT FAKED THEIR WAY TO TRACTION

Case Studies In 'Growth Faking'

There were several factors that contributed to YouTube becoming the #1 video-sharing platform. However, initial adoption was significantly driven by the fact that the platform allowed pirated content to be hosted. If you wanted to watch the latest episode of a sitcom for free, YouTube was your best bet. Kim Dotcom noted how pirated content was driving YouTube's adoption. As a late follower in the online video category, Dotcom's Megaupload seeded the platform with pirated content, as a means of solving the chicken-and-egg problem. This strategy worked for a while, but being involved with pirated content was always likely to result in problems. Megaupload went under when it was alleged that the provisioning and hosting of pirated content was a deliberate part of the platform's strategy. Megaupload's deliberate seeding of pirated content offers a rather brute-force but effective tactic for solving the chicken-and-egg problem, and building network effects. Faking initial supply may often serve as the bait needed to kick-start network effects.

Some platform owners, as in the case of Megaupload, solve this by creating a fake inventory of content, using a variety of methods. The in-house team acts as a substitute for the producer side of the platform. First-time consumers get the impression that the platform is already in business, and continue participating. Over time, the user base grows, users start contributing themselves, and the platform sustains activity without having to fake it. There are three broad approaches to faking traction:

Seeding And Weeding

Dating platforms often simulate initial traction by creating fake profiles and conversations. Users who visit the platform see desirable activity and are incentivized to stay on. Over time, as real users join the service, the fake profiles are removed to reduce the noise on the platform.

Marketplaces may also showcase fake activity, initially, to attract buyers or sellers. Early on, a common tactic is to show top transactions of the day or most recent transactions – to signal high activity – even when very few transactions are taking place on the platform.

Faking usually works only for the first player in a new category. As a late entrant to a category that already boasts players with strong network effects, faking may hurt the platform, instead of helping it. Producers and consumers are unlikely to get onto a platform with fake activity when they already benefit from real interactions on an existing platform.

Seeding Demand

The book, PayPal Wars, talks about how PayPal converted a base of eBay sellers, into PayPal users, by faking buyer-side demand for the service. When PayPal deduced that eBay was their key distribution platform, they came up with an ingenious plan to simulate demand. The company created a bot that would buy goods on eBay, and insist, as a prospective buyer, on paying for those goods using PayPal. Not only did sellers come to know about the service, they rushed onto it, as multiple bots, masquerading as buyers, insisted on using the same service, thereby creating an illusion of ubiquity. The fact that it reduced friction compared to every other existing payment mechanism on eBay, only served to increase repeat usage.

Seeding Supply

To solve the chicken-and-egg problem, marketplaces may also create fake supply, to attract buyers. Lending marketplaces like Australian startup, Rentoid.com, seeded initial activity when the founder himself bought products as they were requested and lent them out to users. In its early days, oDesk hired a captive group of service providers to guarantee service provision and attract an initial set of clients. It subsequently used that initial traction to attract freelancers and set off the virtuous cycle of increasingly attracting more of both demand and supply.

Content platforms often rely on 'faking it', during the initial days. An in-house editorial team works on creation of content, curation of user-generated content and moderation of other actions by users. As the community scales, the editors scale down content seeding and focus on scaling curation. Quora started off with in-house Quora moderators asking and answering questions to generate activity. As community activity increased, the Quora moderators focused more on curation of content and less on creation. Over time, the curation also phased out into the community as user actions helped the platform determine reputed users who consistently curated high-quality content. This helped scale quality during the initial growth of the platform. Like all strategies, there is a method here to the apparent madness, as explained below.

USE USER - FACING TOOLS AND WORKFLOWS WHILE FAKING IT

Even if an editorial team is employed to fake initial activity, the team should focus on using the same tools that the users would eventually use. This ensures a real-time testing of actual activity and ensures that the activity is a fair representation of the eventual user activity desired on the platform. Having editors use community curation tools also helps fine-tune curation algorithms in the initial days.

Fake It Well

Dating communities do not fake it much anymore, but it was not uncommon to see a whole community of models 'hanging out' on dating websites some time back. Signaling high-quality production, initially, often helps to attract high-quality production from producers on the platform.

It is equally important not to indulge in any unethical behavior while faking traction. Apart from the legal implications involved, poor ethics, on the part of the platform manager, may discourage users from participating, and impact the community's culture adversely.

Encourage Behavior That Is Desired On The Platform

This is, by far, the most important principle in getting this right. Reddit cofounder, Steve Huffman, has gone on record stating that the link-sharing platform was initially seeded with fake profiles posting links to simulate activity. The links were posted by fake profiles and the vote counts assigned, to indicate activity, were fake as well. This fake activity was based on one principle: to ensure the seeding of content that the founders wanted the community to eventually discuss. As Reddit gathered traction, the initial content signaled high quality and encouraged user-producers to contribute content of similar quality, eventually creating a culture of such content in the community. Reddit is often criticized for encouraging a hive mind but there is no denying the strong network effects that the platform has succeeded in building.

PLATFORM SCALE IMPERATIVE

Platforms that try to create entirely new consumption behaviors may benefit from faking production initially. Platforms that require new consumption behaviors will often find it difficult to attract producers. Producers will likely be skeptical of participating in an interaction without a proven consumption behavior. Faking initial supply may work for platforms that create a new category and aim to cater to entirely new consumption behaviors. However, all attempts at faking supply – or even demand – should be executed carefully. When not done well, fake activity may destroy users' trust in the platform and wreck it before it even gets started.

EVERY PRODUCER ORGANIZES THEIR OWN PARTY

The Mechanics Of Producer-led Traction

Some platforms may be designed to benefit from the actions of a few power-producers: producers who individually attract a large number of consumers. Designing your platform so that your producers can bring along consumers helps to solve the chicken-and-egg problem, while concentrating solely on one side of the market. This strategy works when the following design considerations are satisfied by the platform:

1. The platform offers a compelling organic incentive for producers to bring consumers onto the platform.
2. The 'off-platform' influence and following of the average individual producer is significant enough to attract a large number of consumers to the platform.
3. The platform allows producers to interact with their followers (consumers) in a much more efficient way than currently allowed by alternative channels.

TOOLS TO HARVEST FOLLOWERS

One of the most common manifestations of this strategy is seen in the launch of platforms like Kickstarter and Udemy. These platforms allow producers to 'harvest' their existing connections and followers on other networks like email, social networks, and blogs. Kickstarter allows project creators to raise funding from their connections and followers. Skillshare allows teachers to teach a course to their followers (and subsequently others). These 'follower harvesting' use cases offer compelling incentives for producers to bring in their following. Over time, as different producers bring in their followers, the platform builds out a network of all producers and consumers, allowing followers of producer A to consume from producer B, and so on. Eventually, a small group of power-producers help such platforms solve the chicken-and-egg problem within a short period.

FROM LOYALTY TO MARKETS

This model works equally well for retail loyalty platforms. Merchants may use loyalty platforms to offer discounts to their existing customer base. In turn, these customers stay more engaged with the merchant. As a result, merchants see value in promoting the consumer-facing applications among their customer base. As a result, every individual merchant brings their existing customer base onto the loyalty platform. As consumer data flows through the platform, the platform learns consumer purchase preferences. This helps the platform 'cross-pollinate' consumers to other non-competing merchants, and the power of the network effect sets in.

THE 'VOTE ME UP' CONTEST GONE VIRAL

Platforms that provide production and marketing tools benefit from this strategy as well. One of the widely discussed anecdotes surrounding early traction on YouTube suggests that the platform conducted contests among its user base, asking creators to create videos. Creators were then encouraged to invite their friends to 'upvote' these videos. The videos with the maximum upvotes would win a prize. This strategy has been repeatedly applied by platforms like Binpress and Txtweb. The brilliance of this strategy lies in the fact that producers are naturally motivated to not only bring the consumers on board but actually have them pass through a whole loop of consumption and curation, which fully acquaints them with the platform's value proposition. As with other examples above, some such consumers stay on to become producers themselves and start the virtuous cycle afresh. Once users produce, they become marketing agents for the platform to attract other consumers. We discuss the details of executing such strategies more closely in the next section, on viral growth.

THE FLY-ATTRACTING BEACON

Malls have been doing this for the last fifty years. Attracting a marquee tenant, by offering prime real estate helps to attract consumers to the mall, subsequently exposing them to smaller merchants as well. This strategy works equally well for kicking off network effects on digital platforms. Ad networks use this strategy by getting exclusive access to premium 'eyeballs' and using that to attract advertisers. While AdMob and other US-based ad networks took over the mobile advertising space, India-based InMobi emerged as an unlikely contender by getting access to developing market eyeballs and selling them to advertisers in developed markets. As already mentioned, education platforms like Udemy and Skillshare also try to use the star power of certain teachers (think Seth Godin) to attract students in droves.

PLATFORM SCALE IMPERATIVE

Identifying a group of power-producers and providing them with tools to better 'harvest' their following can solve the chicken-and-egg problem very effectively. Relying on power-producers is especially attractive because a relatively small number of producers can help to solve the chicken-and-egg problem by attracting a large base of consumers. As social platforms proliferate, allowing users to build large followings, new platforms will increasingly rely on this strategy to encourage users to bring in their off-platform following.

BRINGING IN THE LADIES

How Dating Sites Work

In the heyday of online dating services, most dating platforms faced a unique version of the chicken-and-egg problem: an inability to get enough women on board. While young men signed up for dating websites in droves, these platforms encountered far greater difficulty in getting women to sign up. Dating is a market with a 'hard' side problem. It is 'harder' to get in one side than the other. Members of the 'hard' side are more likely not to show up. Given the lack of quality interactions on most early dating platforms and the unpleasantness of being stalked, women were a lot more wary about joining.

THE LADIES' NIGHT STRATEGY

Getting the 'hard' side in almost guarantees the 'easy' side following in, although getting the 'easy' side in, exclusively, may yield little value. Dating platforms are not made successful purely on numbers. Women do not sign up just because there is an army of available men on the platform. A dating site with real women, on the other hand, almost always, attracts men. When it comes to network effects, the dating use case is won on quality rather than quantity. In such scenarios, women need to be incentivized to join in. This is often referred to as the Ladies' Night strategy, a hat tip to the strategy used by bars and pubs in holding a weekly 'Ladies' Night', where women are offered free drinks, tapas, in order to gather a critical mass of women, which would then attract men all the more. What works for a singles bar often works remarkably well for any other social system focused on bringing men and women together! Many dating platforms offer inorganic incentives to women to get them on board.

WHEN CUPID GOES CURATING

Dating platforms often have a quality problem. Without appropriate curation, some of the most active members often tend to be the most undesirable ones: stalkers and spammers. CupidCurated tries to solve this by letting 'real women' curate the membership and determine the men who are allowed to register on the platform. Advance curation reduces search efforts for women using the platform, who do not need to invest quite as much in background checks and potentially unpleasant experiences.

In a similar vein, Sittercity curates babysitters that get listed on the platform. Finding babysitters is a high-risk interaction. Much like dating, advance curation helps separate the best from the rest. The platform's ability to attract quality supply, and signal this quality to the demand side, enables it to get demand on board. On Sittercity, parents – consumers on the platform – pay a subscription fee for access to a curated list of babysitters.

Several B2B-application platforms also follow this model. While consumer-facing app stores allow for abundance, business-facing platforms like SAP and Salesforce are very selective about the types of apps that are selected for their app store. The tolerance for a low-quality app is much lower in the case of business app stores. Advance curation guarantees the quality and reliability that is needed to appeal to a business customer.

PLATFORM SCALE IMPERATIVE

Platforms that facilitate high-risk interactions often find it more difficult to attract the side that bears the risk of participating in the interaction. These platforms need to rely on one of two strategies. They can initially incentivize the side that is more difficult to attract, much like the Ladies' Night strategy used by bars and pubs. However, to sustainably encourage high-risk interactions, these platforms must invest in curation, and must signal high-quality supply to the demand side. Solving the chicken-and-egg problem on such platforms requires solving quality control issues rather than gunning for a critical mass of users.

THE CURIOUS CASE OF NEW PAYMENT MECHANISMS

Why M-Pesa Works

Finding adoption for a new payment mechanism has always involved solving a chicken-and-egg problem. Ranging from the introduction of new forms of currency in medieval to early modern times, and the adoption of credit cards to the rise of PayPal (as alluded to in many of the strategy discussions in this section) and the recent rage around Bitcoin, new payment systems have regularly offered some of the most complex chicken-and-egg challenges. Both buyers and sellers need to adopt the same exchange mechanism, almost simultaneously. The staging that is possible in some platforms – attracting one side first and then the other – does not work in the case of payment mechanisms. *In such scenarios, the solution to finding adoption often lies in providing backward compatibility with existing solutions.* While most social networks, like Facebook and Twitter, are walled gardens, a new email service is compatible with existing email services and does not need a closed network to be valuable. This principle applies more generally to all types of platforms, and specifically to payment solutions. New payment mechanisms succeed in gaining adoption when they are compatible with existing payment mechanisms. As an example, the lack of backward compatibility in NFC-enabled payment mechanisms has hindered the adoption of such systems. Consumers may not go out of their way to get NFC-enabled phones unless there are enough merchants accepting them, and merchants do not want to invest in terminal hardware unless enough consumers start using the network. Getting both sides to change behavior compounds the challenges associated with launch and adoption.

BACKWARD COMPATIBILITY IN TANDEM WITH THE STANDALONE MODE

Square solved the chicken-and-egg problem by targeting the merchants with an app and dongle that converted their phone to a standalone payments terminal. They allowed a new mechanism for accepting payments for merchants while leveraging existing payment behavior on the consumer side. Merchants, especially those who were interested in accepting payments on the move, and who could not afford to carry clunky POS terminals around, took to the new mechanism. Gaining adoption among merchants creates traction on one side, allowing the platform to potentially bring consumers onto Square as well.

Companies like CheckFree have provided a comprehensive payment mechanism to consumers while allowing merchants to either migrate to a new system (online payments) or receive checks in the mail like they already do. CheckFree successfully changed behavior on the consumer side because the consumer had the advantage of making one-stop, one-click payments. Merchants were allowed the option to continue with the old behavior or adopt a new, more efficient one. If CheckFree had insisted that all merchants accept e-payments from the outset, it would not have been able to build a comprehensive portfolio of merchants, which would have prevented it from gaining traction among consumers.

EFFICIENT REINTERMEDIATION OF A TRANSACTION

Over the last decade, mPesa has established itself as a revolutionary payment mechanism in Kenya. North and East African nations already had a system of money transfer, inherently linked to the Islamic business order, known as Hawala. In the Hawala system, the sender asks a Hawala agent to transfer money to an acquaintance in another location, who then contacts another Hawala agent in the new location to pay the receiver. The sender then pays the sum to the first agent along with a small fee. The debt between the agents is logged and settled at a later date. MPesa adopted this behavior, without trying to introduce new ones, and made it more efficient by tracking the movement of money. The user-agent relationship remained the same while the agent-agent relationship improved significantly. Instead of logging in transactions in a book and settling them at a later date, the payments system allows the agents to settle money transfers instantly, over the network. While reintermediating an existing payments business, mPesa brings in added efficiency to the transaction, without reinventing the end-user behavior.

BACKWARD COMPATIBILITY AS A ROAD TO GRADUAL BEHAVIOR DESIGN

Any form of payment has to combat a behavioral problem. Hence, building in some form of 'backward compatibility' helps spur adoption because users have the choice to continue with the existing method or transition to a new one. Visa and MasterCard have extensive experience regarding disrupting the payments space. When Wave and Pay were first introduced, the new cards that were issued supported both swipe (existing) and wave (new) modes of payment. Consumers could continue using swipe until merchants set up enough wave terminals. Additionally, a string of incentives to early adopters of wave helped increase the adoption of wave.

PLATFORM SCALE IMPERATIVE

Platforms that require near-simultaneous adoption by two markets may find it difficult to achieve traction if they try to create new behaviors on both sides. Such platforms may often benefit from backward compatibility that helps the platform remain compatible with old systems while changing behavior on one side.

DRINK YOUR OWN KOOL AID

The Platform Is The Producer

The most obvious way to never have the chicken-and-egg problem, in the first place, is to start as the producer and open out the platform, over time, to other producers. Unlike the 'fake-it-till-you-make-it' strategy, the platform owner explicitly declares their its role as the producer.

When the iPhone first launched without the app store, it had a basic set of apps from Apple, which gave it the minimum functionality required from a high-end phone at that time. Apple, acting as a producer on its platform, launched the iPhone with a few apps, which, along with the superior design and hardware, attracted an initial base of users. This initial base of users, and a simplified set of developer tools, helped attract developers to the iOS platform, eventually expanding the app store with apps.

Amazon adopted a similar strategy in launching as a retailer and gathering consumer traction, before opening out the producer end to other merchants, via the Amazon marketplace.

When platforms become producers, other producers need to be assured of the non-competitive participation of the platform. The platform owner owns the curation and discoverability algorithms that connect consumers to content and applications. Hence, other producers, competing directly with the platform's role as a producer, may run the risk of not getting enough traction, as the platform promotes its apps, creations, and inventory.

PLATFORM SCALE IMPERATIVE

Starting as the first producer on your own platform may help solve the chicken-and-egg problem but it often places the incentives of the platform owner (as a producer) at odds with those of other producers. Platforms have been known to bait and switch, in such scenarios. As a result, producers may be hesitant in participating on such platforms. While effective, this strategy needs to be executed with care if the platform wants to eventually build a large ecosystem of co-producers.

BEG, BORROW, STEAL AND THE WORLD OF SUPPLY PROXIES

The Genesis Of Marketplaces

How does one kick-start a platform connecting service providers to consumers of that service?

Unlike content-intensive platforms, the value in services platforms is not in the availability of content but in the availability of service providers and the platform's ability to match a consumer with a service provider interested in providing a specific service within a certain time frame. This nuance allows services platforms to leverage an alternative strategy to solve the chicken-and-egg problem.

Yelp is an online local search platform that allows consumers to search for businesses, read reviews and make decisions accordingly. Yelp started with not one chicken-and-egg problem but two. As a review site, it needed reviewers as well as readers, but as a local commerce platform, it needed merchants as well as consumers to participate. Yelp's solution to the second problem has served as an interesting lesson for many local commerce startups that followed.

Yelp started with a searchable directory of local businesses and used that to gather consumer search intent. Once there were enough consumers, it pitched relevant consumer interest on the platform to merchants. With numbers backing the sales pitch, the businesses were brought on board to claim their listing and advertise for related search terms. Over time, this built up the producer side of the network.

The Yelp model is particularly interesting because the staging of the two sides did not require expensive incentives, and did not need to be coordinated in quick succession as consumers would get value from Yelp's search engine and reviews, even when the merchants were not on board. In this manner, Yelp offered a compelling standalone value proposition.

The model, however, is not as applicable to most other local commerce platforms because they do not necessarily offer a standalone value proposition like directory search. Most similar platforms exist for the purpose of matching consumers to service providers and having them transact. They need both sides to be on board for interactions to ensue.

However, with a few tweaks, the essential principles of Yelp's model can still be applied to a broader range of platforms and marketplaces.

YELP'S MODEL TWEAKED

Yelp's model can be tweaked to offer a more generalized solution to the chicken-and-egg problem, for any platform seeking to match service providers with consumers. The following strategies emerge as we tweak this model:

- *Step 1. Source supply proxies*
  Supply proxies are data points that represent true supply but which are not created by the producer. The platform, hence, does not own the supply side yet. Instead, it intends to have producers come in and claim their supply proxies, eventually creating true supply on the platform.
- *Step 2. Provide a superior interaction experience*
  The platform does not simply act as a directory of service providers. It provides a superior producer-consumer interaction – discovery, navigation, personalization – which is handled much more elegantly

than at the source, from which these supply proxies are picked. Yelp provided a better search experience than yellow pages, and overlaid that with high-quality user-generated reviews and, hence, a reliable mechanism for ascertaining merchant reputation.

- *Step 3. Gather consumer activity*
  Unlike Yelp, these platforms cannot afford to wait till consumers come on board and remain engaged. Consumers are looking to interact with the producer right away. To stage participation, these platforms should try to encourage actions that allow consumers to stay engaged and express their interest in a particular service without requiring a service provider instantly.
- *Step 4. Invite producers showing them relevant leads and activity*
  Producers come on board when they see activity and indication of intent from consumers. To ensure they do, the friction required for the producers to come on board should be as low as possible.
- *Step 5. Provide a better transaction experience*
  As in step 2, ensure that the post-discovery transaction is a more desirable experience than the experience through substitute channels. This ensures that both consumers and service providers repeatedly participate on the platform.

Startups often employ this model to piggyback off Craigslist's listings to start new platforms, as we note in the case study that follows. In an inadvertent comedy of errors, Justdial, India's largest local commerce platform, sued rival, Infomedia, when it found that Infomedia was stealing listings from Justdial. It figured this out by deliberately introducing false listings into its database that did not exist elsewhere. Once those listings showed up on Infomedia, Justdial had enough evidence to back its claim.

PLATFORM SCALE IMPERATIVE

Platforms often leverage supply from existing sources to power a better interaction between producers and consumers. This strategy works best when a platform is the first player in a new category. If the platform is a follower, consumers are unlikely to wait for producers to show up on a new platform when producers are already participating on another one. This strategy also does not support on-demand use cases very well. Such use cases are best supported by the platform itself, acting as a producer through a captive base of partner producers.

DISRUPTING CRAIGSLIST

Quality As A Competitive Advantage

Question: Why does Craigslist refuse to get disrupted, despite poor user experience and an utter lack of innovation?
Answer: Strong Network Effects

THREE FACTORS GOVERNING PLATFORM ADOPTION

The success of platforms depends on the following three factors:

1. *Network Effects.* The single most important factor for a platform is its ability to build the network effect. Without a minimum number of buyers and sellers, platforms simply are not valuable enough. With network effects, a platform continues to attract producers and consumers sustainably.
2. *Curation Of Content.* The platform should have a mechanism for separating signal from noise. Owing to network effects, platforms encourage abundance, and users need a mechanism to sift through the abundance and find the most relevant items. Platforms should have a mechanism

to reliably and credibly signal quality to consumers.

3. *Curation Of Participants.* Platforms may need to have a mechanism for determining the reputation of participants. This is especially true for platforms that mediate high-risk transactions.

As we note from the points above, platforms need a healthy balance of quantity and quality to sustainably enable interactions between participants. Craigslist's (largely) free offering, and the fact that it started in the early years of the Web, have allowed it to build tremendous network effects. Strong network effects guarantee that Craigslist is unlikely to be disrupted purely on the strength of a cleaner user interface, better features, and superior technology.

WHY IS CRAIGSLIST SO PARANOID ABOUT PROTECTING ITS DATA?

Craigslist is known to have played the villain with startups, doling out cease-and-desist letters to any startup attempting to build a better interaction experience, leveraging its data.

If Craigslist's network effects are so strong, and a competitor with better features and design is not reason enough for users to switch, why has it been so paranoid about other emerging platforms leveraging its data and content? Network effects, after all, would prevent users from moving to a new platform en masse, in spite of better features.

ACHILLES' HEEL: QUALITY AND NOT QUANTITY

To answer this question, let us revisit the three parameters mentioned above. Craigslist scores very high on network effects, although it does need a better mechanism to separate signal from noise on the platform. The platform has been taking some measures towards that by curbing sexually explicit listings and cutting down spam in some categories, by charging for listings.

However, Craigslist's real weakness lies in the third parameter: curation of participants. Marketplaces are built on trust and thrive on trust. High-risk interactions require participants to trust each other. Parents looking for a babysitter need a mechanism to ascertain their credibility. Hosts need to know that travelers staying at their apartment are reliable, and vice versa.

Craigslist, the king of quantity, suffers on quality. It does not have a reliable method of determining a user's reputation. While a low-trust environment may be acceptable for certain categories (e.g. renting low-value goods), it can be an important decision criterion for categories with high risk or high investment. As a platform, Craigslist does not allow producers to build reputation over time. As a result, it does little to aid a buyer's decision-making

THE CHALLENGE OF HORIZONTAL REPUTATION SYSTEMS

Craigslist is a horizontal platform, a one-stop source for listings across categories. This compounds the problem of setting up a reliable reputation system. Trust and reputation tend to be very contextual. Factors that contribute to reputation in one interaction or use case may be irrelevant in another.

Craigslist, arguably, may not have high activity per category outside the top few verticals so a category-specific reputation system may work reliably only for a few categories. A horizontal reputation system, on the other hand, while feasible, would not be very useful because of the contextual nature of trust.

Craigslist's inability to cater well to high-risk interactions makes it especially susceptible to competition in these categories.

ANOTHER AIRBNB?

Airbnb famously leveraged Craigslist to solve its chicken-and-egg problem. It allowed hosts to post their listings to Craigslist and directed travelers back, from Craigslist to Airbnb, for the transaction. Additionally, it also lured sellers on Craigslist to list on Airbnb, offering a better transaction experience.

More importantly, Airbnb has built a strong reputation system to build a worldwide community of travelers and hosts. It allows both parties to rate each other and has focused on building a huge corpus of reviews. Additionally, it offers verification services to verify hosts, where a photographer visits the actual listing and takes representative photographs. It also looks at implicit signals in the data that it captures to determine actions that reputable hosts perform regularly and those that are often associated with disreputable hosts.

Craigslist understands the importance of online reputation in high-risk interactions. Its paranoia, and relentless drive to protect its content, stems from a constant threat from emerging platforms, which may provide better trust and curation mechanisms in these categories. These competitors can leverage Craigslist's activity to build network effects of their own, while adding the security and trust layer to gain large-scale adoption.

Airbnb effectively used the strategies that we discussed in the previous chapter. Zaarly, Swappel, Krrb and many others have used these strategies to get traction for their own platforms.

If an emerging platform can own a category with the effectiveness that Airbnb has, it is potentially creating a dent in Craigslist's user base, and a very small dent in its network effect. Craigslist understands that multiple startups repeating this feat in multiple categories could potentially create a dent sizable enough to weaken Craigslist's network effects entirely.

PLATFORM SCALE IMPERATIVE

Network effects rely not only on ensuring quantity and availability but also on ensuring quality and reliability. An upcoming platform can compete credibly with an established player if it offers superior reputation systems in a high-risk category.

4.10

STARTING WITH MICROMARKETS

A Leaf From Facebook's Playbook

Building user bases of millions of users, all actively engaged and interacting with each other, may sound daunting. Many startups struggle with balancing the, often conflicting, priorities of user growth and engagement, especially since many run-of-the-mill growth hacks sacrifice one for the other. This is a bigger challenge for platforms that rely on network effects and virality for scale. Since users themselves drive growth, they need to be engaged and interacting, for the platform's user base to scale sustainably. How does a platform balance the conflicting priorities of scaling user bases, and sustaining interactions that deliver value to users and keep bringing them back? An enduring principle for growth on platforms is the following: *Start with interactions and scale interactions.*

Many platforms scale well by focusing on encouraging value-creating interactions before they scale their user base. To achieve this, platforms often target a micro-market, a very small market representative of the overall market and containing both production and consumption activity.

Facebook targeted Harvard, gradually moved on to other schools in the US, then on to companies and, eventually, opened itself up to the world. At a time when Myspace was big in the US and Friendster in other parts of the world, most other attempts at starting social networks were fading away because they failed to build meaningful interactions between users in their early days. Had Facebook launched throughout the world as a general purpose network, it would possibly have suffered a similar fate.

Quora and LinkedIn targeted entrepreneurs and investors in the valley where their respective founding teams had significant influence. Both platforms are, respectively, global brands today.

Local platforms always start by targeting a micro-market, by design. Yelp started by focusing on restaurants in San Francisco, Foursquare focused on New York City, and Groupon on Chicago.

Pinterest offers an object lesson in succeeding as a follower by targeting a micro-market. Pinterest started at a time when Facebook was already huge, users were developing 'social' fatigue, and all the pundits of user experience were advocating real-time text feeds. An image-based social network was not exactly a venture capitalist's dream. Pinterest grew slowly initially, but started gaining traction among designers, especially designer-bloggers, who started using Pinterest to promote themselves. Gradually, the design-centric community and culture that was created on the platform attracted other creative types, leading to rapid growth.

Massive networks have often been built on the back of small starts. As far as network effects are concerned, small user bases with thriving interactions trump large user bases with low activity.

FACEBOOK: A TALE OF MANY MICRO-MARKETS

> *"The reason [Facebook] went in through college was because college kids were generally not Myspace users, college kids were generally not Friendster users... Nobody actually believed... that you could enter the market through this niche market and gradually through this kind of carefully calculated war against all the other networks become the one network to rule them all."* – Sean Parker, on Facebook's micro-market strategy

The odds were stacked against Facebook when it launched. Friendster was already a big social network and Myspace was growing fast. Of all platform businesses, social networks are probably the most unforgiving of late market entrants. Why would someone, who was already on Myspace or Friendster, get onto Facebook? In hindsight, Mark Zuckerberg's decision to launch Facebook in closed campus clusters, whether borne of calculation or convenience, was a master stroke. It helped achieve early network effects for what would ultimately become the Internet's largest network.

SOLVE A PAIN POINT FOR A NICHE SEGMENT

Facebook focused on serving 'underserved' university students, to start with. Social networks existed and were already finding large-scale adoption but were flooded with fake profiles. University students wanted a network with real people, perhaps to improve their chances at dating (and that is where Tinder comes in, as we observe subsequently). Facebook solved both these needs, first by focusing on identity (it required signing up with a Harvard email address) and then by focusing on the profile picture (a reasonably important input to the dating decision). It solved a clear need which helped it find rapid adoption.

TARGET A MICRO-MARKET WHERE SMALL IS GOOD

Facebook gave the students at Harvard the exclusivity they valued, at least initially. High-end commerce marketplaces often build traction relatively fast by catering to an audience that values exclusivity.

In its early days, the small size of Quora helped. The high quality of discussions and the absence of 'trolling', initially prompted the who's who of Silicon Valley to come on board and help build an incredible resource. Subsequently, invite-only networks like Quibb and Medium also built a culture of quality by staying small, initially.

LEVERAGE EXISTING INTERACTIONS IN THE MICRO-MARKET

Facebook leveraged a community with strong offline ties. This helped build critical mass rapidly. Online interactions were built on top of offline interactions.

In a similar way, PayPal found early adoption among eBay buyers and sellers who were already engaging in transactions but wanted a simpler and more reliable mechanism to transfer money.

FIND A MICRO-MARKET THAT ENCOURAGES SPREAD

University students love self-expression, networking, and self-promotion. Facebook helped them do all three. A lot of early evangelism for Facebook was driven by existing users who wanted to get the word out as the platform opened up. Yelp started in San Francisco and targeted lifestyle categories. It was a unique city-category combination which led to early adoption among technology users who incidentally also travelled a lot, all of which helped spread the word to other locations as Yelp expanded.

FIND A MICRO-MARKET THAT IS REPRESENTATIVE OF THE FINAL MARKET

The key question when starting small is "Does this scale?" If it works here, will it work elsewhere? While user focus is critical, over-catering to the needs of one micro-market can come in the way of effectively spilling over to other adjacent micro-markets. Also, the micro-market itself should be representative of the larger whole and should not offer advantages that will not stay relevant with a larger audience. Many platforms that launch and find traction in Silicon Valley often face a moment of truth where they need to prove their ability to spread to an audience beyond the early adopters of technology.

A MICRO-MARKET MAY BE A THIN-SLICED USE CASE

What is as big as Facebook but relatively unknown? Most people outside China have never heard of Tencent. Yet, at nearly 800M users, Tencent QQ is probably the second largest social network in the world. While there are many factors that led to Tencent's domination of the Chinese market, its focus on gaming and dating, on an otherwise general purpose communication network, was a key reason for early growth. Tencent exploited the popularity of gaming and dating among Chinese youth and, in fact, created all the tools required for these use cases. This focus helped the company differentiate its services from competitors, which were too busy trying to be everything to everyone. Over time, the platform spilled beyond the initial use case to accommodate many different use cases.

MAKE A TWO-SIDED MARKET ONE-SIDED

The micro-market strategy works especially well when both production and consumption functions can be performed by the same target user. On Facebook, the same user creates and consumes content. On Yelp, the same user base would create and read reviews. The platform can target a single closed market and guarantee interactions. However, this does not work as easily for platforms that need two different markets to come on board. In such cases, the best solution to the problem of getting two different roles onto a platform is to find an existing community or group of potential users that already contains both roles.

Etsy, a niche marketplace for arts and crafts, figured an elegant solution to this problem. Etsy is a two-sided market of buyers and sellers. The founders of Etsy, who had earlier built thriving forums and communities for arts and crafts creators, discovered that people who make crafts, also like to buy from other craftspeople. This insight helped them precisely target one group and spark transactions within that successfully. The buyers and sellers were part of the same community and users who came in as buyers started selling, and vice versa.

Platforms, that need to turn two markets on simultaneously, may benefit immensely if they can identify a single market that contains both sides.

PLATFORM SCALE IMPERATIVE

Large network effects are built by scaling interactions. Platforms that enable thriving interactions within a small user base scale much faster. In order to do this, platforms may often have to start by targeting a micro-market, a small, contained market that encourages production and consumption at low scale. Over time, as existing users bring in other users from adjacent markets, the platform scales further, strengthening network effects.

4.11

FROM TWITTER TO TINDER

The Science Of Launching At Industry Conferences

Launching at conferences seems attractive because it satisfies all the wrong metrics with very little effort. It generates buzz, drives visitors, and downloads and may even lead to good PR and an award or two. However, these users tend to be distracted and often 'hop-click-jump' to the next fad. Many are the tales of woe of startup founders who woke up to a blip in their analytics the day after the conference launch, before everything went back to being the way it was.

There are exceptions, of course. Technology industry events are a great place to launch if your pitch can succinctly demonstrate the value that your offering provides (especially if you have a SAAS offering), if your key user base will actually be other startups (again, especially for SAAS offerings) or if your goal in launching is to generate interest among investors rather than among users.

In the specific case of networked platforms, launching at a technology industry event is unlikely to be very helpful. Users who come on board will stay on only if they can participate in value-creating interactions.

For a platform startup to launch successfully at a conference, or any time-bound event for that matter, it needs to ensure that the users who come on board can instantly participate in meaningful interactions.

THE SXSW FORMULA: ENABLING INTERACTIONS

Twitter's 'breakout' moment was the 2007 SXSW conference. While Twitter had been live for nearly a year, prior to the conference, it was not getting much adoption. Twitter's real-time feed would work best among a small number of users, when most of them were using it synchronously. Twitter needed to build concentration in time, similar to how Facebook built concentration in space by targeting Harvard. It needed a lot of users to come on board at the same time to discuss similar topics.

Twitter chose to launch at SXSW, since an event affords massive concentrations in both time and space. The founders created a Twitter visualizer. They set up flat panel screens in the conference hallways. A user at the conference could text 'join sxsw' to 40404, which would then show up on the screens and have the user automatically follow other active Twitter users at SXSW. With enough users tweeting and following each other, and the screens providing massive feedback to the tweeters in real time, Twitter gained the critical mass and activity required to get the platform going.

As Twitter's launch demonstrates, the *best way to launch a platform business at a conference is to ensure that the core interaction on the platform is organically embedded into the conference experience.*

Twitter did this with its launch. Attendees got more from the conference by participating on the core interaction on Twitter: tweeting about the conference. Just as PayPal and other platforms piggybacked on underlying networks, platforms can piggyback on events by ensuring that their core interaction is embedded into the interactions at the event.

The following year, Foursquare recreated the magic. Foursquare was laser-focused on getting check-ins right and was the only platform to leverage real-time location at that point in time. Again, the core interaction on Foursquare was successfully embedded into the conference experience.

At SXSW 2013, BangWithFriends, a network that allows users to find sexual partners, tried the same strategy but the conference clearly did not approve of the core interaction they were trying to embed into the conference experience.

Twitter and Foursquare targeted SXSW because it helped combine the micro-market strategy (a concentration of activity in space) with a concentration of activity in time. By embedding the core interaction into a contained user base with high activity, both platforms were able to encourage interactions. In fact, in spite of SXSW banning BangWithFriends in 2013, the platform still succeeded in leveraging the conference activity to enable more than 200 interaction matches within the first few days of the conference.

FROM BORING CONFERENCES TO FRATERNITY PARTIES

Tinder, a location-based dating network, launched at a fraternity party in the University of Southern California. Tinder allows users to indicate interest in other users and enables an interaction when both sides indicate interest in each other. By taking the awkwardness out of the whole act of meeting, Tinder's core interaction removed the friction in the core interaction of these fraternity parties. Users could swipe others' profiles, get matched and – being in the same area at the same time – meet up in real life.

Location-based, real-time applications have a unique challenge while getting traction. To enable interactions, a lot of people need to be present at the same place at the same time. Traditional marketing does not help. The best way to develop network effects, in such scenarios, is to launch at an event and ensure the core interaction of the platform fits in with the activity at the event. This is what Tinder did by launching at college parties.

...AND BACK TO BORING CONFERENCES

Finally, Airbnb figured its own way to make conferences work. While an alternative to the traditional hotel industry today, Airbnb gained initial traction by promoting itself around important conferences, in specific cities. This helped the platform aggregate a lot of transactions in a limited space and time. Conference attendees needed a place to stay, and hosts needed to see the platform bring them some business. When hotels would get fully booked, attendees would turn to Airbnb. By launching during events with high accommodation-seeking activity, Airbnb ensured there was enough value created for both sides to keep them engaged, and have them use Airbnb even beyond the conference.

PLATFORM SCALE IMPERATIVE

Concentrating in space and time helps the platform leverage existing offline activity by embedding its core interaction into this activity and making it more efficient. Facebook's launch in Harvard created a concentration in space while Twitter's launch at SXSW created a concentration in space and time. Both strategies, highlighted in the last two chapters, bring out one of the most important lessons in platform scale: A *platform can scale well only if it encourages interactions within a small user base before attracting a large number of users.*

In the next section, we build on this lesson to understand how platforms can scale to develop large user bases after having solved the chicken-and-egg problem and created initial interactions.

VIRALITY: SCALE IN A NETWORKED WORLD

Virality is a business design problem, not a marketing or engineering effort. It requires design before optimization.

INTRODUCTION

The Promise Of Viral Growth

A networked world promises scale that was never possible in the industrial economy. Fifty-employee 'developer shops' break out into billion-dollar valuations within a few years, often without investing much in marketing. Traditional marketing pundits are left scratching their heads at user growth curves, which rise non-linearly for no apparent reason. Conversely, marketing agencies increasingly advertise 'viral marketing' as one of the services they provide. What exactly is virality, how does it take simple ideas on breakneck growth journeys, and can it be engineered, or does it - as many believe - just happen because of a well-designed offering?

Virality is user-generated scale. In a viral system, the more users come on board, the faster can new users come on board, till a market achieves saturation. As the user base grows, so does the ability to grow it further. As a result, the slope of the growth curve constantly increases while an offering is finding viral adoption. The ability to scale becomes a function of the current user base and hence keeps accelerating of its own accord, as the user base scales.

In a networked world, businesses no longer rely entirely on push marketing campaigns. Substantial and sustainable growth comes when users get involved. Viral growth is the promise of the networked age and the only form of scale native to the network. It is also the one lever of platform scale available to all businesses, irrespective of whether they are pipes or platforms.

TRANSITIONING TO PLATFORM SCALE

From Bumps To Engines

> "*A startup is a company designed to grow fast... The only essential thing is growth. Everything else we associate with startups follows from growth.*" – Paul Graham

Paul Graham differentiates between startups and new businesses in one particular parameter, the potential for scale. A startup's potential to achieve hyper-growth and rapid scale is largely dependent on the types of growth strategies it implements. Before we embark on the journey of understanding the elements that contribute to virality, it is important to contrast viral growth with the way we have traditionally seen growth in a data-poor, non-participative world of pipes.

STARTING A CAR?

Scaling a business is a lot like making a car move. There are two ways to start a car and make it run. You can drive another car and 'bump' into the first car to make the first car move. The car moves with that 'bump', but that movement is not sustainable. To make a car run sustainably, you need to fit it with an engine. The need for an engine seems obvious with cars but seems less obvious when running a startup. Most scaling strategies for startups fall into one of two categories: bumps or engines.

Bumps
'Bump' strategies - PR, advertising, events - give a startup some traction and exposure, however, these strategies require commensurate investment of time, effort or money. Advertising works as long as you pump in money. PR and marketing events are not repeatable or scalable; you need to invest time and effort every time you run them.

Engines
In contrast, startups that build growth 'engines' scale rapidly and achieve exponential growth. These startups do not rely exclusively on external marketing channels; they build an engine for growth within the offering itself. *Startups with engines are designed to grow as a consequence of usage.*

GROWTH BY DESIGN

Startups with growth 'engines' demonstrate an ability to scale, which constantly increases with further scale. These startups do not divorce the act of scaling from the actual usage of the offering. As more users use the offering, the offering's growth rate increases. More pictures created and shared from Instagram expose Instagram to even more users. As users create and send out surveys from SurveyMonkey, survey recipients get exposed to the platform and come on board to create their own surveys. Kickstarter's project creators spread the word about Kickstarter every time they promote their project. All these offerings are designed to get greater exposure through usage, and that is a common design pattern that we see repeated across scalable startups. As more users use the offering, it gets exposed to new users, leading to greater growth.
These startups implement growth within the offering, much like an engine

sits within a car and powers the car forward. They leverage users to expose their offering to more users. Many startups erroneously believe that getting users to send out invites equals creation of such a growth engine. On the contrary, startups designed for platform scale rarely rely on invites. Instead, they rely on users to share elements of the offering – core value units created on top of the platform – with their network. YouTube users share videos, Kickstarter users share projects and Airbnb users share listings.

PLATFORM SCALE IMPERATIVE

A startup can never achieve platform scale purely on the strength of strong marketing budgets and external 'bump' strategies. It needs a growth 'engine' that powers growth from within. It needs to design growth that accelerates with usage. Finally, it needs to create the hooks and motivations that will enable and incentivize users to expose the offering to others, every time they use it.

Every platform scale marketer should differentiate between bumps and engines. Bumps are important to get initial traction, which then acts as fuel for the engine, but a marketing plan that relies only on bumps is unlikely to help achieve platform scale.

The subsequent chapters in this section break down the constituent elements that power the creation of these growth engines.

INSTAGRAM'S MOONSHOT MOMENT

Deconstructing Luck

Instagram is as famous for its rapid user growth as it is for its billion-dollar acquisition by Facebook. What is less known is the fact that Instagram achieved platform scale without hiring a single traditional marketing manager. At the time of acquisition, Instagram was a 13-employee-strong company without any dedicated effort towards traditional marketing. Started in October 2010, the company took 19 months to reach 50 million users, acquired the next 50 million in 9 months and reached 150 million users in another 6 months. And if the billion-dollar valuation was largely seen as Facebook overpaying for a competitive app, Instagram's valuation skyrocketed to 35 billion dollars within the next 20 months, according to Citigroup Inc. How did a company, without any substantial advertising spend or dedicated marketing resources, succeed in gaining such rapid traction?

Instagram presents a case for scale that was never possible in the industrial economy. In a networked world, businesses no longer rely entirely on push marketing campaigns, or bumps, as we noted earlier. Platform scale is achieved only when users get involved. Viral growth is the promise of the networked age and the only form of growth native to the network. Instagram's success was not accidental. On the contrary, it was carefully designed. Unlike its competitor, Hipstamatic, Instagram did not stop at taking pictures and applying filters onto them; it encouraged the photo creator to share the photo on an external network like Facebook. Converting a single-user activity to a social, multi-user activity was the key reason for Instagram's growth. Leveraging Facebook, a network where users interact with photos, furthered the cause. A user would take a picture on Instagram and share it on Facebook. Viewers on Facebook, intrigued by the effects generated by Instagram filters, would move over to Instagram, try it for themselves and share their own pictures, thereby restarting the cycle repeatedly. Every time users used the app, they shared their creations externally. Every point of app usage worked as an instance of app marketing. In essence, Instagram achieved something quite remarkable – it succeeded in converting most of its users into marketers. In the process, it never needed to hire marketers of its own.

PLATFORM SCALE IMPERATIVE

Instagram's viral growth, as we explore through this section, breaks down into a series of repeatable design patterns. While these patterns do not guarantee viral growth in every instance, they increase the odds of achieving it, if implemented well. A platform scale marketer should look to implement these design patterns that repeatedly convert users into marketers and scale the offering's ability to grow.

THE FOUR MOST COMMON MISCONCEPTIONS ABOUT VIRALITY

Unpacking anecdotal truths

Gaining viral adoption is every marketer's dream in a networked world. However, few understand what virality really entails. Through this chapter, we explore the four most common misconceptions about virality.

MISCONCEPTION #1: VIRALITY AND WORD OF MOUTH ARE TWO NAMES FOR THE SAME PHENOMENON

Virality and word of mouth are two concepts that are often conflated and confused. Word of mouth is a phenomenon where people love an offering so much, they just cannot stop talking about it. Word of mouth is fueled by a company's ability to deliver user delight and its ability to convert users into passionate fans. Nurturing passionate communities helps to drive word of mouth, but the company, or brand, cannot explicitly structure or encourage the process. It can maximize the chances of generating word of mouth by delighting users, but it cannot, directly, get them to start talking about it.

Organic virality, on the other hand, is a phenomenon where users spread the word about an offering, in the context of using it. Unlike word of mouth, virality is not a consequence of users loving the offering, it is a consequence of users using it. As noted earlier, when a Kickstarter project creator spreads the word about their project, the platform achieves greater adoption. The existing users gain value out of taking an action, which, in turn, exposes the underlying platform to new users. Virality does not need fans: it merely needs users, who are encouraged to bring in other users. Word of mouth works effectively both online and offline. Virality works only for networked businesses, and can scale only on digital platforms. Users need to be connected to each other over a network for virality to take place.

MISCONCEPTION #2: VIRALITY AND NETWORK EFFECTS ARE THE SAME AND LEAD TO RAPID GROWTH

Both network effects and virality tend to magnify value and scale, respectively, as more users use the platform. This is probably why the two concepts are often confused. Both are explored in detail in Section 1 as factors that power platform scale. However, there are many businesses that exhibit virality without exhibiting network effects.

Email services and cross-platform communication products serve as a case in point. Email services are interoperable across different email providers. A sender using Gmail can send an email to a recipient using Hotmail. Gmail users do not need to have other users using Gmail to see the value in the email service. This explanation may seem obvious given the ubiquity of email, but it helps to contrast this with a closed network like LinkedIn, where users need other users to join the network before they can communicate with them. Both email providers and closed social networks like LinkedIn, benefit from virality, but email providers do not benefit from network effects, whereas closed networks like LinkedIn do.

Services like SurveyMonkey and Eventbrite leverage external networks for viral spread. SurveyMonkey surveys are answered, and Eventbrite events find registrants only when they are spread on external networks, thereby exposing the respective services to new users. These offerings exhibit virality but have no network effects. The fact that more users use the service does not necessarily add value to other users of the service.

There are many others that exhibit network effects without exhibiting virality. Some marketplaces, for example, may not grow virally but may still benefit from network effects. Sellers may be discouraged from bringing in other sellers, because of competition, and may play no role in inviting buyers either. Likewise, buyers may not invite other buyers into the network without any clear incentive. Craigslist, arguably, has very high network effects but very low virality.

MISCONCEPTION #3: VIRALITY IS ALL ONE NEEDS FOR A GROWTH STRATEGY

Virality involves users bringing in other users. By definition, this form of user growth requires some users at the start. Viral acquisition of users works in tandem with other user-acquisition models, which bring in the first few users to start with, who then bring in other users. Relying on virality as the only source of user acquisition is a flawed strategy.

MISCONCEPTION #4: VIRALITY INVOLVES MANIPULATING USERS TO SEND OUT INVITES TO OTHER POTENTIAL USERS

Virality is a design challenge. Viral mechanics need to be built into the user experience and workflows. Poorly designed viral mechanics lead to a poor user experience. All too often, the numbers-focused obsession of most marketers leads them to optimize a poorly designed viral mechanic, which, in turn, makes a bad user experience worse. In the early years of the Facebook App Platform, apps would often encourage users to send irrelevant invites and notifications into their network. This notion continues to persist even as Facebook has tightened its policies. Startups still implement virality as an invite loop that can be slapped onto any offering. More often than not, this approach spams recipients and gets in the way of good user experience. The single most important element of getting virality right is to understand virality as a design challenge and to deconstruct it into its constituent building blocks. The keys to this, as we observe in the following chapter, may lie in understanding the spread of diseases and epidemics.

ARCHITECTING DISEASES

How To Engineer An Epidemic

Viral growth derives its name from the viral spread of diseases. Platforms like Pinterest and Twitter grow at a non-linear rate, in a manner similar to the spread of diseases through a population. Users 'infect' other users, while they are 'infected' with the usage of a certain platform.
The design principles for unlocking viral growth, unsurprisingly, lie in understanding the fundamental factors that lead to the spread of diseases.

NETWORKS SPREAD LIKE DISEASES DO

The mechanics of disease spread require four key elements operating in a cycle:

1. *The Host*: An infected host sneezes and spreads the germs out in the air.
2. *Droplets*: Sneezed droplets carry the germs that spread the infection.
3. *Air*: Air acts as a medium to suspend and transfer these infected droplets.
4. *The Recipient*: Someone breathes in these droplets and gets infected, in turn.

Subsequently, the recipient becomes the host and the cycle repeats. Removing even one of these elements from the mix can stop the spread of viral diseases. Quarantining, for example, removes hosts. One could speculate, similarly, that sneezing in a vacuum may not have quite the same effect, owing to the lack of air as a transporting medium.

Viral growth works in a very similar manner. On revisiting the Instagram example, mentioned earlier in this section, the following four elements are observed:

1. *The Sender.* A user on the platform sends out a message about the platform.
2. *The Core Unit.* The message is typically the core value unit that the user creates or consumes on the platform. A user taking a picture on Instagram shares it on Facebook.
3. *The External Network.* These units spread on an external network, connecting people. For Instagram's growth, Facebook served as a very effective external network, enabling the spread of pictures (units) created on Instagram.
4. *The Recipient.* Finally, a recipient on the external network interacts with the unit and is brought back to the original platform. At this point, the user from Facebook gets intrigued by the picture and visits Instagram to potentially create photo.

The cycle repeats with The Recipient now acting as The Sender. This cycle, driving viral growth, is repeatedly observed across diverse startups. In a move that is now a part of startup folklore, Airbnb reverse-engineered an integration with Craigslist that allowed hosts on Airbnb to post their listings (value units created on Airbnb) simultaneously on Craigslist. Travelers on Craigslist (the external network, in this case) would see the listing and join Airbnb to make a booking. Over time, this integration, in combination with several other initiatives from Airbnb, created the repeatable cycle mentioned above and led to Airbnb's rapid growth early on.

INCENTIVES FOR VIRAL GROWTH

An ongoing theme that we note through most of this book is the design of incentives for users. The design of incentives (both organic and inorganic), and consequently, of new behaviors and habits, is core to the creation of network effects, and it is also central to the generation of viral growth. Most mobile apps and Internet services are self-serve, opt-in systems. Users need to be incentivized to repeatedly participate in the platform and take actions that lead to stronger network effects and higher virality. These behaviors need to be explicitly identified and designed for users.

Startups – as well as enterprises – building platforms, often make the error of engineering viral growth before designing the right incentives for users to stay on in an engaged fashion. Such growth is rarely sustainable, as demonstrated by the rapid growth of applications like BranchOut, leveraging Facebook as an external network. BranchOut gained users rapidly, through a viral mechanic that spammed a user's network on Facebook, but lost all those users just as fast. Many applications built on Facebook tried to harvest Facebook's user base by flooding users' newsfeeds with invitations but most such attempts failed to design the right incentives for users to come in and stay engaged. Hence, even the ones that briefly succeeded in stimulating rapid scale, saw rapid decline in usage, as users who came in without intent, failed to stay engaged.

PLATFORM SCALE IMPERATIVE

Viral growth can be reduced to the following four design questions:

1. *Sender Incentives.* Why will the sender send units out of the platform?
2. *Spreadable Unit.* What is the minimum transferable unit on the platform that can move on an external network?
3. *External Network.* Where will the unit from the platform meet current non-users?
4. *Recipient Incentives.* Why will a non-user on an external network convert to a user on the platform?

A DESIGN-FIRST APPROACH TO VIRAL GROWTH

Because Design Is The Future Of Marketing

Virality is a design problem, not an optimization problem. It is more the prerogative of the product designer than of the marketer. Unfortunately, it is often treated as a marketing or 'growth hacking' problem, with an inadvertently high focus on optimizing the likelihood that viral cycles get started. Instead, virality should be solved as a design problem. This chapter lays out a framework for designing offerings for organic virality.

SENDER INCENTIVES

Why will users spread the word about the platform?

Sender incentives need to be aligned with the core interaction on the platform. As noted in the preceding chapter, virality is kick-started when the sender sends out value units from the platform onto an external network. This act, which drives virality, should not distract users from the core interaction on the platform. Instead, where possible, spread of the units should enhance the value that the user gets from the core interaction of the platform. The more closely this action is aligned with the core interaction on the platform, the more likely is the platform to succeed with crafting the right sender incentives for achieving viral adoption.

Instagram, YouTube, Kickstarter and SkillShare are all examples of platforms where users gain greater value from the core interaction by spreading the word about their creations – the core value units – on external networks. A user uploading a video on YouTube is likely to be motivated by the potential for self-expression or self-promotion (or both) on that platform. The user benefits further by spreading the video on an external network, like Facebook. Project creators on Kickstarter want their projects to be seen by as wide an audience as possible. This encourages them to spread the project page on their personal social networks.

Conversely, many gaming applications fail to grow virally by asking users to invite other users. On these applications, the act of sending invites does not align with the reason the user plays the game. Some games overcome this by crafting inorganic incentives for the user. Some games may enable users to unlock game levels or weapons if they comply by sending invites. In contrast, turn-based games have a more organic viral dynamic. A user plays their turn and invites their opponent to play the next turn. Playing a turn constitutes the creation of a unit of value that can be consumed by someone else. The action of inviting an opponent (the sending action), using this value unit, is aligned with the core interaction of gameplay. If the recipient accepts the invitation, the sender's experience is enhanced, and the game acquires a new user, virally. These sending and receiving actions are often designed to work asynchronously on turn-based games. This ensures that multi-player gameplay can continue, without requiring both players to be playing at the same time.

This pattern is repeatedly observed across platforms that achieve rapid viral growth. Senders are appropriately incentivized (usually organically), and the act of sharing these units externally enhances the value derived from the core interaction on the platform.

Sender motivations may vary across producer and consumer roles. Producers may be driven to share their creations for the purpose of self-expression and self-promotion. Consumers may be driven to share content they associate with. Both roles may respond to inorganic incentives, in the form of payments or coupons. The incentives that work vary with the type of platform and the context of usage. Zeroing in on the right incentives, and the optimal workflows, which prompt users to share, may often require several rounds of testing different incentives and workflows with users.

In general, producers spread self-created value units for social feedback. Whether for self-expression or self-promotion, producers tend to be the most active 'senders' and regularly contribute to viral spread. As a result, the most viral platforms often have two things in common:

1. *Low friction in creating core value units*: The easier it is to create units, the more often producers produce and share.
2. *High percentage of producers*: The most viral platforms have a high percentage of their user base creating units.

This is one of the reasons why simple applications, like Instagram and WhatsApp, tend to spread virally.

Aligning the sharing act with the core interaction is the first key principle to building for viral adoption. Question askers on Quora want to get their question answered. They often share the question on Facebook or Twitter, at the time of creating the question. Channel owners on YouTube spread their videos on multiple external networks to gain an audience. Survey creators on SurveyMonkey spread their surveys via email, blogs and social networks as this helps them get responses. Authors seeking funding on Kickstarter also spread their project page on their social networks. Two key insights emerge across these examples:

- Producers never spread the word about the platform: they merely spread the word about their creations
- Platforms that succeed with viral growth reward users with accelerating social feedback

The second point above is worth noting, as accelerating feedback encourages users to keep repeating their actions. Platforms like YouTube and Quora perform because of social curation. The videos and answers that get higher upvotes get greater exposure on the platform. While on-platform discovery of content leads to higher upvotes, sharing the content on an external network helps to gather a few initial upvotes. This initial curation leads to greater consumption, and hence, further curation on the platform. This, in turn, kick-starts a virtuous cycle, leading to accelerating feedback

and resultant higher exposure of the content.
In a similar vein to the producer-as-sender use cases, consumers may also spread value units when they find them relevant, interesting or intriguing, or if they feel the unit can give rise to new interactions on another network. Media companies like Upworthy and Buzzfeed scale solely on the strength of consumer-initiated viral spread. These outlets focus on creating content and headlines that inspire shock and awe among content consumers, encouraging them to spread the word on their respective social networks. Much of 9GAG's viral growth also stems from consumers sharing creations on the platform, rather than the producers alone sharing those creations.
Platforms that require users to explicitly connect with each other, before they experience network effects, grow virally through invites. Communication networks, like Skype and Facebook, require users to explicitly connect with others. These platforms rely on local network effects, where users benefit only from having more friends within their immediate network. In contrast, every user on YouTube or Airbnb benefits when there are a greater number of users using the overall network. Sending invitations aligns with the core interaction of connecting and communicating.
Platforms may also use inorganic incentives, but these incentives need to be carefully structured, to scale well. Poorly structured monetary incentives may lead to high burn rates on a rapidly scaling platform. Inorganic incentives should also be contingent on the final outcome. Groupon gifts Credits to a user, only when friends invited by the user purchase a deal. Finally, inorganic incentives should encourage both senders and recipients appropriately. Dropbox increases the likelihood of virally acquired sign-ups, by offering free space to the Sender as well as the Recipient, when the Recipient signs up.

SPREADABLE CORE VALUE UNITS

Are units on the platform designed for spread on an external network?
The most misunderstood contributor to viral adoption is the core value unit created on the platform. The fastest growing platforms have a core value unit that is easily spreadable on an external network. The video on

YouTube, the room listing on Airbnb, the game state in a turn-based game or the question on Quora are all examples of spreadable core value units that are created on the respective platforms, and that are then sent out on an external network.

Word of mouth can work for any offering, irrespective of whether it is physical or digital, but viral adoption only occurs in the case of networked systems, where core value units, created on the system, can be spread on an external network.

The value unit is a representation of the platform that can spread on an external network and act as a demonstration for the platform. When the founders of Hotmail inserted: "P.S. I love you. Get your free email at Hotmail" at the bottom of every email generated on Hotmail, they were adopting a design choice that would be repeated across multiple viral platforms. Every email (unit) created on Hotmail would travel to users of other email providers and act as a demonstration of the free email value proposition that Hotmail championed. YouTube videos embedded in Facebook feeds have accounted for the rapid spread of viral successes like Psy's Gangnam Style, the many Harlem Shake videos, and the ALS Ice Bucket challenge, to name a few.

However, not all value units on all platforms are spreadable. A business exchange platform enabling exchange of proprietary documents may not have units that are spreadable. Users are unlikely to be interested in sharing confidential documents the way they would share photos on Instagram. A spreadable unit has the following characteristics:

1. *It triggers an interaction on an external network.* YouTube owes much of its early growth to MySpace. During its heyday, bands would use MySpace to interact with their fans. Bands, however, had no easy way of sharing videos of their performances and bootlegs with their fans. YouTube explicitly created the functionality to embed videos onto MySpace, allowing bands to host videos on YouTube and embed them on their MySpace profile. These videos helped start an interaction on MySpace, an important requirement for a spreadable unit. Ironically, while MySpace remains a mere footnote in the history of social networking, YouTube, meanwhile, has grown to become one of the most relevant platforms of our time.

2. *It plays on the producer-as-sender dynamic.* Encouraging producers to spread their creation at the point of production drives growth for many content platforms. Some platforms like Instagram, Kickstarter and SurveyMonkey actively encourage this as part of the user workflow.
3. *The spread of the unit helps to complete an incomplete interaction.* An unanswered question on Quora is a spreadable unit demanding social feedback in the form of an answer. A fresh survey on SurveyMonkey needs responses. A Kickstarter project is a bid to potential funders to come over to Kickstarter and fund the project. While not necessarily a requirement for all spreadable units, the incompleteness of the interaction creates an active call to action for the recipient, prompting them to act.

Spreadable units remain the most important, yet least understood, element of designing for viral adoption.

EXTERNAL NETWORK

What is the external network on which the unit spreads? Networks grow on top of other networks. Instagram leveraged Facebook, as did Zynga. There are countless examples of viral growth, leveraging Facebook as an underlying network.

For quite some time, startups building new platforms saw Facebook as their savior for solving launch and adoption problems. For many marketers, implementing viral growth translates to little more than a simple introduction via a share button and an integration with Facebook. However, an inadvertent focus on the tools available often distracts platform builders from the right design decisions. There are four key decisions that determine success of viral growth while leveraging an external network:

1. *Choice of network.* The choice of network is an important consideration. One is often tempted to believe that an effective external network for viral growth is likely to be one that publicly offers sharing buttons. Hence, Facebook, Twitter, Google + and their ilk are the first networks that often come to mind. However, any network where users are explicitly or implicitly connected, and which would allow an external party to insert

a unit, is a possible choice for an external network. Email and the mobile phone contact list are implicit networks, as is the blogosphere (when imagined as a network connecting blog writers and blog readers, many of whom are writers as well). Viral applications and platforms have long leveraged chain mails, contact list integration, widgets, phone notifications and newsfeed updates to spread the word on an underlying network. The choice of an underlying network is governed by three considerations:

a. Relevant interactions: Airbnb reverse-engineered an integration with Craigslist despite the fact that Craigslist does not encourage integration by offering any public APIs. The interactions that Airbnb wanted to facilitate on its platform were already happening on Craigslist. It simply focused on providing a better platform (with better reputation, trust and transaction mechanisms) for those interactions and users switched over.

b. Relevant connections: In another example of an intelligent choice of network, LinkedIn chose to integrate with Microsoft Outlook, even though most other social networks opted for the easier integrations with Yahoo and Gmail. Users' business connections, the ones that LinkedIn wanted to create, already existed on Outlook. The integration, though time and cost intensive, played out well for LinkedIn.

c. Relevant look and feel: Pinterest is one of the largest external sources of traffic to Etsy. On an Etsy profile page, users are explicitly encouraged to share on Pinterest, over other networks; the absence of a cluttered buffet of sharing choices is worth noting. Juxtaposing an Etsy profile page and a Pinterest board helps us understand the reason for this choice of underlying network. Etsy's profile pages are photo-centric, especially since the marketplace is used by artists and craftspeople to sell their wares. These pictures work well with Pinterest boards and get spread around on Pinterest.

The connections and/or interactions you want to enable on your platform may already exist elsewhere. Look for external networks that facilitate similar connections/interactions.

2. *Add value to users on external network.* As with all other decisions related to platforms, a favorable and compelling user experience is also key to

successful viral growth. Flickr's initial growth ensured that it added value to users on an external network. Flickr grew largely because it allowed bloggers a better alternative for hosting their pictures for blog posts. Both bloggers and blog readers benefited from the value. PayPal added value to users on eBay by providing them a safe and secure payments mechanism. As a result, much of PayPal's initial growth was achieved on eBay. While using an external network, one needs to add value to users on that network to achieve sustainable scale.

3. *Unfair advantage*. Companies that are first to leverage a new network often benefit from an unfair advantage. Zynga, RockYou, and Slide used Facebook for viral growth more effectively than others, because they were among the first to use it. WhatsApp used the phonebook, Airbnb used Craigslist, and PayPal used eBay. All three platforms were the first to use the corresponding external network. In most cases, these external networks step up governance and restrictions as more applications start leveraging them for growth. Users may also get sophisticated over time and stop clicking on, and responding to, invite messages.
4. *Ease of integration*. Finally, as a platform builder, the ease of integration is an important factor when choosing an external network. Today's social networks actively encourage such integrations through single sign-on mechanisms and sharing widgets.

RECIPIENT INCENTIVES

Why will the recipient perform the desired action?

In this stage of the viral cycle, the platform's business goal is to drive as many conversions as possible on an external network. Unfortunately, interestingness and relevance are characteristics of the unit (often created by a user) and a platform has limited control over it. YouTube does not control the kinds of videos users create. It plays its part in ensuring that the best videos get greater exposure, and hence, spread further. However, as a platform, it cannot itself introduce interestingness and relevance into the content of the video in the way a publisher like Buzzfeed or Upworthy can. Instead, the platform owner can incentivize conversions through ancillary content that travels with this unit. There are two elements that need to be incorporated into a spreadable unit to incite conversions:

1. *Pitch.* The unit should serve as a compelling pitch for the platform. It should act as a demonstration of the platform and should show the recipient what to expect from the platform. A shared project from Kickstarter shows what users can do on Kickstarter. Each of these is a compelling pitch for the respective platform.
2. *Call To Action.* There should be a targeted and compelling call to action, inciting conversions. When Hotmail first went viral, it carried the message: "P.S. I love you. Get your FREE email at Hotmail" at the bottom of every email. Free email was a new and compelling pitch at that point in time and the call to action ensured that recipients of the message converted in droves. Hotmail was probably the first consumer Internet application that achieved viral growth through a simple tweak in its messaging.

Finally, as noted earlier, a call to action may be implicit, when the spread of the unit helps to complete an incomplete interaction. An unanswered question on Quora, an open survey on SurveyMonkey and a Kickstarter project waiting to be funded are all incomplete interactions, with a clear call to action for the recipient. The call to action is organically embedded within the unit.

PLATFORM SCALE IMPERATIVE

The viral spread of any digital offering requires all four elements, working in tandem. An inability to enable any one of these can break down the entire viral spread cycle. To achieve Platform Scale through virality, a platform needs to watch out for four key considerations:

1. Alignment of the sharing action with the core interaction of the platform.
2. Spreadability of the core value unit.
3. Choice of an external network that encourages spread and enables similar or complementary interactions already.
4. Design of a clear pitch and call to action, which travel with the spreadable unit.

5.6

BUILDING VIRAL ENGINES

Moving From Design To Optimization

Viral growth needs to be designed before it is optimized. Poorly designed but well optimized viral invites can transform into a glut of spam, irritating users and inviting the ire of the external networks that one leverages. This chapter explores four key optimization priorities, for achieving sustainable viral growth.

1. *Send: Maximize Outflow Of Units From The Platform*
The platform should constantly – and explicitly – promote the creation as well as the spread of new units. As more producers create and share from the platform, new cycles of viral growth get started. Producers need to be encouraged to create new units more often. Moreover, sharing actions should be a part of the creation workflow, where relevant, to ensure that new creations are shared. Instagram's creation flow clearly demonstrates the importance of this, seemingly simple, design principle.
It is equally, if not more, important to identify triggers that lead consumers to share the content that they consume.

2. Spread: Ensure That Units Spread On The External Network.
The next priority for the platform is to maximize the spread of the unit on the external network. To a large extent, this spread is determined by the design of the external network. Facebook's Share, Twitter's Retweet and email's Forward functions make units easily spreadable within these networks. However, spread on another network, say the blogosphere, may not be quite as frictionless. Hence, a network's ability to encourage spread of units may be a key consideration when choosing an external network.

3. Click: Maximize Clicks On External Network.
This requires the platform to incentivize conversions through testing different pitches and calls to action. A/B testing multiple messages may yield different results, and may help the platform to zero in on the right messaging.

4. Convert: Minimize Cycle Time.
Virality works as a cycle with a sender sending out units, the receiver clicking, visiting the platform and eventually converting to the original sender, and starting a whole new cycle. The longer the time this cycle takes on average, the slower is the growth rate of the overall platform.

MINIMIZING CYCLE TIME

It is important to ensure that the number of steps between first exposure to a unit on an external network, and the start of a new cycle, is minimized. This ensures that users move from being recipients to initiators of a new cycle without much friction. Chain emails are the best example of content going viral because the effort required to start a new cycle is minimal. Of course, the ominous footnotes foretelling death and other mishaps on a user who does not spread the word, definitely help start new cycles at an alarming rate.

Sometimes, newly acquired users may start a new cycle instantly, as in the case of Instagram or WhatsApp. In other cases, users may need a few visits to the platform before they are nudged towards a new viral cycle.

PLATFORM SCALE IMPERATIVE

Much as managing a platform involves repeating a well-designed core interaction efficiently, managing towards viral growth involves repeating the viral cycle efficiently. The fastest scaling platforms achieve both through one specific mechanism: Focusing on the core value unit and structuring the core interaction as well as the viral cycle around it. Growth, engagement and value creation work in tandem on such platforms.

THE VIRAL CANVAS

A Tool For Marketers To Think Like Designers

The design elements that make an offering viral, as well as the key managerial priorities discussed in this section, are fairly straightforward, when understood and yet, they are often ignored. This chapter presents a visual tool, bringing together the concepts discussed in this section in one cohesive framework, to ensure that managers and entrepreneurs have a ready reckoner for building such businesses and a tool for brainstorming with teams.

THE VIRAL CANVAS

The layout of the viral canvas is based around the sharing action between the sender and the recipient. The four design elements needed to structure this sharing action are laid out, aligned with the sender and the recipient. The inner core of the viral canvas lays out the optimization cycle. This representation serves as a planning tool to plan viral growth for different platforms and offerings. The next two pages lay out the canvas for three case studies, discussed earlier in this section.

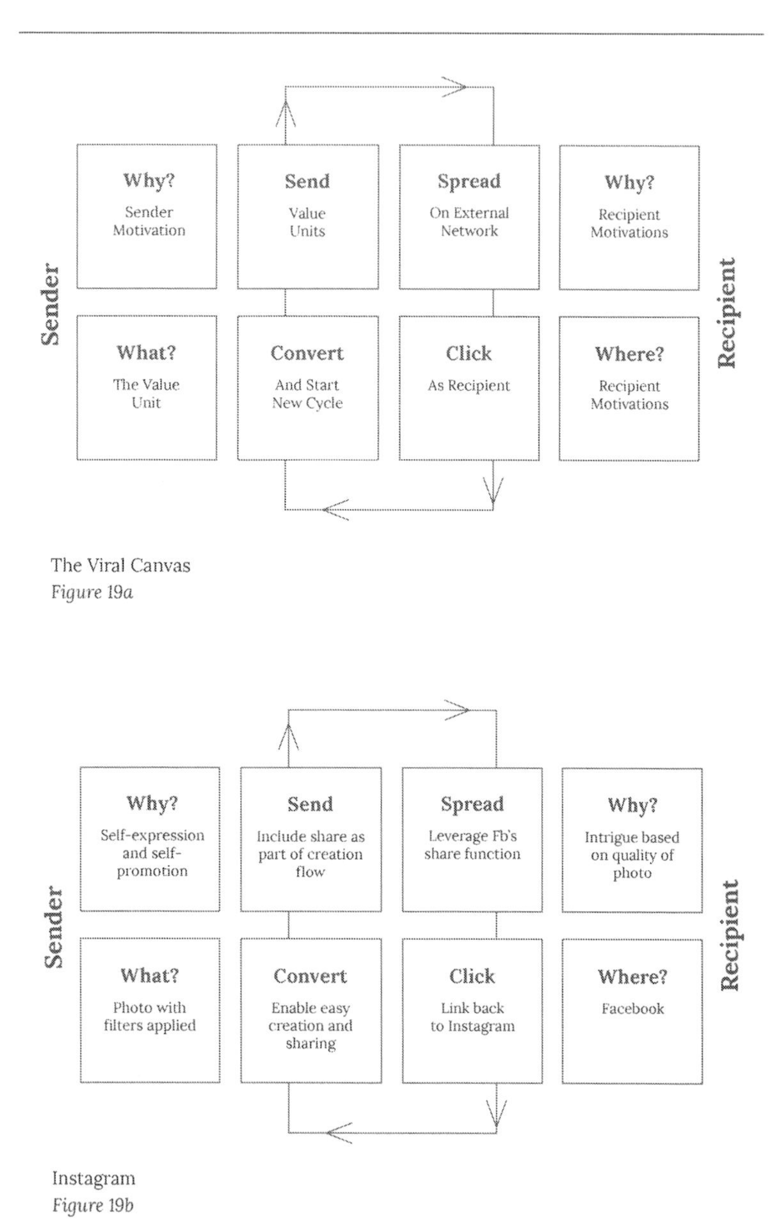

The Viral Canvas
Figure 19a

Instagram
Figure 19b

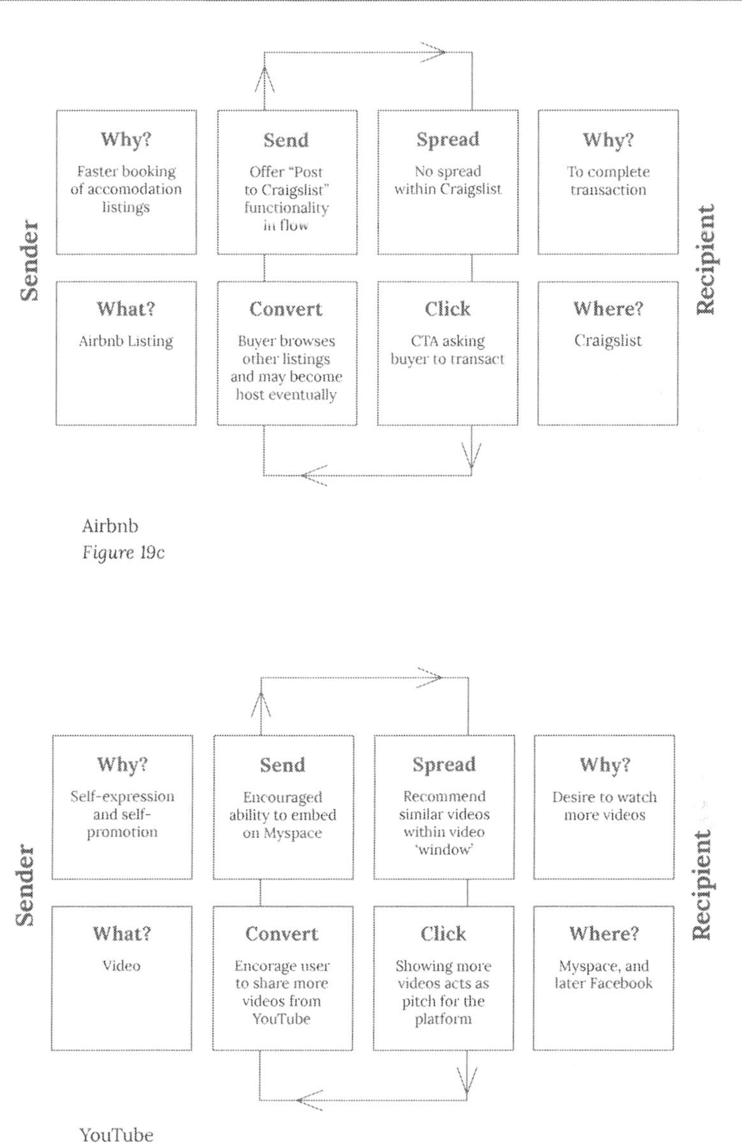

Airbnb
Figure 19c

YouTube
Figure 19d

Section
6

REVERSE NETWORK EFFECTS

The goal of platform scale is to ensure the simultaneous scaling of quantity and quality of interactions.

INTRODUCTION

Too Big To Fail?

The era of big corporations may be drawing to a close, but much of this book makes the case for a new form of big: the era of big ecosystems, built around networked platforms. As the world gets more networked, harnessing the principles of platform scale to our advantage is going to present opportunities to transform entire industries and shape business models that would not have existed before. However, there are limits to platform scale. This section explores the opposing view to platform scale.

The network effect argument posits that platforms should improve in their ability to create and deliver value as they gain greater adoption, however, under certain conditions, scale may work against the platform.

To understand how platforms fail with scale, it is important to revisit the principles that enable platform scale, in the first place. Platform scale is achieved as internal processes are transitioned to external interactions. Platforms that enable highly efficient and repeatable interactions scale faster than those that do not. As a result, if higher adoption gets in the way of interaction efficiency and repeatability, the platform may lose value with scale. The first part of this section lays out a framework for understanding the scalability of network effects.

The latter half of this section explores two key considerations that limit platform scale. The first is a design constraint that sets a natural limit to network effects. This may apply only to certain types of platforms and networks. The more interesting - and often overlooked - consideration discusses a unique phenomenon that leads to depleting value and loss of network effects, with an increase in scale.

6.1

A SCALING FRAMEWORK FOR PLATFORMS

Creation-Curation-Customization-Consumption

The chicken-and-egg problem of kick-starting new platform businesses gets a lot of attention in every discussion of platform scale. Most startups pursuing platform scale fail at this point. As a result, this book devotes an entire section to understanding this. A frequent misconception, though, is that managing platform growth is fairly straightforward once the initial chicken-and-egg problem is solved. Popular wisdom dictates that the engine fuels itself once enough producers and consumers are on board.

Ironically, as networked platforms become more ubiquitous, the support infrastructure needed to kick-start platforms is increasingly making it easier to solve the initial adoption challenge. The ability to piggyback a variety of open user networks like Facebook's social graph and leverage phone book contacts have simplified some of the challenges of initial adoption. As more businesses get started on the path towards platform scale, they are beginning to encounter important platform management issues further down the line. Users are increasingly distracted, and may migrate to other alternatives, thereby leading to fewer interactions on the platform. Investing in behavior design and building cumulative value, as described in Section 3, helps retain users and increase the quantity of interactions. However, as quantity increases, platform managers often have to tackle a second issue: the quality of interactions may fall with increasing scale. Quality issues are often glossed over in most discussions of scale. Dashboards are conveniently created to demonstrate graphs that scale numbers without tracking metrics that indicate the quality of scale.

To achieve sustainable scale, a platform needs to scale both the quantity and the quality of interactions that it enables.

A FRAMEWORK FOR SCALING INTERACTIONS

A platform needs to ensure that its core interaction is repeated as often - and as efficiently - as possible. More rides on Uber, more payments on PayPal and more tasks booked on TaskRabbit, are good news for the respective platforms. To craft a framework for scaling interactions, it is helpful to revisit the structure of the core interaction, as discussed in Section 2. The core interaction consists of four key actions: Creation, Curation, Customization, and Consumption. Depending on the type of platform and the stage of evolution it is in, scaling interactions may involve scaling one or more of these individual actions.

SCALING QUANTITY: CREATION

Some platforms scale by focusing solely on scaling new value creation. A classifieds platform like Craigslist focuses entirely on the depth and breadth of listings across its categories. A platform can stall despite building strong network effects if producers stop creating value on the platform.

To scale creation, the platform needs to focus on fostering an active producer base, not merely an active user base. Where relevant, the platform also needs to ensure repeat participation by producers. Medium, the blogging platform, encourages frequent and repeat contributions from writers by constantly conveying feedback about the performance of their existing articles on the platform. This feedback encourages writers to create more content and to participate more often.

SCALING QUANTITY: CONSUMPTION

Scaling creation often works in tandem with scaling consumption. Producers are likely to participate on a platform only when there is active participation from consumers as well. No one wants to speak to an empty room.
For demand-driven platforms like UpWork and 99Designs, where the value is created in response to a consumer-driven request, scaling demand – and, hence, consumption – is a critical first step to scaling interactions. On marketplaces, scaling consumption leads to greater commercial activity, thereby fueling greater seller (producer) participation. On creation-centric platforms, like YouTube and Medium, scaling consumption provides ongoing feedback to producers, encouraging them to produce more often. Scaling consumption is also important to guarantee some level of platform performance to producers. Sellers on a marketplace may get disengaged if they fail to see their listings generate purchases.

SCALING QUALITY: CUSTOMIZATION

To scale consumption, the platform needs to strengthen its filters. It needs to capture better data about the consumer and use that data to make more relevant recommendations. The strength of filters, along with the consequent relevance of recommendations, is the single most important driver of value for consumers on the platform.
To strengthen filters, platforms need to constantly acquire data about users. A scaling strategy for platforms is incomplete without an ongoing data acquisition strategy. Data acquisition must start right at the point of signing up, and must continue as the platform scales. For example, Pinterest asks users to 'like' a few boards and a few topics, as part of its on-boarding flow. This data helps Pinterest build out the initial filter. This filter needs to be strengthened throughout the life cycle of the user, through the explicit and implicit capture of data.
Increasingly, buyer-seller marketplace platforms are not focused on transactions alone. Many such marketplaces encourage buyers to follow topics and listings, thereby capturing buyer interest data. Creation of these interest-based filters helps provide opportunities for transactions in the future,

without the buyer explicitly initiating one. Marketplaces like The Fancy allow buyers to create wardrobes, wish-lists and collections of items, which they may want to follow. In doing so, the buyers indicate their interests to the platform, which gradually nudges them towards an eventual purchase.

SCALING QUALITY: CURATION

The platform needs to constantly improve its ability to differentiate high quality from low quality. It needs to encourage actions that result in high-quality creations, and discourage actions that result in low-quality contributions.

Wikipedia blocks IPs and accounts, which generate a lot of suspicious activity, in its bid to discourage undesirable actions. It also scales an editor's rights on the platform as they perform desirable actions, to further encourage such actions. Encouraging desirable actions and discouraging undesirable ones should be implemented, as feedback loops, into the mechanics of the platform.

Both Sittercity, a platform connecting babysitters with parents, and Task-Rabbit, a platform aggregating service providers, invest in intensive background checks on service providers on their platform. A combination of ongoing social feedback, and occasional editorial screening, helps the platform scale and manage quality.

Curation is managed in one of three forms:

1. Editorial: An editor, administration or community manager approves or rejects contributions to the platform.
2. Algorithmic: Algorithms take decisions on what is desirable and what is not, based on certain parameters.
3. Social: The community curates through signals about quality; signals may include rating and voting.

Scaling editorial curation.

The traditional approach to scaling editorial curation has involved getting more editors on board. This never works well for a network effects platform. These platforms gain adoption at non-linear rates, whereas editorial actions, reliant on a limited in-house editorial team, can only scale at a linear rate.

On platforms, editorial actions scale well only when they are gradually moved out to the community over time. The editors do not become redundant; they simply take on more abstracted roles. These new roles may involve educating the community on how to curate and ensuring that the tools of curation (e.g. rating, reviewing, and reporting) are being used correctly and often enough.

Scaling algorithmic curation.

Algorithmic curation scales best on networked platforms, however, algorithmic curation should be implemented with care. A common approach to implementing algorithmic curation is to look for frequently repeated curative actions among editors, and identify repeated actions that can be automated as algorithms. With every iteration, algorithms take on repetitive curative actions and editors elevate themselves to a higher level of abstracted curation. For instance, algorithms may uncover all undesirable activity above a certain threshold and editors may exercise judgment to take the final decision.

Scaling social curation.

Social curation scales in two ways. Social curation mechanisms, especially on platforms needing strict curation, may scale by permeating a reputation model through the community. As a consequence of this reputation model, the opinions of experts are given more weight than that of novices. On platforms with lower curation needs, and those that gain traction faster, social curation may rely merely on the strength of numbers. On such platforms, all opinions have the same value. It is important to note that reputation models may be implicit or explicit, or a combination of the two. Explicit reputation manifests itself as a badge, score, level, rating or some other form externally, while implicit reputation is used solely within the mechanics of the platform to differentiate highly reputed users from others. A platform's decision to choose one form of social curation versus another depends on sampling costs and interaction risks involved, as discussed in Section 3. If sampling costs – the costs involved in evaluating one unit of value – and interaction risks are low, many and diverse opinions may be

more important. In situations with high sampling costs and high interaction risk, permeating a reputation model may be critical to scaling social curation. The choices are not binary; a platform may implement a combination of the two choices. The more the expertise required to make a judgment on curation, and the higher the risk involved in the subsequent interaction, the more likely is the platform to rely on a reputation model. Users who have curated well in the past have greater influence on future curation.
Viki is a platform that leverages an engaged community of translators to add subtitles to Asian soaps and movies. In Wikipedia-like fashion, translators add subtitles to videos and highly reputed translators moderate these insertions. Viki has created a virtual hierarchy across its community, to differentiate the actions of highly reputed subtitle creators from those of less reputed ones. Privileges on the platform are gradually phased out, from internal editors to highly reputed user-editors, and so on.

SCALING QUALITY: CORNER CASES

A corner case is an undesirable usage of the platform that is an exception rather than the norm. Every platform may have a different degree of tolerance to the existence of corner cases.
To eliminate corner cases, or minimize their occurrence, the platform needs to identify undesirable interactions and needs to ensure that they are not repeated. A murderer using a dating site to find their next victim is engaging in an undesirable interaction, as is a contributor defacing the Wikipedia profile of a public figure. These corner cases can often be resolved through a combination of advance screening of producers before they access the platform and by allowing consumers to flag inappropriate actions. These can be implemented in tandem with a reputation model that carefully guards privileges on the platform and rewards users with privileges only when they have exhibited a successful track record on the platform.

SCALING QUALITY: MITIGATING INTERACTION RISK

As platforms scale, they need to manage the risk inherent to either side, in participating in the core interaction.

Not all interactions are created equal. Some are riskier than others. Participating on Twitter does not involve much risk for either side, but participating on a platform for discovering – and ordering – home-cooked food may have higher associated risks. Depending on the degree of risk involved, the platform may have to invest heavily in offering centralized guarantees and insurance. Most 'sharing economy' platforms, like Airbnb and Uber, invest in creating insurance and trust mechanisms to ensure that users are not discouraged from participating.

PLATFORM SCALE IMPERATIVE

A scaling strategy cannot be restricted simply to acquiring new users and keeping them engaged. A scaling strategy for platforms should involve:

1. Scaling of production
2. Scaling of consumption
3. Strengthening of filters through ongoing data acquisition
4. Scaling social curation
5. Scaling community culture
6. Minimizing interaction risk

There are significant management challenges when scaling a network effects platform, which are often underestimated. The above framework helps platforms scale in a manner that ensures repeatability and sustainability of the core interaction.

6.2

REVERSE NETWORK EFFECTS

Why Scale May Be The Biggest Threat To Platforms

Platforms may lose value as they scale. Scale, in fact, may be the greatest threat to platforms, if not managed well.

As noted in the previous chapter, a failure in any one of the four actions - Creation, Curation, Customization, and Consumption - may lead to a failure of the core interaction. When one or more of these actions start to fail with increasing scale, we see the onset of reverse network effects.

Network effects make a platform useful as more users use it, however, beyond a certain scale, network effects may work against the platform. Beyond this point, further scale may make the platform less useful for every individual user. At this point, reverse network effects set in.

ACCESS, CREATION AND CONNECTION FAILURE

Reverse network effects may set in due to failure of access control. New users joining a platform may lower the quality of interactions and increase noise on the platform. Slackening control at access points can lead to an abundance of noise, instead of the abundance of value that the platform manager may have hoped for.

Dating websites often suffer from reverse network effects. As they scale, new users joining the network may lower the value for existing users. Dating platforms need stringent curation, either at the point of access or when users try to connect with other users. On dating sites, women often complain of online stalking, as the community scales. Some women, eventually, abandon the community. Sites like CupidCurated have tried to solve this problem by curating the men that enter the system, in a manner similar to restriction of access at a singles bar.

Professional networking platforms like LinkedIn exhibit similar dynamics. As more users join the platform, the number of unsolicited connection requests increases on the platform. This may irritate sophisticated users and may discourage them from continuing to participate on the platform. To counter this, LinkedIn creates friction by preventing users from communicating with distant connections. It also marks out users whose connection requests have often been denied. This ensures that users do not receive unsolicited messages, and the ones who are sending unsolicited messages are appropriately discouraged from repeating the act. This also allows LinkedIn to offer frictionless access (InMail) as a premium value proposition.

ChatRoulette, an online anonymous video chat network, failed because of its inability to manage access control. Users used the platform without the need for a login and were connected at random, anonymously, over a video chat. This lack of friction led to ChatRoulette's stellar growth but also led to reverse network effects. User anonymity, in tandem with random matching, encouraged certain users to show up in 'various states of undress', driving genuine users away from the network.

Early social networks, like Orkut, also imploded in a similar manner after reaching scale, owing to noise created by fake profiles. Orkut allowed users to communicate with each other frictionlessly, irrespective of whether they knew each other or were connected over the network. This led to a rapid escalation in unsolicited messages, driving its once engaged user base away. The fact that Facebook implemented higher friction, in comparison, and was rapidly developing network effects itself, provided users with an alternative as they fled Orkut.

Platforms that fail to regulate access may end up with reverse network effects. However, frictionless access and creation may continue to work at scale if the platform scales its content curation well. One of the most important reasons for reverse network effects is the inability of the platform to scale its curation.

CURATION AND CUSTOMIZATION FAILURE

Content platforms like YouTube or Flickr allow content creation with low friction, to encourage activity from producers. To ensure that the content stays relevant and valuable to consumers, these platforms need to scale curation (the ability to distinguish the best from the rest) and customization (the ability to filter the most relevant content to consumers).

Curation failure occurs when the platform fails to manage the abundance of content created on it. It fails to distinguish the best from the rest. Customization failure may result from curation failure. It may also result from the platform's inability to create strong consumption filters, as discussed in Section 2.

Reverse network effects set in if the content curation systems do not scale well or if the customization filters fail to improve over time.

As noted earlier in this section, platforms may curate through a combination of editorial moderation, algorithms, and community-driven tools (like voting, rating and reporting). Voting on YouTube, flagging a post on Facebook and rating on Yelp are examples of curation tools. Curation mechanisms may break down as the volume of content increases. This may happen because of one of the following reasons:

1. Excessive reliance on editorial moderation that fails to scale as the platform scales.
2. Curation algorithms that are too customized to the initial use cases of the platform, and do not scale well, as the platform expands to include more use cases.
3. A failure to spread the culture of curation throughout the user community as the user base scales.

Platforms that rely heavily on editorial moderation, often choose to institute a high degree of friction at the point of access, so that the platform scales (relatively) slowly but steadily.

Medium, the blogging platform, has scaled its curation very effectively. In its early days, when Medium was an invite-only platform, it relied heavily on editorial moderation. As Medium opened access to all writers, it transitioned the editorial function to the community. Writers now had to submit their creations to collections, moderated by user-editors, before the article could be published. In doing so, Medium moved the editorial function from a centralized, non-scalable model to a decentralized, scalable model. The editorial power of every user-editor was determined by their ability to gather a following for their collection.

Platforms may experience reverse network effects owing to customization failure if the consumption filters are not strengthened over time. An inability to maintain a highly customized experience, as the platform scales, may lead to lower relevance for consumers, eventually leading to reverse network effects.

The user experience on Facebook is centered around the newsfeed. However, Facebook's insistence on frictionless sharing and its tendency to clutter the newsfeed with promotional posts, especially those from brands, may lead to lower relevance for users, as the network scales. Several factors contribute to this:

1. When a user adds friends indiscriminately, their newsfeed may become cluttered with irrelevant posts, at least initially.
2. Noise is further increased when marketers and app developers get access to the newsfeed.
3. When networks like Facebook and Twitter implement monetization models like Promoted Posts/Tweets, noise increases further as promoted content is often less relevant than organic content.

Facebook has, thus far, tried repeatedly to ensure that it performs well at customization. It has repeatedly restricted access and spread for marketers and developers on the platform.

Quora has a similar problem. Quora is a Q&A platform that has scaled curation very well. The community bubbles the best answers to the top. For a brief period, Quora users experienced customization failure.

People follow topics on Quora. These topics serve as filters that customize the user's experience on the platform. A user who follows the topic 'Startups' may get the latest questions and answers, tagged with that topic, delivered to their feed. This worked very well when the platform started in Silicon Valley. As Quora expanded beyond the US and gained rapid traction in India, users in the US started experiencing customization failure. As an example, users in India would tag their questions and answers with the 'Startups' topic and this content would be delivered to readers in the US. Some questions would be so specific to Indian startups as to be irrelevant for a reader in the US. This was a problem that was eventually fixed, but not before a significant amount of backlash and abandonment from users.

PLATFORM SCALE IMPERATIVE

The indiscriminate quest for platform scale may often work against itself. Quality needs to be constantly scaled along with quantity. To ensure that reverse network effects do not set in, platforms need to ensure that access and creative control, as well as curation and customization, scale well as the platform scales.

MANIFESTATIONS OF REVERSE NETWORK EFFECTS

The Many Roads to Failing With Scale

Reverse network effects may get kick-started because of small mistakes in architectural decisions. However, their ramifications on the growth and evolution of the platform can be massive. Feedback loops serve to power platform scale and lead to rapid traction. Conversely, they also serve to magnify poor design decisions in a manner that can eventually wreck most platforms. This chapter explores seven specific manifestations of reverse network effects, and how they can potentially ruin a networked platform.

#1: UBER-ABANDONMENT

The exponential forces that power platform scale may also lead to an equally rapid abandonment of the platform. As noise increases on a platform, credible producers start to abandon the platform. This leads to an even higher proportion of noise on the platform, which leads to consumers abandoning the platform. As a result, a feedback loop sets in, where greater noise discourages high quality producers, leading to a further increase in noise on the platform. This leads to a poorer consumption experience, discouraging consumers from returning to the platform. This, in turn, leads to lower value production, as producers feel discouraged by lower consumption and ever-increasing noise.

ChatRoulette, a network of video chatters that connects users with anyone across the world at random, saw uber-abandonment play itself out on the platform within a very short period. Since ChatRoulette had absolutely no checks and balances to screen users, it encouraged a range of pornographic and deviant use cases. As the network grew, unpoliced, an increasing number of deviant users joined in, leading to an exodus of genuine users. As legitimate users fled, the relative noise on the platform increased, further fueling a feedback loop that saw the site lose traction at nearly the same skyrocketing pace that it had gained it.

Myspace went through a similar cycle of uber-abandonment. Users fled the social network faster than they had signed up for it. There were multiple factors that led to this, not least of which was the presence of a better substitute in Facebook. Myspace's relatively poorer privacy guidelines led to undesirable experiences for many users. The site also allowed users to play around with the HTML and customize their respective pages. By giving users too much power over the platform, the social network ended up compromising the navigation experience. The social network's focus on advertiser benefit, over user experience, did not help either. A combination of these factors drove users away en masse. As users fled the platform, the users who remained saw diminishing value in their network of friends, all of whom were leaving to sign up elsewhere.

Platforms are often as valuable as the participants they connect. Quora, as we noted in the previous chapter, found rapid adoption in Silicon Valley as it connected highly successful early technical adopters, who were experts in their field. Quora's strong curation also ensures that the best answers get showcased invariably. The Quora community has created a deep repository of knowledge, thanks to these experts. As Quora scales, many worry that less sophisticated users, entering the system, may increase noise, leading to similar uber-abandonment scenarios.

In every story of platform scale lies the hidden potential for uber-abandonment. Platforms need to ensure that they scale their ability to create value and monitor early signs of reverse network effects setting in.

#2: OUTPUT ABUSE

When platforms organize producers to create a specific output, their ability to create that output increases as the producer base scales. However, if reverse network effects set in, the platform's ability to create high-quality output may diminish with scale.

Wikipedia demonstrates that an online platform is open to abuse. The platform has often been criticized for allowing incorrect information. The presence of incorrect articles demonstrates the vulnerability of a user-powered platform, as much as the volume of the correct ones demonstrates its strength.

The problem of poor quality increases as platforms scale, as policing these platforms becomes more complicated with scale.

Over time, Wikipedia has strengthened the governance of its platform to prevent abuse. However, it has ended up creating a virtual, centralized hierarchy, while managing the quality of its output. This prevents it from being as flexible and open as many other decentralized platforms.

#3: ECHO CHAMBERS

Echo chambers may form when filters get too efficient for their own good. When exposed to a lot of information, users are likely to consume what they already agree with. Filters that customize the experience of every consumer on the platform can lead to inadvertent reinforcement of what they already believe in. YouTube, for example, serves videos based on past views and interests. Facebook's newsfeed works on similar parameters and is often criticized for reinforcing an echo chamber.

As a system scales, over-customization may lead to a constant plethora of information that is geared to what its users already believe in, not necessarily what they need. This can prevent those seeking a solution, from being served a solution that is radically different (and effective), and may over-serve obvious solutions.

#4: THE HIVE MIND

Most platforms start within a small micro-market, as we noted in Section 4. Once the micro-market is saturated, these platforms spillover to adjacent micro-markets. Sometimes, the culture developed while saturating the initial micro-market may become so strong and insular that it may discourage adjacent micro-markets from coming on board.

This problem is compounded because of a platform's need for governance. If certain forms of behavior are encouraged during the early days and certain others are discouraged, the platform runs the risk of creating a hive mind. With scale, certain behaviors get reinforced and established as desirable behaviors. The governance on Reddit and Hacker News is so stringent that it overtly favors existing users (who have earned their karma) over new ones. These communities are often criticized for developing a hive mind.

#5: CROWD-AS-A-HERD

On platforms, reputation and influence are often conferred by the community. The best answer to a question on Quora is decided by the community through upvotes and downvotes. The best restaurants are determined by user-curators on Yelp. Value is dynamic and constantly evolving, best exemplified by a Wikipedia article in constant flux.

Curation by the crowd is often shown as being superior to that by experts, but it comes with its unique set of disadvantages. If enough curators accept something as true, it becomes the new truth, even if it is untrue. As a community scales, user-curators tend to help the rich get richer. A restaurant that is already rated well on Yelp may continue to get high ratings even if a patron's experience may not be quite as good.

#6: THE RICH BECOME RICHER

Consider an online platform that enables sharing of knowledge globally and helps those looking for an answer to connect with those who have the answer. The best contributions do not always come from existing experts, neither do the existing experts understand the context of needs in specific niches. Hence, micro-experts are needed to deal with the long tail of problems.

The creation of new niche experts requires a curation model that, effectively, separates the best from the rest. Traditionally, the creation of experts relied on certifications or affiliations with trusted bodies. Creating a similar model of accreditation on an online platform is extremely important if one is to create new experts.

The curation of micro-experts is non-trivial. On Quora, experts are constantly created based on the community's feedback on their past creations. As such platforms scale, they often find it increasingly difficult to identify new experts. Community sentiment tends to be biased towards early participants. The favorably curated invite further favorable curation. Early users on Quora and Twitter tend to have many more followers than those who joined in late, not only because they had more time but also because of two key mechanics in these platforms:

1. One-sided following follows a rich-becomes-richer dynamic. Those with higher counts attract even more followers, thereby growing their follower count further. A higher follower count signals legitimacy and credibility on the platform.
2. The platform itself features users with greater social proof and recommends new users to follow them. New users are prone to get deactivated and abandon the platform. To mitigate abandonment by new users, the platform recommends that they then connect with and follow seasoned users with strong social proof. This, in turn, feeds the rich-becomes-richer feedback loop. As a result, a small group of users rapidly build a high level of influence on online platforms.

This is, ironically, aggravated by focusing on high quality. Twitter recommends super users to prospective followers as these users are likely to create better content. Hence, the platform itself helps separate the power users from the rest.

Users who join later find it more difficult to develop a following and may stop using the platform. These platforms need a mechanism to ensure new users have equal access and exposure to the community, to develop influence. A portfolio-hosting platform for highly proficient photographers, 500px, differentiates Top creations from Upcoming creations, to expose recent activity (often from undiscovered users) to the community.

#7: THE LONG TAIL ABUSE

For all its efforts at curation, Wikipedia successfully controls the quality of only the top 20% of articles that account for 80% of the views. As any platform scales, curation methods tend to work very effectively for the 'Head' but not for the long tail of user contributions. This runs the risk of long tail abuse. While it may be argued that most consumers do not get affected by abuse resulting from the actions of a few producers, the minority that are affected grows as the network scales and as the curation problem itself gets exacerbated.

PLATFORM SCALE IMPERATIVE

Reverse network effects often cause a large and thriving network to implode. Platform managers must watch out for early signs of reverse network effects. This may involve reaching out to abandoners, especially those who were highly engaged in the past. It may also include proactive monitoring of users, whose activity falls drastically, and may involve creation of feed-back loops to encourage them back to the platform. The challenge of orchestrating producers and consumers is not merely restricted to the early days of a platform: it is an ongoing imperative for all platforms looking to unlock platform scale at every stage in their life cycle.

6.4

DESIGNING THE ANTI-VIRAL, ANTI-SOCIAL NETWORK

Networks And Platforms That Refuse To Scale

The growth stories of Facebook, Twitter, Pinterest and others have been repeated often enough to make us believe that all social networks benefit from platform scale. However, there are certain social networks that are inherently designed against platform scale.

THE UNSCALABLE SOCIAL NETWORK

While Facebook, Twitter, and Pinterest have great growth curves to show off, many social networks fail to scale at that rate. There are certain characteristics that structurally prevent such networks from scaling, irrespective of the quality of execution. Networks and platforms that fail to scale, by design, often exhibit one of the following three patterns:

1. The need to solve the chicken-and-egg problem multiple times, not just once: This compounds the challenge of execution, and impedes the platform's ability to scale. In such cases, a typical growth graph looks like a series of steps rather than one that grows non-linearly

throughout. New networks are created from scratch as the chicken-and-egg problem is solved repeatedly.

2. A cap to organic virality: Existing users cannot bring in more than a certain number of other users. This limits the spread of the network.
3. Very low overlap between clusters within which network effects operate: This leads to a low probability of easily expanding from one cluster to the other.

Two key determiners of platform scale are the size of the network cluster within which network effects are observed, and the degree of overlap between clusters.

NETWORK CLUSTERS

Network effects occur when more production leads to more consumption, and vice versa. However, all such effects occur within certain clusters. Within a cluster, producers and consumers benefit from each other.

Geographical limits create a common form of cluster. More Uber drivers in San Francisco do not lead to more rides in New York City. The network cluster for Uber is restricted to a city. In contrast, the network cluster for LinkedIn may not have any geographical limits.

LinkedIn also has network clusters, though not geographical. These clusters are industry-specific. However, unlike geographical clusters, industry boundaries are not quite as rigid. The same agency, for example, may service clients in multiple industries. Hence, LinkedIn's clusters have a greater degree of overlap.

As we note through the case studies that follow, the size of the network cluster and the degree of overlap between those clusters determine a network's ability to expand and achieve platform scale.

PATH: THE ANTI-VIRAL NETWORK

Path is a network that mirrors very strong offline family ties. Every family constitutes a network cluster and Path is made of many such network clusters. Path's network cluster is built around family ties and every user is part of a specific network cluster. There may be some overlap between network clusters as different users may define their family 'boundaries' differently. However, such overlap is likely to be low and a user is likely to be part of only a limited number of extended families.

If one were to visualize different networks, Path would likely have multiple network clusters with low overlap, different family groups with few common relationships. Facebook, in contrast, would have significant overlap between different network clusters (say your college network and your work relationships' network).

Further, Facebook benefits from high virality because a user obtains greater value out of the network by getting all their friends on board. In contrast, Path structurally requires users to invite only family members. The use case itself imposes a natural cap on virality.

NEXTDOOR: SOLVING THOUSANDS OF CHICKEN-AND-EGG PROBLEMS

Nextdoor is a social network for the neighborhood and each neighborhood forms a unique network cluster. Since users are unlikely to be part of multiple neighborhoods, these network clusters do not overlap. Every neighborhood is insular.

Nextdoor faces a unique problem. Since every neighborhood is an independent network cluster, every such cluster needs to be kick-started from scratch. Members in neighborhood A do not have a natural incentive to invite members in an unconnected neighborhood B, even though they may be friends otherwise.

As new neighborhoods come up on Nextdoor, some word of mouth does get generated within the city, which helps to get new network clusters started. However, Nextdoor has a unique problem. Network clusters in Path are family-sized. As a result, getting two members of a family on board is usually enough to get others on board. Nextdoor needs a larger number of active users, before users in a neighborhood cluster start experiencing value. It faces a chicken-and-egg problem every time it spreads to a new neighborhood. The problem is likely to get easier as it achieves greater penetration and ubiquity in a particular city, but it still exists.

CITY NETWORKS: WHEN SPILLOVERS DO NOT HAPPEN

City-specific networks and marketplaces like Uber, Yelp and OpenTable also have fairly insular network clusters. Every city is a network cluster of producers and consumers. There is some cross-usage, e.g. traveler from city A to city B may reserve a restaurant in city B but the cluster, within which network effects are experienced, is city-sized.

Social networks scale when the activity in one network cluster can spill-over to another network cluster. LinkedIn, for example, started out in the US but spilled over to new markets. It also started in the technology or software industry, with its roots in Silicon Valley, but gradually expanded into other industries.

Spillover helps networks scale across clusters. However, spillover is discouraged when a platform encourages the creation of insular non-interacting network clusters like families, neighborhoods or cities.

While Path and Nextdoor have potential for spillover (through word of mouth among users in the same city), city-specific platforms like Yelp, Uber or Foursquare need to start operations from the ground up in every new city, and often build a national brand only after they gain adoption in multiple cities.

EXPANSION OF CLUSTERS

eBay realized that it was a network of country-level network clusters. Buyers in one country were not too likely to buy from sellers in another country. eBay's expansion strategy, in its early days, involved acquisition copycats in different countries. Facebook, in contrast, never followed this strategy, partly because it would have been a product and data nightmare, but also because geographical barriers do not pose a problem to the type of interactions that Facebook enables. eBay experienced very little spillover while Facebook experienced a lot. However, as eBay realized over time, expansion through acquisition prevents integration at the data layer. It is almost impossible to create network effects across two networks without data-layer integration.

GROWTH AND SPILLOVER

Networks that achieve platform scale encourage spillover. Airbnb, unlike Uber and OpenTable, has tremendous potential for spillover. The travel use case makes such spillover organic to the network. The host and traveler will often be part of different cities. Such cross-city interaction allows rapid growth, without the creation of insular clusters, although some clusters may still exist. For example, travelers from Europe may travel more often within Europe, however, many travelers will venture further abroad and clusters will, consequently, show higher overlap.

In contrast, Uber and OpenTable need to start operations from the ground up in every city every time they want to scale geographically. Uber does benefit from a growing brand awareness but that alone is not enough. As a result, Uber's geographical expansion incurs much higher costs than the geographical expansion of Facebook or Twitter.

INFLECTION POINTS

The growth curves of Facebook, Twitter, Airbnb, and Pinterest have well defined inflection points. Social networks, which encourage clusters, may not have growth curves with well-defined inflection points, because of the additional investment in starting up new clusters. Instead, these growth curves are more likely to show step function characteristics.

PLATFORM SCALE IMPERATIVE

Platform businesses that encourage the creation of isolated network clusters may still grow and achieve platform scale by implementing one of two strategies.

1. *Cross-Cluster Interactions*: The platform may create an interaction where a user in network cluster, A, needs to interact with a user in network cluster, B. The more often such interactions occur, the higher is the platform's ability to scale.
   Facebook started out by building standalone campus networks but later allowed cross-campus interaction, and subsequently opened itself completely. In the case of Facebook, cross-university relation-

ships already existed offline. In the case of Path or Nextdoor, some other trigger may be needed, on which two families or two neighborhoods may exchange information.
Platforms with small network clusters may achieve spillover by creating an interaction across these clusters.

2. *Cross Cluster Incentive*: Groupon is another example of a buyer-seller network, where every city is an isolated network cluster. Starting new cities has the same chicken-and-egg problem every time. Groupon combated this by creating national deals – a multi-cluster incentive –that attracted consumers in cities where Groupon had not yet launched. By amassing consumers through national deals, Groupon had an initial base of consumers to start with while kick-starting a new city and just needed to get the merchants and deals on board.

Platforms that encourage the creation of insular network clusters must carefully design a cross-cluster interaction that enables the platform to grow across clusters and achieve scale.

EPILOGUE

Platform Scale For Traditional Pipe Businesses

Platform Scale unpacks the underlying principles that determine business design and direct the growth mechanics of platform business models. While these principles apply equally well to both startups and large traditional organizations, most of the examples mentioned refer to the success of platform startups. Observing startup success is inspirational but not entirely useful while implementing these principles at a large pipe organization. This epilogue addresses this need and lays out a playbook for applying these principles at large pipe organizations.

I work on analyzing the business design and growth mechanics of platform business models because these issues are very poorly understood in business today, but are increasingly important for businesses interested in digital transformation. Much of my work focuses on applying these principles to platform implementations at large pipe organizations, where an understanding of the underlying platform mechanics is especially important. Businesses that fail to understand the underlying mechanics involved try to imitate the poster-boys of platform scale, with little success. Instead, understanding the business design and growth factors involved helps businesses leverage these principles to design new business models most appropriate to them. In this context, the implementation of platform scale at a large pipe organization follows a very different template from the implementation of platform scale at a platform startup. This epilogue lays out a framework that I've repeatedly observed while implementing platform scale at large pipe organizations. It serves as an introductory series of steps for a large pipe organization to embark on the journey to platform scale.

PLATFORM SCALE: A TEMPLATE FOR STARTUPS

The platform stack serves as a helpful framework to understand the evolution of platform scale at a startup, and how that differs from the evolution of platform scale at a traditional pipe business.

Platforms like Uber, Airbnb, Facebook, YouTube, Android, and Upwork always start at the infrastructure layer and take off by launching the infrastructure layer. Apps and websites, external manifestations of the platform, serve as interfaces to this layer. Managed services offered by the platform may also serve as an interface to the infrastructure.

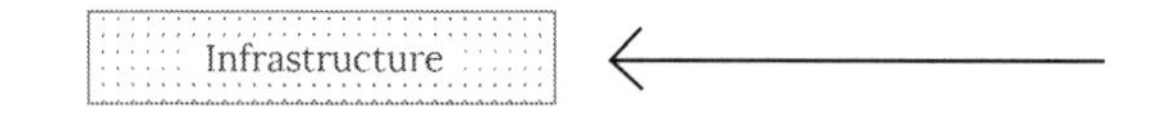

As the infrastructure gains adoption, an ecosystem of producers and consumers starts coalescing around the infrastructure. Drivers and travelers start using Uber, hosts and travelers start using Airbnb, and developers and device users start using Android. This is the next discernible stage in the evolution of the platform. The launch of an infrastructure followed by the coalescence of a vibrant ecosystem around it, engaging in explicit exchanges, is the external manifestation of the platform that we are now familiar with.

Network-Marketplace Community
Infrastructure

Finally, activity by producers and consumers on the platform generates significant amounts of . As noted throughout this book, the data layer serves to make future interactions more efficient and keeps users regularly engaged on the platform. As the data layer grows stronger, the network or ecosystem layer also increases in strength.

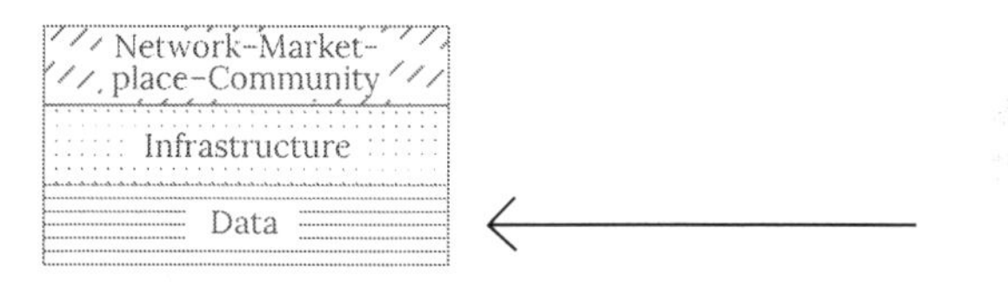

The development of the data layer and its corresponding impact on the platform do not have explicit external manifestations. To the casual observer, the role of data isn't readily apparent. In contrast, the launch of an infrastructure and the coalescence of an active ecosystem around it are readily observable. Moreover, most multi-billion dollar startups achieved platform scale following the above evolution template. As a result of these two factors, it is often believed that any business seeking to build platform scale should launch technology (as infrastructure) and rapidly acquire users of that technology (towards building an active ecosystem).
This template may work for a startup but fails to work for traditional pipe-based enterprises. As a result, large enterprises that try to imitate startups often fail to move forward on the road to platform scale.

PIPES AND THE CHALLENGES OF CORPORATE INNOVATION

Traditional pipe-based businesses face several challenges while innovating. The first and most evident challenge is organizational. Their large organizations, while well designed to enable process efficiency for a pipe business, are slow to respond to environmental input. These organization structures are well structured for maximizing repeatability and efficiency of a well-defined process. But they lack the agility needed to respond to changing usage patterns and to shift direction often while innovating. The second challenge relates to the measurement of platform innovation. Platform scale businesses often take several years to take off, owing particularly to the chicken-and-egg problem discussed in Section four. This does not work well in large organizations where employees are measured and motivated in quarterly and annual timeframes. Owing to the quarterly or annual cycle of measurement, employees working on innovation, particularly on platform scale projects, try to identify metrics that may be effective in demonstrating progress within the specified time period. However, the choice of convenient metrics often obstructs choosing the most appropriate metrics to determine platform health.

Challenges in corporate innovation, particularly the two mentioned above, are well understood and acknowledged. However, it is equally important to appreciate the unique advantage that large pipe businesses possess. Unlike startups, these businesses have been around for decades and have successfully built large pipes that serve millions of users. These businesses have unique market access that they may well leverage towards platform scale. Pipes pursuing platform scale need to contend with a third challenge, unique to the pursuit of platform scale. Traditional pipe businesses lack a culture that focuses on the user and on external interactions. More importantly, they lack a culture of data acquisition and management.

When traditional businesses see startups innovating, they tend to imitate these startups in the hope of achieving similar outcomes. Pipes interested in achieving platform scale are likely to follow the above template for platform scale that startups leverage and start by launching a website or an app in the hope of kickstarting the rest of the platform evolution. *In following this template, these large pipe businesses fail to factor in their unique advantage in user access and their unique disadvantage with data acquisition and management.* This leads to a failure to innovate. This failure is all too often blamed on the organizational structures of large companies.

Instead, many of these failures can be avoided by creating an alternate template for platform innovation unique to a large pipe-based enterprise. Understanding the above advantage and disadvantage that a pipe business faces when pursuing platform scale helps to create an alternate template for pipe-based enterprises to achieve platform scale.

PLATFORM SCALE: A TEMPLATE FOR PIPE-BASED ENTERPRISES

The journey to platform scale for a startup starts with the infrastructure layer. The network or ecosystem layer comes in next and the data layer kicks in at the end. *In contrast, the journey to platform scale for a large pipe-based business starts with the data layer.*

1. *Build A Culture Of Data Acquisition*

The first step a traditional pipe-based business needs to take is cultural. It needs to create a culture of data acquisition. Most pipe-based businesses have been designed with a culture of dollar acquisition. Sales representatives who acquire revenue are incentivized accordingly. The key metrics measured are structured around the sole priority of dollar acquisition.

To kickstart the journey towards platform scale, businesses will need to create a culture of data acquisition. Businesses like LinkedIn and Netflix demonstrate that higher data acquisition opens greater monetization opportunities. LinkedIn acquires significantly more data from its users than Monster. This has helped create a larger recruitment market on LinkedIn. Using data, LinkedIn recommends highly relevant jobs to professionals and their network and helps recruiters find the most relevant candidates. This is made possible by a relentless focus on data acquisition. For example, the progress bar on the website constantly urges users to enter more data by showing them how far they are from building a full-fledged profile.

On the road to digital transformation, most current pipe businesses launch a portfolio of digital services - apps and websites - available to users. However, these apparently digital moves are often neither strategic nor transformative. A *digital strategy should be evaluated from the lens of dollar acquisition and data acquisition.* All digital services launched to users should be integrated at the data layer. More importantly, every service should serve either to acquire dollars or to acquire data that can be monetized in some form in the business.

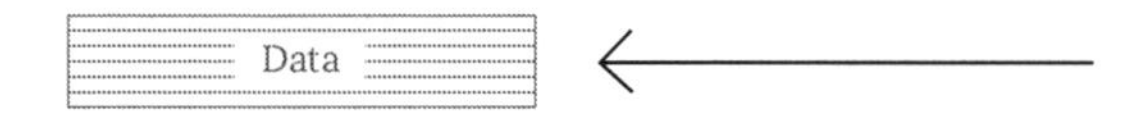

Facebook first launched as a single app on the mobile phone but has gradually built a portfolio of apps. However, this isn't merely a portfolio of disconnected apps launched opportunistically. These apps work together as interfaces for a common platform, all integrated at the data layer.
A *free app is a user benefit in exchange for data.* The app store is flooded with free apps but not all of them are necessarily strategic in intent. To be strategic, a free app should be a data acquisition interface that powers a larger business model. Every app by Facebook is structured as a user benefit in exchange for data. Facebook's news feed itself is the best example of a user benefit in exchange for data. As Facebook and LinkedIn demonstrate, a digital strategy, particularly one that intends to leverage platform scale, should start with a cohesive data strategy. This needs to be executed using a culture of data acquisition.

2. *Enable Data Porosity And Integration*
Platform business models are enabled by platform organizations. *An organization that is not integrated at the data layer cannot enable an ecosystem that is orchestrated by data.*

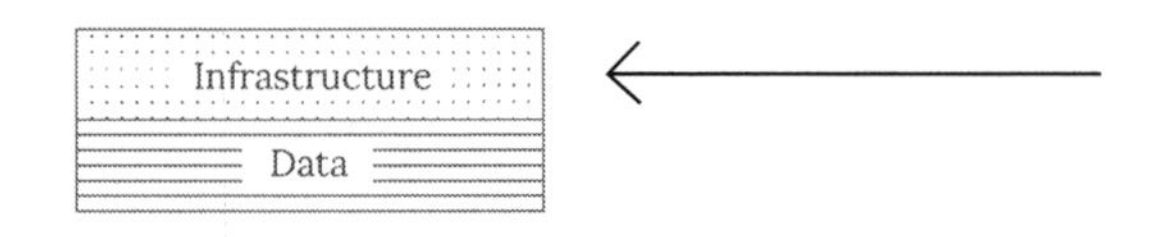

With a clear platform strategy in mind and having set a culture of data acquisition, a pipe organization must institute infrastructural change. It must start integrating its internal organization.

The pipe business must integrate all processes, workflows, and touchpoints at the data layer. Pipe businesses must restructure their internal systems to be more data-porous. This requires the implementation of internal APIs. Today, most organizations leverage IT as a backend infrastructure, but their business units work in silos and do not communicate with each other. There is minimal data exchange between business units. To eventually leverage platform scale, pipe organizations must be data porous. Most importantly, they must have a unified view of the user. Every user should be represented by a unique data entity. Pipe businesses that have never implemented a centralized user focus often struggle with this, but any quest for platform scale will remain incomplete and ineffective without it. *The move towards data acquisition and data porosity signify the two most important steps in the journey towards platform scale.* Businesses that acquire and leverage data will find new ways of understanding their users and moving up the stack to the network layer. Toyota, GM, and Ford are becoming data acquiring companies. Their cars constantly stream data about usage. This helps the businesses better predict after-sales service and also allows them to monetize this data by selling it to insurance companies. Retailers today realize the need for acquiring data and integrating the buying experience across multiple touchpoints. Financial services companies have long been in the information business but are only now realizing the inefficiencies of operating in a data-rich but non-porous internal environment.

3. Leverage Implicit Data-Driven Network Effects

The first two steps in the quest for platform scale were structured to address the disadvantage that pipe businesses face by not having a data-first outlook. The third step leverages the unique advantage that an established business has when compared to a new startup: the access to a large user base.

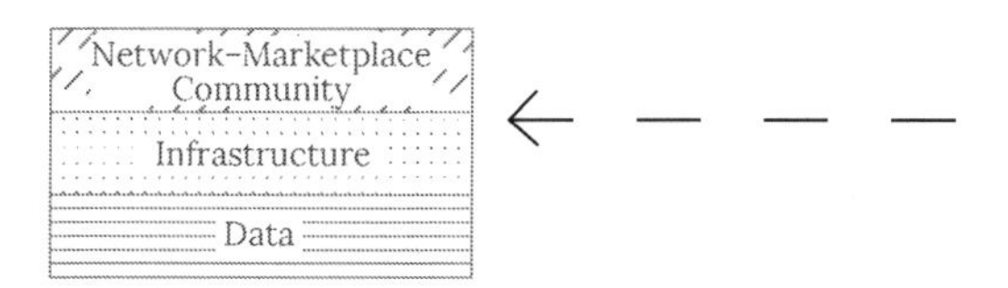

Once the user is uniquely represented at the data layer, following steps one and two above, the business can start benefiting from implicit network effects. Users of Amazon benefited from implicit network effects even in its early days through product recommendations powered by the buying decisions of other users. Amazon's users-who-purchased-this-product-also-purchased-the-following is a mechanism of delivering a benefit through implicit network effects. Traditional branded retailers can provide similar services by leveraging purchase data.

4. Build Explicit Communities

Pipe-based businesses should start building explicit communities among their user base only after the first three steps are well executed. It is only at this point that the pipe's business model starts showing external manifestations of the platform business model. For example, a retailer may encourage

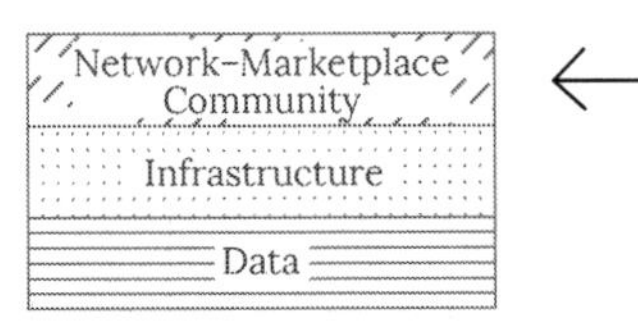

buyers of a brand to connect within a locality. A bank may identify the network of transactions that a small business customer has and encourage the creation of closed industry networks around the bank's products.

In the quest to transform to platform models, pipe businesses often skip the first three steps and move to the fourth. They may be effective in building communities but will fail to leverage the power of data, filters, and intelligence because of poor integration at the data layer. In effect, they will fail to benefit from true platform scale.

5. Enable Explicit Exchange

The final step involves the enablement of the actual exchange. At this stage, the pipe business can move in completely new directions and

fully leverage platform scale.
Users are now connected and are being led to new interactions.

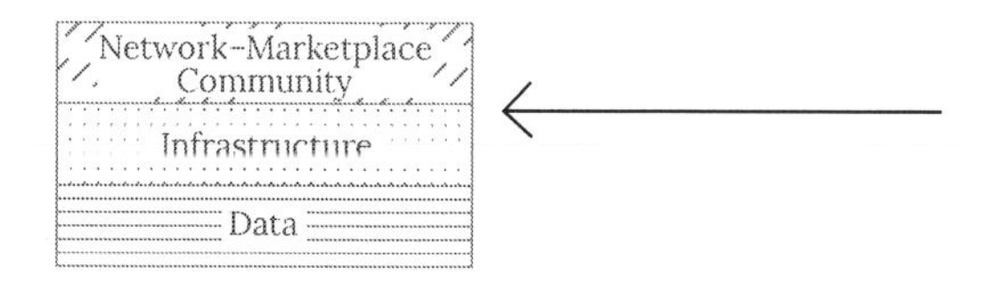

This is the original vision with which most pipe businesses start when they want to realize platform scale. However, the path towards this vision is quite different from the path that a startup would follow. This is needed because a large pipe organization should innovate in a manner that best leverages its advantages - access to a large user base - and acknowledges its disadvantages, stemming from a lack of focus on data acquisition and porosity.

A FINAL NOTE

In the course of my work helping large pipe organizations transform themselves for a platformed world, I regularly observe the above template for digital transformation. It is a slower path to a more sustainable platformed future. Innovation efforts often seem exciting when they deliver rapid results. However, a sustainable shift in strategy and business design is best achieved by building these capabilities in the pipe organization across all layers of the platform stack. Quick experiments to build user communities or launch digital services may seem innovative, but may not necessarily be strategic.

The business design and growth principles in this book lie at the core of the transition from pipes to platforms. Those that understand the underlying mechanics of platform scale will exploit this to their advantage. As the world gets more connected, the businesses that benefit from platform scale will increasingly disrupt and replace the ones that don't.

The platformed world is here to stay.

WHAT'S NEXT

Thank you for investing in this book. Now that you have read it, I would love to hear from you.

If you found this book useful, I would really appreciate it if you could leave a review for the book on Amazon and on Goodreads.

To learn more about platforms, visit the companion blog Platform Thinking at http://platformed.info and sign up for the Platform Newsletter. For an in-depth analysis of the other issues involved in managing platform business models, please check out my forthcoming book *Platform Revolution* (details follow).

For any queries regarding speaking or advisory as well as for any feedback or questions, contact me at sangeet@platformthinkinglabs.com

ABOUT PLATFORM THINKING LABS

Platform Thinking Labs is a C-level advisory and research firm focused on the application of platform strategies across industries. It engages in CXO-level advisory with Global 2000 firms as well as with high growth startups on network effects and platform strategies. Advisory work ranges across diverse industries, with clients in Europe, USA, Australia , South America and Asia.

The services offered by Platform Thinking Labs include the following:

1. C-level executive education on management of platform business models and network effect businesses
2. Platform business design workshops and masterclasses
3. Strategic advisory on platform business design and execution strategy
4. Commissioned research
5. Keynote speaking

All advisory at Platform Thinking Labs is backed by proprietary research, conducted in collaboration with leading thinkers globally, including educators and economists from MIT, Stanford, INSEAD and HBS. Workshops and executive education material have been tested across multiple client engagements, industry workshops, accelerators and business schools globally.

For more details, visit http://platformthinkinglabs.com/advisory

To discuss an engagement with Platform Thinking Labs, please contact sangeet@platformthinkinglabs.com.

What next?

Platform Scale starts a discussion of platform business models and unpacks the factors that drive their scalability. But as these models become more important, they will transform the design and management of many businesses. A whole slate of additional issues comes into focus:

1. Competition: How does competition change in a world of platforms?
2. Governance: How are platforms governed and managed?
3. Regulation: How will platforms be regulated?
4. Metrics: How can we measure platform success?
5. Monetization: Why do traditional monetization strategies fail?
6. Disruption: How can pipes predict disruption and how can they respond to it?
7: Future: What can we say about the platform world that looms ever closer?

My upcoming book *Platform Revolution* (published by W.W. Norton & Company, Inc, February 2016) addresses these questions. Co-authored with world experts Geoffrey Parker and Marshall Van Alstyne from MIT, this book brings together more than a decade of our research and practical applications to answer the most pressing questions about platforms and their future.

To pre-order a copy of the book now, visit www.platformscalebook.com

ACKNOWLEDGEMENTS

The quest to understand business in a world of platforms has captivated me for over three years now. This book is an outcome of many of the ideas that I've developed through the course of this quest. This journey wouldn't have been quite the same without the support and partnership of many people who have made this both an enriching and a hugely satisfying pursuit.

First and foremost, I would like to thank the contributing authors - Geoffrey Parker and Marshall Van Alstyne - for their valuable friendship, support and partnership not just with this book and with other projects we work on together, but through our journey together in better exploring and unraveling platforms. This is one of the many outcomes of that journey.

I would like to thank other colleagues and thinkers who have significantly contributed to the ideas that I've developed over the last three years or have helped them reach the right audience, in chronological order of their involvement - Nir Eyal, Martin Bryant, Mark Bonchek, Hugh Mason, Meng Weng Wong, Ashish Sinha, Ryan Hoover, Patrick Vlaskovits, Simone Cicero, Hemant Bhargava, Andrew Chen, Christian Printzell Halvorsen, JP Rangaswami, Vallabh Rao, Andrew Karpie, Andrei Hagiu, Michael Karnjanaprakorn, Epi Ludvik Nekaj, Sean Moffitt, William Mougayar, Brian Solis, Marvin Liao, Amit Kapoor, Peter Evans, Adrian Turner, Sharad Sharma, Jon Shieber, Bronson Taylor, Haydn Shaughnessy, Julia Kirby, Jeff Epstein, Jon Oringer, Chris Dixon, Sonal Chokshi, Nanette Byrnes, and Shlok Vaidya.

I would also like to extend my heartfelt thanks to the team that worked on this book, as well as the larger group of contributors and patrons. I am in awe of their passion and interest in contributing to making this book what it is. I would like to specifically thank the following people: Gary Percy for his tremendous dedication in planning the book launch, Michael Silverman and Raji Gogulapati for their notable contributions to the book, and Ideactio and Nav Qirti's team for their valuable contribution to book design.

Finally, I would like to thank the person, who has played the most significant role in my journey into the world of platforms, my wife Devika. She has remained both a pillar of strength and an equal collaborator in developing many of the ideas that you see take shape in this book. Above everything else, she is the reason I have confidence in believing that this is but the first of many.

THE PLATFORM SCALE BOOK TEAM

Author

Sangeet Paul Choudary

Contributing Authors

Geoffrey Parker

Marshall Van Alstyne

Overall Project Manager

Gary Percy

Section Leads

Section 1: Michael Silverman

Section 2: Raji Gogulapati

Section 3: Griffin Anderson

Editing

Evelyn Shilpa

Design, Ideactio

Elisa Raciti

Nav Qirti

Rebecca Yong

Marketing And Promotion

Charis Rafailidis

Gaurav Lakhani

Prashant Chamarty

Anuj Adhiya

Karim Pearson

Guy Vincent

Designed by ideactio

Ideactio is a Singapore-based business + design consultancy rooted in principles of design thinking. We enable organizations to employ innovation as a critical driver for sustained business growth.

www.ideactio.com

LIST OF PATRONS*

The author wishes to thank the following patrons of the book for their support and early backing for the Platform Scale book project.

Jon Oringer
Emanuel Sugar
Joy Hou
Tim Knowles
Chris Schneider
Fan Jin
Jonathan Mundy
Julian Origliasso
Larry Zimbler
Peter Lehrman
Mark Bonchek
Mike Cannon-Brookes
Sandro Pugliese
Stephane Kasriel
Tom Maduri
Wiebke Liu
Gregori Pesci
Guy Vincent
Muhamad Rasyid
Robert Richman
Steve Shipley
John Philpin
Albert Canigueral
Antonio Tombolini
Artem Tutov
Banoyi Zuma
Brad Parsons
Martijn Arets
Bryan Greenpal
Daniel Scott
Eric Saint Andre
Fang Soong Chou
Floyd D'Costa
Giuseppe Costabile
Jaryl Sim
Laure Reillier
Michael Lachapelle
Nagarajan M
Nick Katsivelos
Raphael Dana
Alan Turner
Shana Ferrigan Bourcier
Yooni Suh

*List of patrons ordered by award type and date of pre-order

LIST OF CONTRIBUTORS*

John Philpin
Alexander Barge
Thomas Meijerink
Kevin Furbish
Albert Wieringa
Matt R. Tucker
Sinan Deniz
Ilkka Kakko
Philippe Chetrit
Massimo Chiriatti
Sophie-Charlotte Moatti
Rush Carskadden
Anuj Adhiya
Nir Eyal
Rainer Bareiss
SB Chatterjee
James Nanscawen
Evandro Inada
Barbara Thornton
Justin Coetzee
Gunnar Eensalu
Jerome Bell
Teddy Ho
Edson Rigonatti
Shabbir Khan
Nikhil Patwardhan
Venkat Balasubramanian
Luis Muller
David Smith
Ciprian Timofte
Emil Davityan
Peter Lehrman
Nagarajan M
Matt van Wyk
Eric Saint-Andre
Lloyd Fassett
Abhinav Soni
Raju Varanasi
Chirag Dani
Peter Byebierggaard
Guy Vincent
Sagun Garg
Jolly Jose
Arun Raj
Brad Parsons
Amit Pathak
Philip Polaski
Sudhanshu Ahuja
Cynthia Siantar
Samip
Michael Lam
Leon Lim Jiu He
Sameer Gautam
Inder Raj Singh Virdi
Sanjay Rathi
Sandeep Todi
Apurva Jalit
Saravana Kumar M
Timo Fritsche
Dhruv Sahgal
Kevin Carroll
Neeraj Sanghani
Margaret Saizan
Tahsin Mayeesha
Nikolay Vyahhi
Simon de Haast
Paras Chopra
Michael Lachapelle
Alex Shevelenko
Ashish
Mario López de Ávila Muñoz
Antonio Tombolini
Manfred Bortenschlager
Alex Broudy
Oscar Sastron
Freek Smoes
Henri Isaac
Femi Oni
Thomas O'Duffy
David Weingartner
Bernd Amin Out
Giuseppe Catalfamo
Ron Williams
Carlos Sierra
Bert Cattoor
Christoph Nieberding
Andreu Castellet
Mariliese Tan
Kristian Collin Berge
Arek Dymalski
Stewart Mackintosh
Stefan Fountain
Ross Alderson
Geoff Hurst
Mark Jones
Atish Davda
Shams Juma
Mark Slaughter
William Sager
Yeh Diab
Espen Grimstad
Kevin Bradshaw
Glenn Ericksen
Nikolai Bratkovski
Neil Soni
Srinivasan.G
Fabian Szulanski
Jan Choma
Ken Carroll
Bryan Clayton
Sari Azout
Wilfredo Cocco
Oscar
Peter Klamka
Pramod Raheja
Val Kharkover
Naren Bansal
Stephen Reed
Daniël W. Crompton
Dan Perlman
Sam Lindsay
Martijn Arets
Terry Yelmene
Nick Daigle
Josef
David Melamed
Ricardo Duarte Duarte
Ebrahim-Khalil Hassen
Andraé McGary
Jon Neiditz
Chee Wan Ng
Stéphane Frénot
Ram Viswanadha
Pramod Dikshith
Kshitij Gupta

Mohan Reddy
Conor Cusack
Ville Kairamo
Lawrence
Ursula Morgan
Joel Modestus
Luis Andres
Hemant K. Bhargava
Richard Cartwright
Carrie Jones
Peter Armstrong
Mark Elszy
Luciano Lima
Raji Gogulapati
Rufin Tshinanga
Barbara Tien
Chris Aitken
David Marquardt
Jim Bloedau
Tom Tabor
Saker Ghani
Brahma Tangella
Michael Salerno
Jason Mariasis
Antonio
Brendan Benzing
Mark Bonchek
BeiBei Que
Arlie Peyton
Ben McMann
Abhishek Jindal
Andrew Zallie
Khai Yin
Thomas Kohler
Solomon
Daniel Ripoll
Ashita
Rita Zerrizuela
Rajat Wadhwani
Sridhar Machani
Daniel James Scott

Mike Lerner
Prabhu Soundarrajan
Daniel Barnett
Venky
Sunil Gupta
Anastasia Ashman
Bhavin Kothari
Vishal Biyani
Fayyaz Hussain
Greg Spillane
Brenton Thornicroft
Michael Sacca
Karim Pearson
Vardhan Koshal
Anurag Baveja
Josh Blandy
Jamey Merkel
Eddy Sabbagha
Tommy Darker
Hugh Mason
Andre Ribeiro Winter
Sistla V Abhishek
Daniel Bentes
Larry Lawal
Ayoub Mohammadian
Raul Tiru
Merja Kajava
Karl Täuscher
Simon Torrance
Inbal Leshem
Jacob
Robert
Itai Talmi
Albert
Robert Williger
Vishnu Venkataraman
Jeff Epstein
Trevor Scott
Abhishek
Sundar
Elisha Tan

Brett Meyers
Lars Oliver Mautsch
Anandh Sundar
Alexandre Rocha Lima e Marcondes
Victor Schmedding
Gary Percy
David Aidekman
Ranganathan B
Stéphane Grumbach
Dr. Karl Popp
Michael Radke
Steven Arjonilla
Edmar Ferreira
Prem Sharma
Patrick Liu
Hai
Athena Lee-Colmagro
Rajesh Lingam
Constantine Anastasakis
Leon Rubinstein
Kerrie Holley
Chandra Dorai
Cooper Marcus
Bastian Buch
Birgitta Edberg
Marcos Eguillor
Charin Polpanumas
Varun Raj
Kamil Szybalski
Michael Silverman
Erik Suhonen
Robin Alter
Alessandro Castiglioni
Kathy Kitts
Pieter van Herpen
Laure Claire Reillier
Alex Linley
Arun Ned
Jim Passmore
Niklas Larsson
Steve Townsend

*Contributors listed in order of sign up.

www.platformscalebook.com

Made in the USA
Coppell, TX
28 August 2022

82206884R00186